MW01485007

RISK MANAGEMENT FOR OUTDOOR PROGRAMS

A Guide to Safety in Outdoor Education, Recreation and Adventure

Jeff A. Baierlein

Viristar LLC
Seattle, Washington

VIRISTAR

Viristar, Seattle Washington 98155 USA
© 2019 Viristar LLC

All rights reserved. No part of this book may be used or reproduced in any manner whatsoever without written permission, except in the case of brief quotations in critical articles and reviews.

For more information, contact Viristar, 19551 38th Ave. NE, Lake Forest Park WA 98155, info@viristar.com.

Published 2019
Printed in the United States of America

DEDICATION

To those who have experienced serious illness, injury or other loss on an outdoor program,
and to their family members and loved ones.

And to those who have worked to prevent such losses,
and when they have occurred
have responded to them
with care, skill and commitment.

BRIEF CONTENTS

CONTENTS

PREFACE

The ten-day backpacking trip through towering trees and past sparkling streams was supposed to be a highlight of the school year. For students who didn't do well in traditional schools, the outdoor-focused alternative school provided hands-on learning and wilderness adventure. Only things didn't go as planned.

The final night of the expedition, while the adult trip leaders were away, strangers wandered into camp. Students got into a fight; the campsite was destroyed, and frightened students scattered into the darkness. The next morning, at the bottom of a cliff, two students were found, dead.

If you were the manager of the outdoor program where this terrible tragedy occurred, how would you respond? Could you have prevented this? Is this just an example of the inherent risk of outdoor adventure? Or is it a sign that trip organizers failed to act appropriately? These are questions I was asked to address as an expert witness in a legal proceeding following the tragedy. It was one of the many incidents to which I have responded that helped propel the writing of this book, so that tragedies like this would happen never again.

This book emerged out of my more than 30 years as an outdoor professional, both field leader and administrator. My hope is to share guidance useful to outdoor program managers based on my experiences with multiple wilderness fatalities and lawsuits, and work with dozens of outdoor organizations on four continents.

In 2017 I was asked by my good friend and colleague John Lin (林政翰) to provide a risk management training for outdoor professionals in Taiwan. After the two-day course, John suggested to me, "You should write a book!" Here it is.

Interest in outdoor activities is growing around the world. Leaders of outdoor programs face pressures to minimize costs, but social tolerance for injury and other losses while outdoors is decreasing. How to balance these competing demands?

Standards, technologies, and activities are ever-changing. New outdoor organizations and program managers are emerging. Although most outdoor experiences end safely and successfully, preventable accidents still occur. What are the best practices for appropriately managing outdoor risks?

Happily, established safety standards, accreditation of outdoor organizations, and information-sharing are all on the rise, and provide responses to some of these questions. This book aims to add to that network of support for both new and experienced leaders of outdoor programs around the world.

Like many others, as a youth I found time outdoors with others to be among the most fulfilling and joyful experiences of my life. Outdoor experiences have an extraordinary power to offer fun, rejuvenation, self-awareness, and community. Well-facilitated experiences in nature can also inspire people to work towards environmental sustainability. And high-quality cooperative outdoor adventures can help people build strength of character and admirable human qualities, above all, compassion.

The vast majority of outdoor experiences are safe, positive and successful. The very best ignite caring for the beautiful blue-green planet that sustains us, and light a spark that leads towards a more compassionate world. If this book fosters more safe and successful outdoor experiences that lead to that better world, then it shall have succeeded.

Jeff A. Baierlein

Seattle, Washington USA

March 2019

ACKNOWLEDGEMENTS

I would like to thank Bill Reller and Michelle Palmer at AAA Printing in Seattle for printing this book, and Jessica Kelso of Blue Petal Designs for her skillful layout and design work.

Many thanks to Xiao ming of Yangshuo, and Jamie and the team at 遠東翻譯社 in Taipei City for providing expert translation services.

My appreciation and sincere thanks to 林政翰 Lin Cheng-han for suggesting I write this book and providing encouragement and support.

I wish to thank Outdoor Adventures by Boojum Executive Director Carol Popejoy Davis and Director of Program Gayle Hilgris for permission to use Boojum materials.

To those who graciously provided permission to use their images in figures and illustrations: thank you. These generous persons and organizations are listed in the Image Credits.

Thank you to Mr. Ted Pease of Classical High School in Springfield Massachusetts for inspiring generations of authors.

Finally, a thank you to my parents, Ralph and Jean Baierlein, for their many years of encouragement and support.

Note: this book is written for the benefit of the outdoor community. Comments and suggestions are gratefully welcomed for the next edition. Feedback should be sent to: publications@viristar.com.

DISCLAIMER

The information contained in this book is intended to support outdoor program administrators in appropriately managing risks in their outdoor programs.

However, not every hazard, risk, or management approach is covered in this text. Other or additional risk management measures may be necessary for appropriate management of outdoor risks.

Following recommendations in this book does not eliminate the possibility of injury, illness, property damage, death, or other loss.

Reasonable efforts have been made to ensure the accuracy and correctness of information provided, but the information may not be accurate or free of errors.

All reasonable attempts have been made to ensure that material in this book is current as of the date of publication. Information in this book, however, may not be up-to-date, as laws, standards, technologies and practices are ever-changing.

The material in this book is general in nature and may not be suitable for all contexts. The information in this book should be used as a guide only, and is not a substitute for the judgment of qualified persons in assessing and managing risks relevant to each unique situation.

The publisher, author, and those who have contributed to this publication, to the maximum extent permitted by law, disclaim all liability and responsibility for any direct or indirect loss, damage or liability which may be suffered or incurred by any person as a consequence of reliance upon anything contained in or omitted from this publication.

Part One

GETTING STARTED

CHAPTER 1

INTRODUCTION

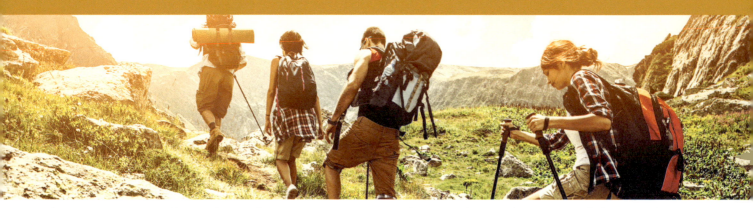

Adventure. Joy. Personal growth. Outdoor programs provide these, and more. But there are risks. Any person who holds a responsibility for the well-being of participants on outdoor programs may wonder, are we safe enough? How can we tell? When it comes to providing great outdoor experiences that meet risk management standards, are we the best we can be? This book can help you answer these questions with confidence.

Risk Management for Outdoor Programs: a Guide to Safety in Outdoor Education, Recreation and Adventure offers an in-depth view of risks faced in conducting organized outdoor programs, and how those risks can be managed appropriately. The book covers risks associated with participants, staff, activities, equipment, activity areas, transportation, organizational culture, and more. Chapters show how to identify risk management standards that should be met for each of these areas. And the book introduces a variety of tools for managing risks appropriately. Finally, readers are given ideas on how to put all the elements of effective risk management together and view them from a systems perspective.

The book is written to be useful in any country and any outdoor environment. Since not every possible situation can be addressed, of course, the book provides general guidance and tools for making good risk management judgments in any context.

This publication is suitable for use as a textbook in academic classes on outdoor program risk management at the university level. It's also designed as a textbook for risk management trainings. And it can be a desk reference for anyone who has a professional responsibility for managing risk in the outdoor context. Therefore, it can be read front to back, or readers can skip to the chapters

most relevant to their needs. But since all elements of a quality risk management system are interconnected, the book is best when treated as a whole.

The book is built around four fundamental approaches to risk management: Eliminate, Reduce, Transfer, or Accept risk, to socially acceptable levels. Each chapter begins with a list of learning objectives, followed by the chapter content, and ends with a chapter summary. The narrative format contains recommendations for appropriate professional practices, but is not structured to serve as a staff field handbook or list of procedures. Leadership of any organization wishing to develop a manual of policies, procedures, and guidelines for staff use based on the information here will need to use their own judgment about how best to construct such a manual.

Risk Management for Outdoor Programs: a Guide to Safety in Outdoor Education, Recreation and Adventure is written for use by anyone with a responsibility for the well-being of those involved with outdoor programs. This includes managers of outdoor organizations such as program coordinators, program directors, human resources leaders, gear and logistics managers, safety or risk management officers, and members of a safety or risk management committee. It also will be useful for executive leadership such as senior executives, the CEO, and Board members.

The book is designed to apply to outdoor programs that are independent businesses or nonprofits, within a university or grade-school setting, or part of a government agency. It covers a wide variety of contexts, including outdoor education, outdoor recreation, and healthcare settings such as wilderness therapy programming. While written primarily for those with administrative leadership responsibilities, it can also be informative for guides, facilitators, instructors, and other activity leaders working directly with students, clients, or other participants. And, it can be an important resource for those conducting risk management reviews, incident reviews, or safety inspections.

From long expeditions in a remote and glaciated wilderness to a walk in the local park, *Risk Management for Outdoor Programs: a Guide to Safety in Outdoor Education, Recreation and Adventure* provides guidance for a wide range of outdoor settings. Each chapter is targeted towards the small to mid-sized outdoor program that is typical in the industry; tiny and very large programs should scale the principles introduced here to meet their organizational size. (For example, a very small organization might not have a dedicated risk management officer; a large entity might have a multi-person risk management department headed by a Vice President or Chief Safety Officer.) While the book has a global perspective, it may be most useful in countries without comprehensive, nation-wide legislation covering outdoor adventure safety, and the supporting national-level regulatory, auditing, incident reporting, best practice guideline and related infrastructure.

The content of this book represents one approach to excellence in outdoor program risk management. There are others, equally valid. In an industry that is ever-evolving, the principles here should be considered ideas to consider and build upon, rather than the final word.

After reading this book and absorbing its contents, the goal is for you to have the information necessary to build and maintain organization-wide risk management systems for your outdoor program that meet outdoor industry standards. You should know where and how to access additional information and stay current with best professional practices. Ultimately, the successful application of the material in this book should lead towards outdoor programs being more safe and more effective in meeting their goals.

Managing risk appropriately in outdoor settings is not a mystery to be viewed with apprehension, but a subject that—with diligent study and the benefit of experience—can be approached with confidence. Here we hope to offer you not the final answers to every outdoor safety question, but tools to help you apply sound judgment to important risk management decisions.

Risk management, like much else, is a journey rather than a destination. *Risk Management for Outdoor Programs: a Guide to Safety in Outdoor Education, Recreation and Adventure* invites you to travel along that path. This book is offered to you as a trusted companion on your journey, to support you in providing excellent, fulfilling outdoor programs to satisfied participants. Let us begin, together.

CHAPTER 2

AN APPROACH TO RISK MANAGEMENT

LEARNING OBJECTIVES
1. Reducing the probability and magnitude of risks to socially acceptable levels
2. Prerequisites for building a risk management system
3. Identifying risk management standards
4. Domains of risk
5. Policies, procedures, values and systems to meet standards
6. Field Manuals and administrative risk management documents
7. Risk Management Plan document
8. Implementing risk management systems
9. Continuous improvement of a risk management system
10. Risk management techniques: eliminate, reduce, transfer, accept
11. ISO 31000 standard for risk management
12. Legal and other risk management requirements
13. Sources of support for developing risk management plans

2.1.   INTRODUCTION

Good outdoor programs provide adventure, fun, and personal growth. Yet outdoor experiences come with risks. These risks, however, can be managed to stay at acceptable levels. In this chapter we'll look at over-arching approaches to appropriately managing the risks that may be experienced in outdoor programs.

We'll focus here on an organization-wide approach to risk. Addressing activity-specific risks is covered in Chapter 4, Activities and Program Areas.

Outdoor programs have a responsibility to reduce the level of risk to one that is acceptable by society. To do so, the organization must understand the risks that might be reasonably foreseeable in an outdoor program. The organization then must ensure that the probability and the magnitude of the risks are within socially acceptable limits. These limits can include legal regulations and a comparison with what a reasonable and prudent person in a similar situation would do.

For instance, a risk in rock climbing is loose rock falling and injuring a climber. The expectation is that this would rarely occur, and that if it does occur, serious injuries are unlikely.

To reduce the probability to a level of a rare occurrence, an organization would only select climbing sites that have minimal loose rocks. Each climbing route might be given a close, hands-on inspection and cleaning each season to remove loose rocks. And before each climbing session, a climbing site manager would assess site conditions, visually inspect the routes, and only use those considered reasonably free of loose rock.

To reduce to magnitude of the risk, climbers would be required to use helmets, and would be instructed on protective procedures in case of rockfall.

These common practices, along with others, can bring the risk of injury from rockfall to an acceptably low level. Risk is likely to remain after risks are addressed, but the residual risk is within the risk tolerance of the legal, social, cultural, and political environment in which the organization operates.

2.2. BUILDING AND IMPLEMENTING A RISK MANAGEMENT SYSTEM

Any approach to managing risk fundamentally employs a simple, common-sense structure. It is the same structure each of us uses every day in managing day-to-day risks that are a part of life. In this case, it's adapted to the context of an outdoor program.

Managing for risk in an organizational context is like managing for any other business objective, such as quality or financial performance. It can be considered, then, an issue of management systems.

A standards-based model for developing a risk management approach and integrating it into an outdoor organization's practices is outlined here. This is an approach employed in some accreditation and risk management review models.

2.2.1. Meet Prerequisites

As with any business planning process, certain prerequisites must be met before beginning.

1. **Support from top leadership**. The top leadership of the organization, such as the Board and CEO, must value safety and good risk management that meets reasonable community standards, and brings risks as low as reasonably practicable. Leadership must also be committed to ensuring that the necessary resources are available to develop and continuously manage the organization's risk management systems.
2. **Availability of practical resources**. In addition to political support, sufficient practical resources—financial, intellectual, material and personnel—to initiate and complete a risk management planning process must be available.
3. **Clarity of organizational identity**. The enterprise should answer two questions, and ensure there is shared agreement throughout the organization on the responses:
   a. *What is our purpose?* Why do we exist? Specifically, what are the organizational outcomes we seek? This informs everything the organization does.
   b. *How do we achieve our outcomes?* What is the program we offer participants? What are the activities that comprise that program? (As mentioned in Chapter 4, Activities and Program Areas, the activities with the lowest risk that meet organizational outcomes should generally be the ones selected.)

This creates a linkage from the overarching purpose of the organization to the outdoor programming it offers. Thus, risk management of the outdoor program can be clearly linked to serving the organization's mission.

With these prerequisites in place, we're now ready to develop and implement the risk management structure.

2.2.2. Identify Standards

In this step, we identify the expectations for managing risk that apply to each of the risk domains present in an outdoor program.

Risk Domains. Risk domains, or "risk reservoirs," are the locations in an outdoor program where risk is found. There are multiple models for the risk domain concept, with more or fewer categories depending on the taxonomical preferences of the model creator. The risk domains used here are covered in Part II of this book, and are:

1. Culture
2. Activities and Program Areas
3. Staff
4. Equipment
5. Participants
6. Subcontractors
7. Transportation
8. Business Administration

The risks in the domains all interact with and affect each other, however. Participants well-suited for one activity area (the local park) may run into trouble in another (high-altitude mountaineering). We illustrate the interconnected nature of the domains in Figure 2.1.

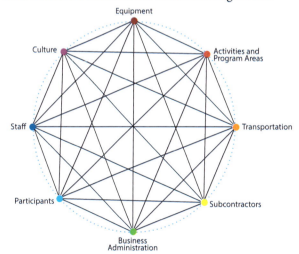

Figure 2.1. Risk Domains. Each is connected to, influences, and is influenced by the others.

Standards in Each Risk Domain. Next, in each risk domain, we identify standards that, when followed, will lead to appropriate management of risks in that domain. Correct identification of standards that comprehensively address all reasonably anticipated risks must be done with care. A team of seasoned, capable outdoor professionals with diverse and extensive experience with the activities, participant populations, staff, equipment, and activity areas applicable to the outdoor program must be employed. The team must also have a background in understanding and managing corporate culture, subcontractor management, and administrative aspects as outdoor programming.

Happily, some of this work has already been done. Examples include:

- Outdoor industry groups have developed risk management standards, such as the Australian Adventure Activity Standard (AAS) and the Association for Experiential Education's Accreditation Standards for Adventure Programs.

- Good practice guides and similar instruments, such as the Good Practice Guides of the Australian AAS project and the Activity Safety Guidelines published by the New Zealand outdoor industry, provide guidance on activity-specific risk management.

- Activity leader qualifications are well-developed in many countries by leading outdoor industry groups. Some of these groups are known in the UK and Ireland as National Governing Bodies. Examples include British Canoeing and the British Mountaineering Council. Some are known in Australia as peak bodies. An example is the Outdoor Council of Australia. It's relatively simple to understand that a staff person with the relevant qualification (such as an award, diploma, or certificate) is likely to be competent in the technical skills required to conduct the relevant activity.

- Equipment manufacturer recommendations are available for care and management of vehicles, outdoor gear, and other items.

- Organizations such as the Wilderness Medical Society provide guidance on standard medical protocols for outdoor contexts.

Examples of standards are offered below. Note that these compilations may not be suitable for your particular context, and explanatory detail is not included. Other standards that might apply to these areas but may instead have been placed in different categories (such as international considerations, documentation or program management) are not listed. In addition, the specifics of precisely how to meet each standard are not specified; developing and demonstrating those specifics is the responsibility of the outdoor program.

Standards Related to Staff

1. Qualifications for field and management staff are communicated and adhered to.
2. Each staff member is aware of their risk management responsibilities; accountability for risk management outcomes is clear.
3. Staff hold appropriate emergency medical training certifications; certifications are on file.
4. Staff have appropriate knowledge of program areas, including risks and emergency response.
5. Staff are appropriately trained for the activities and participant populations; documentation of training is on file.
6. A system for appropriately assessing and supervising staff is in place.
7. Staff are appropriately rested and refreshed prior to work, especially regarding long programs and times of heavy workloads.
8. Staff are apprised of changes to policies, procedures and other expectations.
9. Subcontractor suitability is assessed prior to and throughout subcontractor hiring.

Standards Related to Transportation

1. Only individuals meeting established eligibility requirements serve as vehicle operators.
2. Vehicle operators receive adequate vehicle operator training.
3. Vehicle operation policies and procedures are established and adhered to.
4. Vehicle occupants are aware of and comply with established safety policies and procedures.
5. Vehicles have appropriate licenses, registrations, inspections, and any similar requirements.
6. Vehicles have appropriate insurance.
7. Vehicles are appropriately maintained and repaired.
8. Vehicle operators appropriately inspect vehicles before use.
9. Vehicle loading standards and weight ratings are adhered to.
10. Vehicle trailers, if employed, are used appropriately and by qualified staff.
11. Vehicles are stocked with appropriate emergency supplies.

12. Appropriate risk management practices for use of personally owned vehicles for program purposes are established and maintained.

2.2.3. Establish and Document Policies, Procedures, Values and Systems to Meet Standards

Now we have identified standards for professional practice that demonstrate acceptable management of risks. The next step is to integrate these standards into organizational practice. To do this, policies, procedures, values and systems should be incorporated into the organization.

This, too, is made possible through the wisdom of experienced and capable outdoor professionals. In organizations providing multiple activity types, documentation can easily run to hundreds of pages, and must be precisely crafted to provide properly framed guidance.

Policies, as described in the Glossary, are over-arching mandatory directives or high-level rules. An example might be that required first aid and emergency response equipment is available at all times.

Procedures are established way of doing thing, and should be followed, unless it is evidently safer or superior not to do so. An example is given here for lining a canoe. (Lining refers to walking a boat downstream while holding on to guide lines, for instance past a dangerous rapids without a portage trail.) The procedure is: when lining a canoe down a rapids, the person should stay between the boat and the shore, rather than on the river side of the boat.

Values refer to prized ideals. In this context, values might include having a conservative approach to taking risks, following established policies and procedures, treating others with care and respect, or taking initiative to assess and manage risks at all times. Chapter 3, Culture, explores values in more detail.

A **system** is a set of interacting things that form a complex whole. A medical screening system, for example, could consist of a trained medical screener, medical or health history forms, a medical screening manual, one or more consulting physician medical advisors, a set of policies and procedures regarding screening processes, communications protocols between screeners and other staff members, and documents such as specialized questionnaires and physician referral forms.

Documentation. Policies, procedures, values and systems should be documented. This helps to ensure there is widespread awareness and a shared understanding of expectations. (Training, coaching and enforcement may also be necessary to ensure that behaviors match expectations established in documents.) Rather than having a risk management book that sits on a shelf and is rarely consulted, risk management should be suffused throughout the organization and its documents and practices.

Documentation comes in three forms: field manuals, administrative documentation, and a risk management plan.

Field Manual. This document is a handbook used by activity leaders. It lists policies and procedures applicable for working directly with participants in outdoor activities. Subjects might include an introduction to the organization's risk management approach, hazardous conditions, incident reporting, emergency response (including medical protocols, evacuations, missing persons, local medical facilities, and search and rescue), activity-specific protocols, and an emergency call guide.

Care must be taken to ensure that essential safety items are highlighted and easy to find. The manual must be formatted for maximum readability, and be available as a resource to activity leaders at any time.

Administrative Documentation. This refers to documents for administrators and managers as well as information for volunteers such as Board and committee members. It also includes sales, marketing and enrollment documents. Examples include medical screening manual, incident report form, Risk Management Committee charter, and staff training and evaluations schemes. Marketing materials discussing safety, and forms for participants such as equipment lists, written behavior expectations and contracts, pre-program training recommendations, and medical forms, are also included here.

Risk Management Plan. This is a document that outlines all aspects of the organization's approach to risk management. It discusses the organization's commitment to risk management, briefly describes the major risk management systems, and references other documents such as the field handbook and important administrative documentation.

(This document is variously known as a safety statement or safety management plan. The names, organization and structure of any of the elements of an organization's approach are less important than their ultimate functionality in appropriately managing risks.)

Every employee and volunteer should be provided with the risk management plan, review it thoroughly, and be given the opportunity to ask questions about it.

Various formats can be used. One template is as follows:

1. **The purpose of the plan**. For instance, to document why and how risk is to be managed.

2. **The goals of the organization's risk management program**. This shows what successful management of risk looks like. This section might include a risk management mission statement. A mission statement can provide overall direction and inspiration, and a vision for what all protocols, strategies, and actions should work towards.

   One organization's mission statement includes the following:

   In all of its programs and practices the organization seeks to eliminate fatalities, disabling injuries, and serious illnesses. In addition the organization is committed to reducing other property damage, lost participant hours and participant program days, injuries, accidents, and illnesses, including those that may have behavioral causes and those involving emotional and psychological harm.

   Another organization's risk management goals are precise, seeking an accident rate lower than that of certain motor vehicle accidents in the region.

3. **The organization's philosophy of risk management**. This may include ideas such as that the organization does not seek to take risks for their own sake.

4. **A demonstration of top leadership commitment to risk management**. Written endorsement of the plan by the CEO and Board, or equivalent leadership, provides vital credibility to the plan. This can be in the form of a written and signed statement at the beginning of a plan, or other means.

5. **Roles and responsibilities**. Each person and job position in the organization, including that of volunteers, has an important role to play in risk management. These responsibilities should be summarized here. This reinforces a culture of safety and increases accountability.

6. **Risk management methodology**. Risk management principles and processes can be summarized. This can include a summary of approaches to risk management in each of the risk domains:

   1. Culture. The importance of a safety culture, and how it is established and maintained
   2. Activities and Program Areas, including applicable policies and procedures
   3. Staff, including training regimes and certification requirements
   4. Equipment, including medical, emergency and rescue gear
   5. Participants, including screening and supervision
   6. Subcontractors and their assessment, selection and supervision
   7. Transportation, summarizing risk management approaches
   8. Business Administration, including workplace health and safety, insurance, and a reference to relevant items of the Employee Handbook such as drug policy and harassment policy

   This can also include approaches to the risk management instruments in Part III of this book:

   1. Risk Transfer instruments such as liability wavers
   2. Incident Management. A summary of the field-based emergency response procedures can be provided. A detailed description of how to manage the administrative aspects of incident response should be included here.
   3. Incident Reporting, noting the existence of incident reports and summarizing the system for analyzing them and making changes based on the analysis
   4. Incident Reviews, including when these are triggered, and summarizing how they are conducted
   5. Risk Management Committee, referencing its existence, describing its purpose, and summarizing its activities
   6. Medical Screening, referencing the medical screening manual and processes
   7. Risk Management Reviews, including internal and external reviews, when and how frequently

they are conducted, who leads them, and how the results are dealt with. Periodic inspections, such as for challenge course installations, can be included here.

8. Media Relations, particularly for crisis situations
9. Documentation, briefly discussing the major risk management documents such as the field manual, personnel records, inspection reports, and the like
10. Accreditation, covering any accreditation held by the organization
11. Systems thinking, summarizing how the organization uses systems thinking to manage risks

2.2.4. Implement Policies, Procedures, Values and Systems

What's written on paper needs to be brought to life, and kept thriving. Employees and volunteers should be given the time and opportunity to read the risk management plan and other documents relevant to their position. They should sign and date forms stating that they have read, understood, and agree to abide by the requirements of the Risk Management Plan and other applicable documents (such as Employee Handbook and Field Manual).

Employees and volunteers should go through regular trainings where risk management information is covered, and a culture of safety is reinforced.

Staff should also be given ample opportunities to provide input on the organization's management of risk. The organization benefits from staff wisdom, and staff increase their psychological commitment to a process if they have helped build it. This can be done by a variety of methods, including involving staff in debriefs, incident reviews, risk management reviews, policy development, New Element Readiness Assessment planning (covered in Chapter 6, Activities and Program Areas), and elsewhere.

2.3. CONTINUOUS IMPROVEMENT

The organization should strive to continually improve its management of risk.

A common-sense process can be as follows:

1. **Develop a risk management approach**. The standards-based model above can be used.
2. **Implement the approach**. Put into action the policies, procedures, values and systems that comprise your management plan.
3. **Assess the approach**. How well have things

worked? Assess the results of risk assessments, program evaluations by clients and staff, activity and program debriefs, Risk Management Committee proceedings, incident reports, inspections, accreditation reports, incident reviews, and risk management reviews. Review the results of risk management initiatives—for example, if an effort is made to improve staff qualifications by reducing turnover, examine staff retention statistics or employee survey results. Compare results to standards and your risk management mission.

4. **Improve the approach**. Use information from your assessment to strengthen the organization's management of risk.

The process is then repeated. The improved risk management approach from the fourth step is used in beginning again by assessing standards and conformity to those standards.

This reflects the plan-do-check-act management method (Figure 2.2), of which there are many variations.

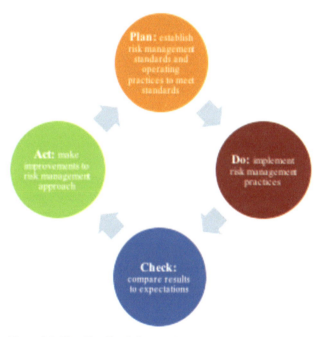

Figure 2.2. Plan-Do-Check-Act continuous improvement management model.

2.4. CATEGORIZING RISK MANAGEMENT TECHNIQUES

Risk can be managed by four methods:

1) Eliminate
2) Reduce
3) Transfer
4) Accept

Eliminate. For example, one could completely eliminate the risk of altitude sickness by not traveling to high altitudes.

Reduce. This approach is often the one that receives the most attention in program operating procedures. Risk reduction can be accomplished by many methods, such as:

- Staff selection, training and supervision
- Equipment management
- Participant screening and training
- Activity location selection
- Subcontractor assessment
- Emergency plan development

Transfer. Approaches for risk transfer vary widely by legal jurisdiction. Methods include:

- Insurance
- Subcontracting
- Agreements with participants:
  o Indemnification and hold harmless
  o Release of liability
  o Assumption of risk

Accept. Some risk is inherent, unavoidable, and acceptable, in every human activity. Both participants and the organization can choose to accept certain risks.

After being suitably informed of the risks, participants can give consent to taking those risks. These might be risks inherent to the activity (such as hypothermia when winter snow camping). They might include simple negligence on the part of staff. This may also include accepting the risk, although low, of significant illness, injury or death.

(When a participant signs a document acknowledging these risks, agreeing to assume them, and releasing the organization from liability arising from them, this risk acceptance on the part of the participant can technically be considered risk transfer on the part of the organization.) Organizations generally accept outdoor program risks

once they have fallen to an acceptable level. For example, injury from rockfall may exist, but it can be brought to an acceptable level by inspecting and cleaning climbing routes, keeping unhelmeted persons out of rockfall zones, and using other good institutional climbing practices.

Variations. In addition to the eliminate-reduce-transfer-accept model described above, other ways of categorizing risk treatments exist and may be suitably employed.

2.5. AN ALTERNATIVE MODEL

An alternative to the standards-based model presented above is the risk assessment-treatment model. This is found in ISO (International Organization for Standardization) standard 31000:2018 (figure 2.3). It provides a detailed process for identifying, analyzing, evaluating, and treating risks. It is designed to be applicable to any kind of business in any type of industry, and provides tools particularly well-suited for large enterprises. The Australian Adventure Activity Standard Core Good Practice Guide follows the ISO 31000 approach.

2.6. REQUIREMENTS

Figure 2.3. ISO Standard 31000, Risk Management.

As a general rule, every organization has a legal and moral obligation to manage risk. More specifically, however, having a formally established system for doing so, including a written plan and supporting documents, is not just a good idea; it's a requirement in some cases. For instance:

- New Zealand's Health and Safety in Employment (Adventure Activities) Regulations require outdoor adventure providers to have a safety (risk) management system, and be audited by an external risk management reviewer.

- In Australia, it is required to have risk management plans for each adventure activity, in order to meet the voluntary Australian Adventure Activity Standard.

- Health and safety regulations may require a documented assessment and control plan for risks, for example, as do the UK's Management of Health and Safety at Work Regulations.

Your organization should check to see what the requirements are for your circumstances.

2.7. GETTING HELP

Support for developing risk management plans is available.

- The SupportAdventure online resource of the New Zealand outdoor adventure industry, funded by the New Zealand government, has guidance on how to create a risk management system.

- The Australian Adventure Activity Standard and associated Good Practice Guides give guidance on how to develop risk management plans.

- Accreditation schemes such as that of the Association for Experiential Education can provide criteria for outdoor risk management that can be used to help form a risk management plan.

- Consulting services will help organizations develop risk management systems, for a fee.

- Health and Safety agencies provide guidance and templates for risk assessment and risk management plan documents. For example, the UK's Health & Safety Executive provides online examples of risk assessments for various business types; it is your responsibility to decide if they are sufficiently comprehensive or applicable to your situation. The Health and Safety Authority of Ireland provides online a sample risk management plan with detailed language that is customizable to your situation.

Case Study: Tick-borne Encephalitis in China

In 2007 a 15-year-old first-year high school student at a prestigious private school in the USA attended a summer program run by the school in China. Students hiked up Panshan, a mountain approximately 100 km from Tianjin in northeastern China, by a paved pathway. Students and teachers split up on the descent, most taking a cable car down the mountain. The student, and a small group of others, decided to walk down the mountain by themselves, and were permitted to do so.

The student left the paved trail and began walking on narrow dirt paths surrounded by vegetation. The student received insect bites during this time. Shortly thereafter, she began to experience symptoms, and was diagnosed with tick-borne encephalitis.

The encephalitis had terrible effects. It gave the student permanent brain damage and left her unable to speak. She is only able to give soft, monosyllabic, childlike sounds. Her fingers have limited ability to bend, which makes activities like typing difficult. She also has limited control of facial muscles, and drools, has difficulty swallowing, and exhibits socially inappropriate facial expressions. Her cognitive abilities are also diminished, particularly in complex problem-solving, and ability to comprehend math and reading. This damage is expected to last her entire life.

Before the trip, the school advised students to visit a travel medicine clinic; the student did not do so. The school listed insect repellent on the packing list. The school warned students about several hazards, but not about the possibility of tick-borne disease in China, or steps to take to avoid tick-borne disease. Insect repellent was brought to the site, but left on the bus. Students were advised to wear long pants but it was not required. The school did not ensure that the student took steps to avoid tick-borne disease such as conducting tick checks.

The school argued that tick-borne encephalitis is rare—the student was the first American traveler to contract tick-borne encephalitis in China—and the risk of contracting the disease was not reasonably foreseeable. The school also argued that it did not have a responsibility to warn against every single possible risk that a student might encounter, including rarely occurring risks.

In a lawsuit, the school's release form was ruled to be invalid. A jury awarded the student USD $41.5 million in damages, which was upheld by the state Supreme Court.

Questions

A risk management system is not required to eliminate all risks, but only to reduce reasonably foreseeable risks to a level as low as reasonably practicable. Based on the information above, did the school's risk management plan work as intended? Was this an example of a non-foreseeable risk and a reflection of inherent risks? Or should something different have been done?

Could your outdoor organization develop and implement risk management systems to keep something like this from occurring? If so, how?

Chapter Summary

1. Outdoor programs have risks, which should and can be managed to acceptable levels.

2. Reasonably foreseeable risks should be managed.

3. The acceptable level of risk is determined by society, including through laws and a reasonable person test.

4. People manage risks all the time in everyday life; managing outdoor risks uses similar approaches.

5. A standards-based risk management model can be used in the outdoors.

6. First, the political, financial, and other resources must be available.

7. Next, the organization identifies standards in the risk domains in which it operates.

8. Risk domains include culture, activities, program areas, participants, subcontractors, staff, equipment, transportation and business administration.

9. Then, the organization puts in place policies, procedures, values and systems to meet those standards.

11. A written risk management plan outlines the organization's approach to risk management and summarizes components.

12. The risk management system should be continuously improved.

13. Risk management techniques are: eliminate, reduce, transfer, or accept risk.

14. An alternative to the standards-based risk management model is a risk analysis-treatment model, as explained in ISO Standard 31000.

15. Having a risk management system, and a written risk management plan, is a requirement in some situations.

16. Outdoor industry organizations and health and safety government agencies provide support for risk management planning.

CHAPTER 3

STANDARDS

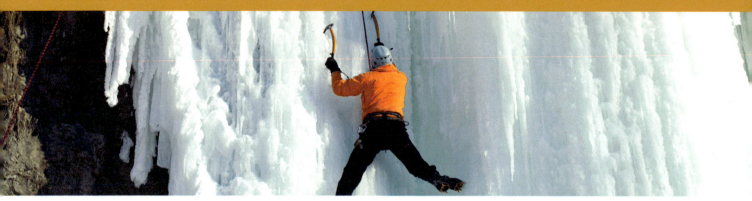

LEARNING OBJECTIVES
1. What standards are
2. The value of standards in maintaining quality and limiting liability
3. Domains in which standards may apply to outdoor programs
4. Sources of standards, including legislation, industry groups and standards-setting bodies
5. Examples of standards that apply to outdoor programs
6. Locating standards applicable to your situation
7. Standards in the institutional context versus on personal time
8. Organizational areas to incorporate standards
9. Limitations of standards

3.1. INTRODUCTION

3.1.1. Defining Standards

Standards are widely accepted norms or expectations. Complying with standards in some cases is voluntary. When they are incorporated into law, standards are legally enforceable (see Chapter 4, Legal Considerations).

3.1.2. Why Standards are Important

Standards, when well crafted and maintained, provide useful guidance on how to conduct outdoor programming in ways that are broadly considered to be acceptable. They are a resource to help you understand and meet established professional practices. By meeting high quality standards, you help ensure that the chance of injury, accident or other loss on your outdoor programs is kept appropriately low, and that you are providing successful outdoor experiences that meet your organizational mission.

Complying with established standards does more than lead to satisfied customers and achievement of outdoor education, outdoor recreation, or other programmatic objectives. Standards conformity can reduce the threat of liability and penalties to outdoor organizations and the individuals associated with them.

Outdoor programs have a responsibility is to manage risks to acceptable levels. Organizations can expect to be held to standards—written or unwritten, legally codified or not—for their industry. Even if you claim no association with standards-setting entities, the standards may still apply to you. Depending on your jurisdiction, standards may be used to establish what is reasonable behavior. This helps establish the duty of care you owe to your participants and others. Outdoor organization staff have an obligation to act in a reasonable and prudent manner. If this does not occur, individuals may be found to be guilty of negligence. Penalties for failing to act reasonably depend on the jurisdiction, the nature of any negligence and other factors, but can run from fines to loss of operating license and imprisonment.

3.2. OUTDOOR PROGRAM STANDARDS

Many standards pertaining to outdoor program safety exist, established by a wide variety of entities. Standards also vary widely in quality. Determining which standards apply to an organization can at times be a challenge.

3.2.1. Areas of Applicability

Standards may apply to several domains, such as:

1. **Jurisdictions.** Standards can apply within certain jurisdictions such as countries, country subdivisions (such as state, province, territory, county or city), or land management agency land units (such as a national park). Outdoor programs may be held to standards set by jurisdictional authorities (such as government agencies) for any jurisdiction in which your outdoor organization is headquartered, has facilities, travels through, or conducts activities, or from which your organization draws participants.

2. **Entire outdoor program.** Some standards are relatively comprehensive and cover many aspects of outdoor safety. These can include accreditation standards, institutional standards from an education institution overseeing outdoor activities in the academic context, or national laws regarding outdoor adventure activities.

3. **Activities.** Standards may be focused on specific outdoor activities such as sailing, rock climbing, scuba diving, or others.

4. **Populations.** Standards may apply specifically to youth, school pupils, wilderness therapy clients, or others.

5. **Practitioners.** Standards may be specific to the conduct of instructors, guides, leaders, facilitators, teachers, or other outdoor leaders. Specific examples include mountain guides, ship captains, or challenge course facilitators.

6. **Equipment.** Outdoor equipment is subject to a number of standards (see Chapter 8, Equipment.)

3.2.2. Where Standards Are Found

Some standards applicable to the outdoor industry are found in laws; see Chapter 4, Legal Considerations. Others are found in materials published by accrediting bodies, as described in Chapter 22, Accreditation. Outdoor industry groups disseminate various standards, as may government agencies.

Standards-setting organizations also publish standards applicable to outdoor programs. These standards-setting organizations provide a forum and a process by which various stakeholders—industry groups, government entities, and others—can come together and arrive at consensus language on accepted norms.

Standards-setting organizations include global and multi-national entities such as the International Organization for Standardization (ISO, figure 3.1) and the European Committee for Standardization (CEN). They also include national standards-setting bodies such the Standardization Administration of China, American National Standards Institute, and Swedish Standards Institute, which often are members of international standards-setting organizations, and which may adopt international standards for their own use at the national level.

Often, standards are developed by a collaboration of these organizations. For example, outdoor industry groups might work with government agencies to establish a standard, which may then be published by a standards organization. Those standards may then stay as voluntary guidelines, or they may be adopted as requirements by government authorities or industry groups.

Figure 3.1. Logo of the International Organization for Standardization.

3.2.3. Examples of Standards

A sample of published standards pertaining to outdoor programming follows.

Example Standards Covering Multiple Operational Areas.

1. **Accreditation Standards for Adventure Programs, Association for Experiential Education.** Standards for receiving AEE accreditation as an experiential adventure programs; see Chapter 22, Accreditation.

2. **British Standards Institution BS8848:** Specification for the provision of visits, fieldwork, expeditions and adventurous activities outside the United Kingdom.

3. **Guidance from the Licensing Authority on the Adventure Activities Licensing Regulations 2004** from UK Health & Safety Executive. Standards certain outdoor activity providers in the UK are expected to meet as a condition of government licensure.

4. **Australian Adventure Activity Standards and Good Practice Guides.** Voluntary best practice guidelines developed by a collaboration of the outdoor industry sector and government bodies.

5. **Safety Audit Standard for Adventure Activities.** Standards for adventure safety set in place by WorkSafe New Zealand, the primary workplace health and safety regulator in New Zealand.

6. **Standards for Industry Practice.** Outdoor safety standards for Singapore developed by that country's Outdoor Learning and Adventure Education Association.

7. **ISO 21101, 21102, and 21103.** International standards on adventure tourism safety management, personnel and participants. ISO standards also exist for specific outdoor activities such as scuba diving, snorkeling, and ropes course facilities & equipment.

8. **ABNT 15334 - Adventure tourism - Safety management system Requirements for auditing skills.** One of a set of 32 Brazilian adventure tourism safety standards developed by the Brazilian government and the Brazilian Association of Ecotourism and Adventure Tourism Companies (ABETA), published by the Brazilian Association of Technical Standards (ABNT), covering a variety of outdoor activities and topics.

9. **ISO 31000 - Risk management – Guidelines** and the related standard IEC 31010 Risk management – Risk assessment techniques can provide a useful process framework for developing risk management systems (for any activity), especially for larger institutions. (The Australian Adventure Activity Standards, for example, were written to comply with ISO 31000.)

Figure 3.2. Outdoor Learning and Adventure Education Association standards (Singapore).

Example Activity-Specific Standards from Activity-Specific Entities. Numerous national-level industry associations (in the UK and Ireland known as National Governing Bodies, and in Australia as peak bodies) and a variety of other standards-setting bodies publish standards specific to particular outdoor activities. A selection follows.

1. **Canoeing and Kayaking.** British Canoeing, American Canoe Association, Paddle Australia, and others publish skills standards for participation in boating activities at various levels.

2. **Mountaineering and Climbing.** The International Climbing and Mountaineering Federation, International Federation of Mountain Guides Associations, and their member organizations, along with national level entities such as Mountain Training UK and the Australian Climbing Instructors Association, have established standards for climbing and mountaineering activities.

3. **Ropes Course/Challenge Course.** Standards include EN 15567 Ropes course requirements (Europe), ABNT 15508 High ropes courses (Brazil), and ANSI/ACCT 03-2016 Challenge Courses and Canopy/Zip line Tours Standards (USA, figure 3.3).

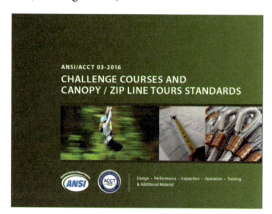

Figure 3.3. ANSI-ACCT 03-2016 Challenge Courses and Canopy/Zip line Tours Standards.

Medical Standards. Organizations set standards for first aid and initial medical response appropriate to the outdoor context, where delayed or prolonged transport, limited or improvised equipment, and extreme environments may be encountered. These standards may be designed for national or multi-national use. Standards may cover how many hours of medical training are required for certain outdoor leader positions, or what medical skills and knowledge the leaders should have. Specific procedures and medications to be used may also be part of these standards. Standards for outdoor or wilderness medicine are evolving. Three examples are provided below.

1. The Wilderness Medical Society publishes Practice Guidelines information regarding wilderness emergency care in its journal Wilderness & Environmental Medicine.
2. The Wilderness Medicine Educators Collaborative has developed Scope of Practice documents for Wilderness First Aid and Wilderness First Responder training courses, both published by the Wilderness Medical Society.
3. The Icelandic Directorate of Health has published wilderness medicine protocols, prepared by the country's national search and rescue organization, for persons certified at the Wilderness First Responder level, using medications and procedures appropriate for the Icelandic environment.

Unpublished Standards. Widely used professional practices, even if not written down, serve as de facto standards. Outdoor organizations are judged against the behavior of reputable outdoor programs operating in similar settings. It is therefore important to understand the practices of high-quality outdoor programs against which yours might be compared. The procedures employed by these other outdoor programs can be established by good networking and conducting appropriate research.

Very large organizations that may have numerous chapters or other subdivisions and many thousands or millions of members or participants may develop and internally publish standards as well.

3.2.4.   Finding Standards that Apply to Your Program

In some situations, identifying applicable standards is relatively straightforward. This may be the case in countries or other regions with established outdoor adventure legislation. It can also be true when authoritative industry bodies (such as an outdoor association, national governing body, or the equivalent) has published standards-related information for specific outdoor activities like mountaineering or canoeing.

It can be a challenge to identify which standards an organization should work to meet, however, in the absence of such unified agreement. This is particularly true when there are multiple sets of standards that could be employed, especially when they have conflicting provisions. In addition, in some cases, standards exist but are not widely known or adopted either within or outside the outdoor industry.

Guidance on identifying relevant standards may be found by when individuals:

1. Network with staff from other outdoor organizations
2. Join industry groups, or attend relevant conferences and similar gatherings
3. Hold safety inspections and risk management reviews by qualified external entities
4. Read industry literature and media
5. Research guidance from relevant government agencies
6. Seek information from insurance agents, legal advisors, risk management committee members, staff, and clients

3.2.5.   Institutional Standards versus Personal Behavior

Expectations for the management of risk are different when one is working for an outdoor program as opposed to having outdoor adventures on one's personal time. Organizations have an obligation to exercise reasonable duty of care for participants (and staff), whereas an individual is generally free to engage in riskier behavior as long as it does not pose an unreasonable risk of harm to others.

It's therefore important for activity leaders to be clear that even though they might not wear a helmet while rock climbing, whitewater paddling or bicycling on their own or with friends, they must do so as part of good professional practice when leading these activities for an organization. An experienced rock climber might feel personally comfortable not being clipped in when less than a body's length from the perceived edge of a cliff. They might even resist admonitions to attach their harness to an anchor, asserting that they feel fine about the risk they're taking. However, in an organizational environment, they—and their participants—should be safely clipped to an anchor when close to the cliff edge.

3.3. USING STANDARDS

Standards are useful only when they are used, and most effective when their application is enmeshed deeply in all aspects of the organization.

These areas include:

1. **Internal program development**. This includes crafting training curricula, program policies and procedures, internal safety checklists, safety briefings, job descriptions, promotion criteria, incident reporting documentation, emergency plans, safety culture surveys, gear management regimes, transportation systems, and more.
2. **Selection of new activities and activity areas**. This includes the generation of New Element Readiness Assessment documents.
3. **Risk transfer**. This includes instruments such as informed consent forms. It also includes sales and marketing materials, which should provide accurate information about program risks and their management.
4. **Risk management and incident reviews**. This includes internal risk management reviews conducted in-house, external risk management reviews led by outside experts, and incident reviews following major loss.

3.4. LIMITATIONS

The contemporary application of standards to outdoor programming has limitations, both for outdoor organizations and customers of outdoor programs.

3.4.1. Limitations for Outdoor Programs

1. *Lack of established, widely adopted standards.* Standards are actively evolving in many parts of the world and in the outdoor industry. There are some national-level standards and legislation, and well-established standards in the EU and elsewhere regarding equipment manufacture. Overall, however—with a few notable exceptions—there is little in the way of definitively settled, well-established standards that are globally accepted, widely complied with, published, and maintained by a credible institution.

2. *Inadequate standards.* Standards may not be complete, well-crafted, up-to-date, or

sufficient. Some standards are thoughtfully developed by skilled standards-developing entities in a deliberative consensus process, with a system for periodic review and update, and are of excellent quality. However, this is not always the case.

In addition, some standards that intend to be comprehensive tend to focus on tangible issues such as staff training and equipment care, but are not robustly developed for systemic and psychological issues such as assessing and maintaining a culture of safety.

3. *Professional judgment still required.* Standards are widely accepted practices. They might be minimum expectations or, at the other end of the spectrum, best practices. The standards you apply to your activities might be higher than those of common practices. In rare circumstances it will be defensible to adhere to a lower standard. In all cases, the interpretation of standards, which often have an element of subjectivity, requires judgment on the part of the outdoor program staff.

4. *Limited portability.* Standards may not be usable universally. What works in one country or region may not in another—a requirement for seatbelt use or a procedure about helicopter evacuation may not apply in a country or region where vehicles typically lack seatbelts or helicopters are unavailable. Medications permitted in one country can lead to imprisonment or deportation in another.

5. *No guarantee of safety.* Adhering closely to well-developed standards does not eliminate the possibility of loss. Standards help keep risk and loss at socially acceptable levels; they don't eliminate them. Some risks are inherent, like slipping and falling while hiking, or being buried by an avalanche while traveling in avalanche terrain. It may not ever be possible to eliminate human error.

6. *Limited protection.* Adhering to standards may not protect you or your organization from liability. If a standard you followed is found to be insufficient, as has occurred in the past, you may be held liable for losses.

3.4.2. Limitations for Consumers.

Those considering enrollment in an outdoor program that states its conformity to certain standards should keep in mind a couple limits to that claim, as below.

1. *Impermanence.* An organization that meets standards today may not meet them tomorrow.

2. *Lack of adherence.* Existing standards may not be adhered to, even if conformity is mandatory or the organization states it is in compliance with the standard. Even when the organization makes sincere attempts to comply with standards, unfailing compliance may not occur.

   In addition, third-party verification of compliance with standards can be of varying rigor, or be absent entirely. And enforcement of adherence to mandatory standards such as legislation regulating outdoor adventures may not evenly occur.

3.5. CONCLUSION

The development of standards applicable to outdoor programs represents a powerful tool for appropriately managing risk and helping ensure that out-of-door experiences are positive and successful experiences for participants. Although the world of outdoor program standards is still evolving, many existing standards offer valuable guidance.

Outdoor organizations should carefully research what standards may apply to them, put careful thought to interpreting relevant standards for their situation, and take reasonable steps to ensure standards are regularly and fully met. When combined with other elements of a comprehensive risk management system, the consistent application of appropriate standards can be extremely valuable in helping an outdoor program meet its safety and programmatic goals.

Chapter Summary

1. Standards are widely accepted professional practices.

2. Standards compliance may be voluntary or mandatory.

3. Standards can guide an organization in providing quality outdoor programs.

4. Compliance with mandatory and voluntary standards can demonstrate meeting the duty to care, and reduce exposure to legal penalties.

5. A wide and sometimes confusing variety of standards, in varying levels of quality, exists.

6. Some outdoor standards apply to specific jurisdictions like a country, province, or state.

7. Standards can be relatively comprehensive, or apply specifically to particular activities, staff, equipment, or participant types.

8. Standards can be located in laws and in publications by accrediting bodies, outdoor industry groups, and standards organizations.

9. Typical behavior of outdoor organizations can be considered an unpublished standard, against which others may be judged.

10. To identify standards applicable to your organization, consult other outdoor programs, industry groups, government agencies, your insurance agent, and legal advisors. Conferences, safety inspections, risk management reviews, industry media, staff and clients can also provide useful information.

11. When working professionally, a staff person should meet high risk management standards, even if they personally choose not to during their free time.

12. The applications of standards should be suffused throughout all aspects of the organization.

13. Standards have limitations; for example, they may not be up-to-date, high quality, or comprehensive, and application of standards may be uneven.

14. Despite limitations, standards offer a powerful and valuable tool for managing risk and providing excellence in outdoor programming.

CHAPTER 4

LEGAL CONSIDERATIONS

LEARNING OBJECTIVES
1. Laws regarding outdoor program risk management
2. Legal requirements from executive, legislative and judicial branches of governments
3. Laws in comparison to voluntary standards
4. Consulting legal experts for relevant specific legal advice
5. National and sub-national laws pertaining to outdoor safety
6. Laws pertaining to specific outdoor activities
7. Duty of care and other general legal requirements
8. Limitations of legal frameworks
9. The need for evidence of legal compliance
10. Approaches for keeping aware of changes in legal landscape

4.1. INTRODUCTION

Laws concerning outdoor safety have been established by a variety of government authorities. When well crafted, they help protect the well-being of participants and carefully balance the benefits with costs of compliance. These legal requirements are enforced by penalties such as fines, loss of operating license, and imprisonment. Outdoor programs should be aware of and comply with the legal obligations that apply to them.

It is straightforward to recognize that when an outdoor program understands and conforms with the laws relevant to their operations, potential legal problems are minimized.

4.1.1. Types of Legal Requirements

Legal frameworks vary widely from jurisdiction to jurisdiction. For instance, in some countries, persons are considered innocent until proven guilty; elsewhere, the opposite is the case, or neither is true.

In settings where a legislature, judiciary, and executive branch of government exist, legal requirements can generally be set by any of the three branches. Legislatures pass laws, also known in some situations as statutes or ordinances. The judiciary interprets law, in the process establishing legally binding "case law." Executive branches establish regulations, also known in some circumstances as rules, codes, or "administrative law," which have the force of law. Accordingly, outdoor programs should be aware of applicable legal requirements that originate in any branch of government.

In this text the term "law" refers to legal requirements generated by any legally authoritative body, including those from legislative, judicial, or executive branches of government.

4.1.2. Comparison with Standards

Laws establish mandatory standards to which an organization and its staff are held. Voluntary standards, discussed in Chapter 3, also set expectations for accepted behavior. As a general rule, compliance with both legally required and well-developed voluntary standards is good idea.

4.1.3. Chapter Limitations

Several limitations to this discussion of legal considerations should be clear.

There are a wide variety of laws applicable to outdoor programs. We will only discuss a small and incomplete sample of them here. It is the responsibility of the outdoor program to determine which laws apply to them.

The legal requirements discussed in this chapter may or may not pertain to your situation. In addition, laws are regularly revised or replaced, so what is described here may not be up to date.

This chapter does not provide legal advice. You should consult qualified legal specialists familiar with your organization and its activities, and the jurisdictions that pertain to your program, for advice applicable to your situation.

4.2. LAWS PERTAINING TO OUTDOOR PROGRAMS

4.2.1. National Laws Specific to Outdoor and Adventure Activities

Many countries do not have national-level laws specific to outdoor and adventure activities. Some countries, generally higher-income nations with either a history of well-publicized outdoor tragedies or an economy based in part on outdoor or adventure tourism, have created such a legal framework. Following are three examples.

In the United Kingdom, the Activity Centres (Young Persons' Safety) Act 1995 requires certain adventure providers to meet safety standards. The Adventure Activities Licensing Authority (Figure 4.1) oversees inspections and issues licenses to approved providers.

Figure 4.1. Adventure Activities Licensing Authority of the United Kingdom.

In Switzerland, under the Federal Act on Mountain Guides and Organisers of Other High-Risk Activities, mountain guides and leaders of other high-risk activities must be suitably trained and licensed, and follow other requirements. Businesses conducting these activities must also be licensed and safety-certified. (Individual cantons in Switzerland also have their own requirements.)

New Zealand's Health and Safety at Work (Adventure Activities) Regulations provide extensive regulation of adventure programming, including on topics such as audits, risk management planning, and safety standards.

When these laws are comprehensive; rigorous; thoughtfully crafted with industry, public, and governmental input, and updated in an inclusive continuous improvement process, they provide an outstanding structure to improve safety outcomes and strengthen the outdoor industry overall.

4.2.2. Laws Pertaining to Specific Outdoor Activities or Sub-National Regions

Some countries or sub-divisions (such as states or provinces) regulate certain outdoor activities. Maritime authorities such as coast guard agencies regulate aspects of sailing safety. Civil aviation authorities regulate airborne activities like paragliding. Health or other government agencies regulate the possession and use of certain medications (see Chapter 8, Equipment.) A selection of specific examples follows.

The U.S. states of California, Washington, New York and others have regulations affecting challenge courses, ziplines, and climbing walls.

Decree 56/2003 in the Spanish region of Catalonia regulates the safety of outdoor activities, including participant screening, informed consent, staff qualifications, and emergency planning.

Commercial wilderness operators in Yukon, Canada must be licensed and fulfill certain safety, incident reporting, and first aid requirements.

The Department of Education and Training of the State Government of Victoria, Australia publishes mandatory safety guidelines for school-based outdoor education adventure activities, camps, and overnight excursions in the state.

4.2.3. General Legal Requirements

Duty of Care. Although legal requirements vary greatly from location to location, a common concept is the duty of care to participants in outdoor activities. This generally means that an organization must take reasonable precautions against a foreseeable harm. This can include conducting risk assessments, selecting activities and screening participants appropriately, having properly trained staff and suitable equipment, providing appropriate instruction and supervision, and the like. Organizations may not be held liable for risks inherent to the activity.

What is a "reasonable precaution?" This is where outdoor safety standards—legally mandated or voluntary, written or unwritten—come into play. A reasonable precaution may be construed as what a reasonably prudent person in a similar situation would do. In many cases, a reasonably prudent person would be expected to adhere to commonly accepted professional practices or industry standards.

This means that although voluntary industry standards are just that—voluntary—they may also be looked at to assess if a person has breached their legal duty of care.

In some legal contexts, a person can be found guilty of negligence if:
1) There was a duty of care
2) There was a breach of that duty—by doing something they should not, or failing to do something they should
3) There were damages (loss), physical or other
4) The damages were caused by the breach of duty

A person found guilty of negligence can be liable for losses and face other penalties.

Risk Transfer. A variety of laws pertain to risk transfer topics such as indemnification, release of liability, and informed consent. See Chapter 13, Risk Transfer, for further information.

Other. There are many other areas of law that may apply to outdoor programs. These include, but are not limited to, occupational safety and health, building codes and safety of premises, transportation and vehicle operations, taxation, equipment manufacture, providing medical and nonmedical emergency care, discrimination, harassment, abuse, human rights, and child protection. In addition, operations of outdoor organizations may be regulated under laws regarding amusement devices; accident compensation; hazardous substances; maritime safety; civil aviation; crimes; food; liquor, tobacco, and drugs; environmental protection and access, and products and trade, among others.

Although unlikely to apply to most outdoor programs, legally binding international law such as applicable treaties, international human rights and labor laws, and the law of the sea may apply.

Outdoor organizations active in multiple jurisdictions should understand the relevant laws applicable in each jurisdiction. In international contexts, research through embassies, legal specialists with local knowledge, or other sources may be helpful.

THE DANGER OF STOPPING TO HELP SOMEONE IN NEED

In 2006, Peng Yu, a 26-year old student in Nanjing China, came to the aid of a 65-year old woman who had fallen at a bus stop. He helped her get up and accompanied her to a hospital. Later, the woman and her family sued the student, claiming he had knocked her down and caused her to break her leg.

The court agreed, saying that no-one would help someone else unless they felt guilty, and so according to common sense, he must have been responsible. Peng Yu was forced to pay over 45,000 yuan (more than $6,700 USD), covering much of her medical expenses.

As a result of the court's decision, Chinese citizens became less likely to help others in need. This led to injured persons dying on the street as others simply walked around them, afraid to provide assistance. In an effort to encourage bystanders to give aid, in 2017 China passed a 'Good Samaritan' law. The law provides protections from civil liability to those who voluntarily give emergency assistance to persons in need.

Elsewhere in the region, however, similar protective legislation does not exist, and stopping to give care continues to carry the presumption of guilt.

Legislation varies around the globe. In some areas of the world, it is a legal requirement to assist. Different versions of 'Good Samaritan' legislation provide varying levels of protection to those who stop to help.

4.3. LIMITATIONS

A few points of caution on limitations regarding laws affecting outdoor programs are in order.

Laws that focus on mechanical aspects of outdoor safety such as skills training, environmental hazard assessment, and equipment management may not completely address all risks if they neglect to pay attention to the sometimes subtle psychological aspects of safety culture. The best rules are of little use if the organizational culture does not support adherence to them.

Laws—including their content, presence or absence, and enforcement—show extreme variance between jurisdictions. Depending on your circumstances, the topics discussed in this chapter may or may not apply to your situation, and additional legal parameters not discussed here may affect your outdoor program.

In areas of the world where application of rule of law is inconsistent, other factors besides strict legal compliance may have an effect on your outdoor program and staff.

4.4. EVIDENCE OF COMPLIANCE

It's often not enough to have complied with the letter and spirit of the law. Evidence sufficient to demonstrate that compliance should be available. Documentation, as discussed in Chapter 21, is one way to establish this evidence.

4.5. STAYING CURRENT WITH LEGAL CHANGES

Laws are regularly changed, repealed, replaced, or otherwise modified. This applies to legislation, executive branch regulation, and judicial case law. Staying abreast of changes in the legal landscape helps an organization maintain a high level of risk management.

Approaches for staying up to date in a dynamic legal environment include:

1. Consult regularly with your lawyer. It can be useful to engage a number of legal advisors with special expertise in areas such as contract law, waivers and related instruments, or litigation defense, as necessary. Some lawyers specialize in outdoor law.

2. Seek out information from industry conferences, media, and credible people in your network.
3. Stay connected with local industry groups. For example, the New Zealand Mountain Safety Council provides general guidance about legal requirements for New Zealand in its Mountain Safety Manual 38. Organizations supporting small businesses and non-for-profits may also have useful general legal guidance.
4. Solicit information from inspectors, safety reviewers, insurance agents, and outdoor safety consultants.
5. Read the text of legislation. Contacting government representatives can provide useful interpretation and guidance.

4.6. CONCLUSION

We began this chapter by noting that well-crafted laws are designed to support the safety and well-being of people. This is a reasonable approach. We can then understand that when we demonstrably take reasonable steps to anticipate and manage risks in line with relevant standards, as would a prudent person in a similar situation, then our risk of incurring legal liability is low—and the probability of providing positive outdoor experiences for customers is commensurately high.

The legal context can seem complex. In essence, however, the law is designed to encourage us to do the right thing, as defined by society—in the outdoor context, by appropriately anticipating and reducing risks, typically in line with widely accepted professional practices.

When you sincerely act in the best interests of your participants, staff, and others; aim your efforts to meet established industry standards, and document or otherwise demonstrate your adherence to relevant laws and standards, you are taking important steps to meet your legal obligations and appropriately manage outdoor risks.

Chapter Summary

1. Laws regarding outdoor safety have been developed to protect persons from harm, and should be complied with.

2. Legal frameworks vary widely in different jurisdictions.

3. Law can be established by legislative, executive and judicial branches of government.

4. Compliance with laws is mandatory; compliance with voluntary standards is recommended but not necessarily required.

5. Organizations should determine what laws apply to them, and seek their own qualified legal advice.

6. National laws about outdoor safety exist in places such as the UK, Switzerland, and New Zealand, and provide significant value.

7. States, provinces and other regions have outdoor risk management laws.

8. Specific activities such as sailing, paragliding, and mountaineering are regulated by laws.

9. In many areas, the legal duty of care for others exists; a breach can result in a charge of negligence.

10. Laws regarding occupational safety, buildings, transportation, finance, equipment, discrimination, child protection and more may apply to outdoor programs.

11. Legal requirements may be incomplete if they do not include a focus on safety culture.

12. In places with inconsistent rule of law, factors other than legal compliance may influence liability.

13. It is important to have evidence of conformity with legal requirements.

14. Stay current with changes in law through research, networking, and consultation.

15. Make verifiable, good-faith, well-informed efforts to manage risks to socially acceptable levels, and safety and liability outcomes are likely to be positive.

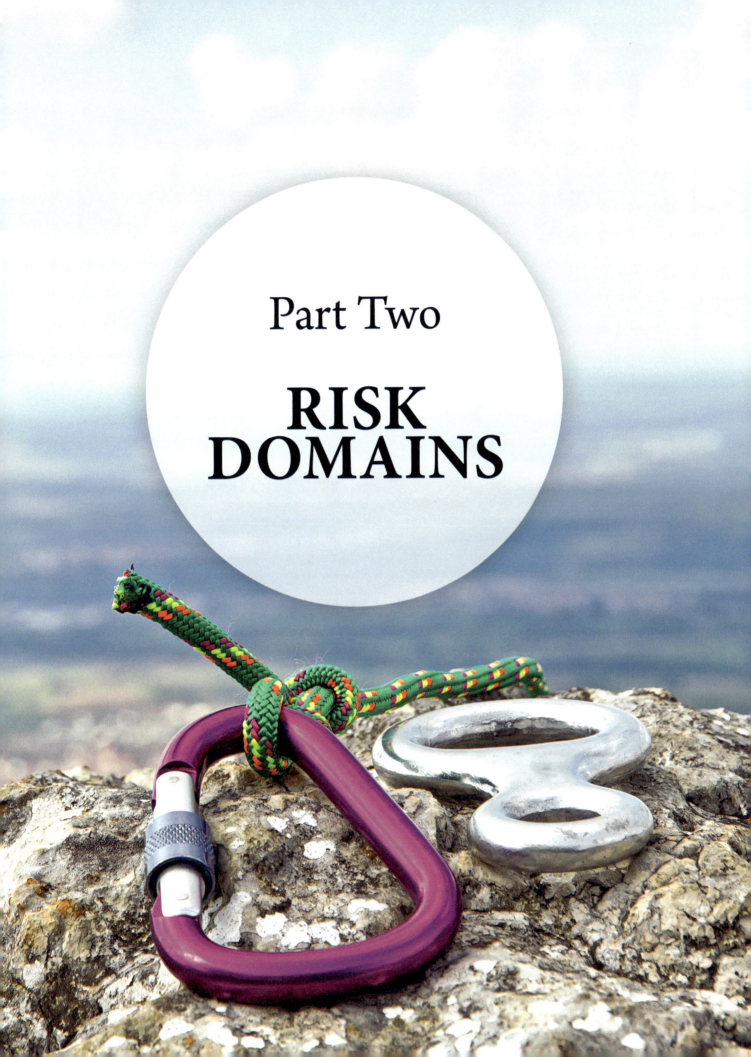

Part Two

RISK DOMAINS

CHAPTER 5

CULTURE

LEARNING OBJECTIVES

1. The importance and benefits of a culture of safety
2. The definition and elements of safety culture
3. Safety culture characteristics unique to outdoor programs
4. Steps for establishing and maintaining a culture of safety
5. Integrated safety culture
6. Safety culture surveys
7. Just culture
8. Additional resources
9. Challenges of change management

The storm moved in quickly, fierce winds lashing tree tops, and sheets of rain pouring from the sky. Trees began toppling in enormous numbers, creating a dense thicket of downed trunks across the trail. One group of students who were huddled under a tree for protection moved to a more sheltered spot, and moments later a tree crashed down right where they had been crouching. Lightning bolts repeatedly struck trees, rocks, anything tall. Flash—BOOM! Flash—BOOM! The group of teens had been traveling through the wilderness for weeks, but this weather was harsher than anything they'd seen before.

The group's trip leaders were camped about a minute's walk away from the student group, leaving the students room to show their independence with camping and wilderness travel skills. As the storm eased, a couple of students walked over to the trip leader's campsite to ask them a question. Both leaders were down on the ground—one moaning, the other not moving. They had been seated on a large rock by the lakeshore, watching the storm, and were hit by lightning. As one trip leader recovered, he helped the students perform CPR on his partner, but to no avail. The body was airlifted out, and the deceased leader's fiancée, who was leading a group nearby, was airlifted out of the wilderness as well.

The initial reports from the outdoor program's administration stated that the bolt of lightning that killed the trip leader

came out of the clear blue sky, from a distant cloud far away. The death was a freak accident—an "act of God"—that no one could have predicted.

The following season, though, the message had changed. A lightning safety group that tracks individual lightning strikes had analyzed the storm and probable time of death, and concluded that the origin of the lightning bolt that killed the trip leader had actually been nearby. It was so close that the trip leaders should have been in a safer location in "lightning drill" formation protecting themselves from the lightning. But they weren't, and the surviving trip leader—who was the supervising leader—was blamed for not following safety rules and causing his assistant's death.

The following season the message changed again. The senior trip leader had not followed the rules, true: but the culture of the program division (at-risk youth) he worked for was known for a certain rebelliousness and disregard for rules. For instance, staff took illegal drugs while in staff housing; this was known and tolerated by administration. Breaking workplace rules was a norm, tacitly approved by management. As the thought process of the organization matured, then, it became clear that blame should not fall on freak weather, or an instructor fault, but that a major cause of the fatality was an issue of corporate culture.

5.1. INTRODUCTION

When we consider outdoor safety, we often think about environmental hazards such as lightning, snake bites, and avalanches. We don't often consider another important influence on outdoor safety: the organizational culture.

However, organizational culture can have a profound impact on successful safety outcomes. The UK's Health and Safety Executive notes that an organisation's culture can have as big an influence on safety outcomes as the organization's safety management system.

5.1.1. What is a Safety Culture?

What is Culture? *Culture* is an integrated pattern of individual and organizational behavior, based upon shared beliefs and values.

Beliefs are things that are accepted as true: for example, "I won't get punished if I speak up about a safety problem."

Values are what are prized: for example, "safety is important."

Behaviors, in the context of culture, are the traditions, rituals and practices that spring from beliefs and values. Examples include following safety procedures, speaking up about safety issues, or organizing an annual disaster drill.

Visible and Invisible Elements of Culture. Behaviors spring from beliefs and values. Behaviors are visible, while we don't see another's beliefs and values. Just as vegetation is brought to life from the interplay of roots and soil underground, the safety behaviors we see spring from the values and beliefs we don't. Strong safety performance ultimately grows from the values and beliefs of a healthy safety culture (see Figure 5.1).

Actions— like leaves and stems, visible

Values and beliefs— like the soil and roots, invisible.

Figure 5.1. Actions, which we see, spring from values and beliefs, which are not visible.

Beliefs and values may not be hidden only to external observers. Just as there can be unconscious bias with regards to sexism, racism, ageism, or other prejudices, employees may not be consciously aware of, for example, their beliefs and values prioritizing production and short-term financial performance over safety.

Safety Culture. Safety culture is the influence of organisational culture on safety. More specifically, safety culture is the values, beliefs and behaviors that affect the extent to which safety is emphasized over competing goals.

As this definition emphasizes, safety is only one of multiple legitimate organizational goals. The safety culture directs how much emphasis is given to safety as opposed to other important—and interlinked— priorities such as financial sustainability, organizational growth, and workplace equity and inclusion.

Therefore, a safety culture sets the conditions so that the organization can manage risks to appropriate standards, and with socially acceptable outcomes. This means that the organization should neither de-emphasize safety such that there are unacceptable losses, nor over-emphasize safety such that the organization is immobilized.

The role of a "safety culture" in preventing accidents came to prominence following the deadly explosion in April 1986 at the Chernobyl nuclear power plant in what was then the USSR. Investigators concluded a safety culture must be created and maintained in order to maintain safety and prevent future catastrophes.

5.1.2. Why Safety Culture Is Important

When stakeholders in an organization have the beliefs and values and show the behaviors commensurate with a healthy safety culture, many benefits follow.

An appropriate safety culture leads to fewer losses: fewer injuries, illnesses, instances of property damage and deaths. These are desirable aims in their own right. They also have business implications: when serious accidents have occurred, outdoor organizations have faced loss of reputation, confronted loss of business, and been forced to close down completely. In some cases, outdoor program managers have been jailed. A strong safety culture makes these outcomes less likely.

The right attention to safety management also provides employees an opportunity to lead a professional life aligned with moral values. This is a good thing in itself, and is a sign of a desirable workplace that employees can be proud to be a part of. Improved employee engagement, productivity and retention may then follow.

These effects can increase the probability of an organization enjoying long-term success.

5.1.3. Safety Culture in the Outdoor Program Context

Outdoor adventure programs, by their very nature, generally involve intentionally exposing participants and staff to risk. We can't seek to eliminate all risk, then, but simply manage it to appropriate standards.

Prospective outdoor adventure program participants may intentionally seek out programs with higher risks, in order to gain the benefits of adventure. Marketers may promote programs with higher inherent risk, figuring that a white-water boating or alpine mountaineering program is more exciting and more likely to sell than a campout in the local park.

And activity leaders may use the workplace to seek out personal challenges, tempting them to take on risks perhaps suited for their advanced skills but beyond participant capacities to handle safely. Many outdoor leaders are young people, no older than their 20's, who by the nature of their stage in brain development seek more and greater risks than do more mature persons.

And with some outdoor activities, such as mountaineering, a macho culture of peak-bagging and mountain-conquering may exist, exacerbating the already greater inherent risks of technical alpine travel.

Those working to influence safety culture in outdoor programs, then, would be wise to be aware of these potential dynamics.

Traditional Masculinity Ideology

In some cultures, the expression of traditional masculinity ideology can lead to increased risk. The American Psychological Association (APA) notes that these cultural values, which include adventure and risk, also lead to suppression of emotions. According to the APA, research indicates that the rigid suppression of emotions is linked to increased negative risk-taking. The World Health Organization also links traditional masculinity and risk-taking. Acculturation to not ask for help, and to not express doubt or confusion, may additionally lead to increased risk. This "toxic masculinity" may not just be present in high-adventure outdoor activities such as mountaineering, but in many settings.

5.2. CHANGING CULTURE

In order to foster an appropriate culture of safety, one has to shift behaviors to ones associated a healthy safety culture. In order to shift behaviors, the beliefs and values of those involved must be suitably aligned with safety aims. How, then, does one going about changing values? In our case, we might ask, how do we increase the amount safety is valued?

Influencing how much safety is held as an organizational value follows the same change management process as influencing any other organizational value: financial performance, innovation, product quality, growth, or equity and inclusion.

Since every organization has a different organizational culture and business environment, there is no one right way for all organizations to go about developing an appropriate safety culture. However, general principles for project management and change management exist. And established standards exist for behaviors, business structures, and ways of thinking that can inform the trajectory of an organization's change process.

It's also useful to remember that an organization doesn't have one safety culture. Instead, multiple safety cultures exist—in different departments, in different levels of the organization's hierarchy, among different demographic groups (for example age or national origin). This diversity should be accounted for when assessing where interventions are most needed.

5.2.1. Articulate Values

Establishment of a safety culture starts with unambiguous and repeated messages from the organization's top leadership that safety is an important value.

Such statements can come in many forms. The importance of safety should be incorporated into the organization's business plan, strategic plans, and risk management plan. It may be a part of the organization's formal mission, vision and values statements. It should be evident in the risk management mission statement that is a part of the organization's risk management plan. It can be stated in company-wide and departmental meetings, announcements, newsletters, and other media.

In order for the messages to have credibility, they must come from the uppermost levels of the organizational hierarchy, such as the CEO and the Board of Directors or equivalent.

It's important to explain why safety is an important organizational priority. Values adoption occurs when individuals examine the value and make a decision to adopt it; it cannot be forced.

5.2.2. Establish Expected Behaviors

After articulating the values expected of staff, the expected behaviors springing from those values are outlined. Behavior expectations are in three categories: policies and procedures, systems and structures, and proactive, dynamic risk management.

Policies and Procedures. Individuals should be directed to follow established policies and procedures. This represents "rules-based safety," as opposed to "managed safety," discussed below; a balanced presence of both is important for an integrated safety culture. For instance, climbers and belayers should be instructed to wear helmets at a climbing site.

Policies and procedures should be comprehensive. However, permitting procedures to not be followed if that is judged to be the safer option (as explained in Chapter, 2, Approaches to Risk Management) helps reduce the risk of creating a compliance culture where safety is reduced to checking boxes rather than thinking independently and using the presence, judgment and initiative of staff to anticipate and deal with unexpected risks.

Many written policies and procedures in outdoor programs are focused directly on outdoor activities—requiring harness double-checks before climbing, for example, or covering incident reporting. However, managerial procedures have an important impact on risk management and should be considered as well. For example, a protocol stating that the sales department cannot sell a group program within, for example, 30 days of the program start without an ok from the staffing department to ensure sufficient staff will be available, helps manage staffing-related risk.

Systems and Structures. This includes the systems in Part III of this book, Risk Management Structures, such as incident reporting, incident reviews, Risk Management Committee, medical screening, risk management reviews, and accreditation. Structures to manage the risks in Part II, Risk Domains, such as subcontractor assessment and equipment management, are also included here.

The expectation should be that these systems and structures are in place, fully implemented, and working

as intended. For instance, with respect to safety issues and incident reporting, it should be expected that:

1. Staff and participants are encouraged to raise safety issues.
2. Issues are promptly reviewed and prioritized.
3. Issues are appropriately resolved.
4. Information about the issue and its resolution is provided to those who raised it and others as appropriate.

Human Resources. Safety performance expectations should be woven throughout Human Resources systems and structures such as hiring advertisements, job descriptions, performance evaluations, promotion criteria, compensation increase criteria, and discipline procedures. In addition, excellence in risk management should be an element in informal recognition systems such as awards and public recognition. Human resources systems should include clear accountability for safety, for the organization as a whole and in each unit. Clear requirements for staff competencies, and contingency plans for backup staff capacity, reduce the probability of poorly trained last-minute hires or "field promotions" leading to unqualified staff in the field. A key element of safety culture in Human Resources is the establishment and maintenance of just culture, outlined later in this chapter.

Mission Integrity. New Element Readiness Assessments, program-level strategic plans, and other necessary tools should be employed to ensure that programs and activities offered stay within the core competencies of the organization. In some settings it can be tempting for the scope of activities to creep outside the boundaries of what the staff and organization are well-qualified to do, in a search for more revenue.

Participants. Communications to participants before program commencement (such as required equipment and training requirements) and during programs (such as safety briefings (figure 5.2), foot checks for blisters, and debriefs) make it clear to participants that safety is a priority. Participant feedback provided during the program, and formally collected at program end, does so as well.

Figure 5.2. Safety briefings before activities reinforce a culture of safety. Here, a safety briefing before rafting a whitewater rapids in Nepal.

Judgment and Managed Safety. Field staff should be encouraged to use their judgment to make safety-related decisions, within appropriate boundaries. This means that operating procedures should generally be followed, but do not have to be, if that is reasonably considered safer. This flexible construction of procedures is intended to create a balance between "rule-based safety" and "managed safety." An integrated safety culture (Figure 5.3, below) strikes this balance, and promotes proactive and dynamic risk management on the part of field staff. This represents decentralized risk management, rather than a top-control model that can falsely give the illusion of control over risk.

Avoiding a compliance culture where risk management is diminished to unthinkingly following rigid rules is particularly important where there is significant risk, and the environment is not under staff's control and can change quickly. Mountaineering in avalanche terrain is an example of this situation. Here, more weight should be given to judgment and taking initiative to identify and respond to risks, and less to compliance to a long list of safety rules.

Extreme amounts of filling out paperwork and completing checklists can lead to a compliance culture in which individuals don't think for themselves or take the initiative to dynamically assess and manage risk. But some documentation is essential, so an appropriate balance must be found.

Integrated Safety Culture

Figure 5.3. An integrated safety culture skillfully balances rules-based safety and managed safety.

5.2.3. Establish Expected Ways of Thinking

Risk assessment spreadsheets and safety checklists, unless used skillfully, or constrained to limited contexts such as evaluating discrete activities or activity areas, can lead to a focus on the obvious operational risks like boat capsizes and sharp knives in the camp kitchen. A broader view that captures a wider range of risks and accounts for their interrelated nature is found in a systems thinking approach to risks.

The most significant accidents—major catastrophes—are often the result of systemic breakdowns, and are hard to predict. This applies to outdoor incidents such as multiple-person fatalities on a boating trip, as well as industrial incidents like airplane or train crashes, nuclear power plant meltdowns, and acts of terror.

See Chapter 23, Seeing Systems, for more on systems thinking.

5.2.4. Invest Resources

Talk is cheap. No amount of rhetoric will make up for a risk management system starved of resources. Even in times of financial stress, the appropriate resource allocation to risk management must be protected.

Time and Attention. What people pay attention to is reflected in what they talk about, and the stories they tell. This shows up in a variety of ways.

1. **Meeting agendas**. Risk management is including in meetings at all levels of the organization: for example, Board meetings, senior leadership team meetings, planning retreats, management team meetings, all staff meetings, program briefings, and program debriefings. One metric used in safety culture assessment is: at Board meetings, time to discuss risk management is equal to or greater than time to discuss financial performance.
2. **Reports**. Risk management is included in reports about organizational performance: for example, annual reports, reports to the Board, reports to funders, and written end-of-program reports.
3. **General communications**. Risk management is presented in newsletters, reference materials made available to staff, posters and bulletin board materials, articles passed around for professional development, and elsewhere.
4. **Safety memos**. Safety memos go out to staff periodically, providing positive reminders about safety practices. A memo might include a case study or narrative of a recently occurring incident, discuss the incident, provide a reminder of important risk management principles, and conclude with an appreciation for staffs' attention to risk management and a positively-worded encouragement to continue efforts in the service of risk management excellence.

5. **Recognitions and celebrations**. When awards for performance are provided, at season-end celebrations, at all-staff meetings, and in similar settings, staff are recognized for superior risk management performance. This can be as formal as an official annual award, or a simple as a few words of recognition.

In addition, sufficient time to perform tasks without rushing or taking shortcuts should be provided. Situations with staff who are exhausted, harried, or overwhelmed are more likely to lead to incidents. Research indicates that stressed individuals tend to make riskier decisions. In addition to having sufficient time for program planning, leading activities, and transportation, activity staff require sufficient dedicated time to handle risk management responsibilities such as writing program-end reports, holding debriefs, and writing incident reports.

Funding. Financial resources sufficient to adequately manage risks—even when money is tight—must be provided. This includes funds for staff (including sufficient compensation and professional development to support good employee retention), training, and equipment. If an accident occurs, a defense of "we didn't have enough money" is ineffective.

Equipment. Safety, first aid, rescue and emergency gear and supplies must be available and in good condition. This includes safety-critical equipment such as vehicles, appropriate clothing and personal protective equipment. Chapter 8, Equipment, discusses details. If safety equipment—such as satellite phones or the next generation of emergency telecommunications technology—is available at a reasonable cost, it should be procured and appropriately maintained and used. Failure to properly purchase, maintain and employ reasonably available safety equipment can lead to charges of negligence.

Staff. All staff should have dedicated time for the management of risks. In larger organizations, this includes full-time positions such as a risk management officer, Vice President of Safety, or the like, and may include a separate department solely devoted to risk management. Organizations of any size should have a person designated as the risk management officer, if not solely then along with other duties. Medical screening staff should also be employed.

Field staff need appropriate training not just in technical skills, but in judgment, communication and decision-making. Board members, committee members and other volunteers should be supported in their safety-related training needs as well.

Investing in preferentially hiring activity leaders whose brain development with respect to risk management has more fully developed than with individuals in their teens or early 20's can be helpful. Establishing, tracking, and working towards employee retention goals can be useful as well.

See Chapter 7, Staff, for more on this topic.

5.2.5. De-incentivize Undesired Behaviors

Enforce behavior expectations by having negative consequences for conduct not commensurate with a culture of safety. This includes enforcing appropriate compliance with policies and procedures.

At one outdoor program, the logistics manager's driver training for activity leaders included a warning to not exceed the speed limit while driving. Asked if the logistics manager always obeyed the speed limit herself, she declined to answer affirmatively. This behavior does not support a culture of safe driving.

5.2.6. Incentivize Desired Behaviors

Here the positive consequences of doing the desired thing are enhanced to reinforce appropriate behaviors.

This includes ongoing communications and leadership by example from the organization's top leadership. Awards, recognition and celebrations of safety success, as discussed above, also have a positive effect. (Care should be taken to avoid perverse incentives, however, such as a goal of reducing incident rates leading to underreporting of safety incidents.)

Principles of social norms marketing can be effective in nudging individuals towards desired behavior. People generally want to do what they believe other people are doing, that is, what they consider to be "normal" or "typical" behavior. Sending messages about how most people are doing a certain pro-safety behavior can increase the rate at which message recipients exhibit that behavior.

5.2.7. Seek Continuous Improvement

An environment in which new and better ways of managing risk are constantly being sought, assessed, and implemented reinforces a culture of safety.

This can include reviewing promising new approaches and technologies, providing continuing education, and conducting surveys that solicit improvement ideas.

It also includes reviewing safety results—including incident report data, incident reviews, inspections, risk management reviews, debriefs, program reports, personnel evaluations, and program evaluations by staff and participants—and following up with improvement actions.

Managing for Continuous Improvement. The plan-do-check-act management method discussed in Chapter 2, Approaches to Risk Management, can also be applied to managing a continuous improvement process for any focus area, including safety culture.

Assessments of baseline status and improvements in safety culture can be done with a variety of tools. Similar to how a risk management review uses document analysis, interviews, and direct observation to assess overall risk management performance, those tools, along with survey instruments, can be used in assessing safety culture.

5.3. SURVEYS

Surveys are a common tool for evaluating the culture of safety. Staff at all levels of the organization, volunteers (including Board and Risk Management Committee members), contractors and participants can be asked about the espoused and lived safety-related values, along with related beliefs and behaviors, at the organization.

Survey instruments provide the most useful data when professionally designed by evaluation experts. Questionnaires and related survey instruments are best when they are both valid and reliable. Validity refers to the degree to which a measurement actually measures what it is intended to assess. Reliability indicates the extent to which the results obtained can be replicated.

Sample sizes, methods of administration, and statistical analysis of results are among other areas of survey design and administration that benefit from skilled expertise.

Surveys should ideally distinguish respondents from different departments and hierarchies of the organization, in order to uncover sub-cultures of safety present in the organization. However, appropriate confidentiality and anonymity should be retained in order to obtain the most candid feedback.

Although surveys developed, administered and processed by evaluation experts are optimal, in some cases simple questionnaires distributed to staff can provide useful information.

Survey instruments are often re-administered every 12 to 18 months to review progress.

5.3.1. Safety Culture Survey

Questionnaires are often organized as a series of questions covering certain topics. A response scale such as the following is often used:

1 – Never true
2 – Rarely true
3 – Sometimes true
4 – Almost always true
5 – Always true
0 – Unsure

A focus group can be used to develop themes and subjects for survey.

Since the needs of each organization differ, a complete survey is not provided here. Examples of topic areas and sample questions, however, are provided. For each topic area, multiple questions should be asked, dispersed throughout the questionnaire. To improve validity, some questions should be framed positively (where a response of 'true' indicates an appropriate safety culture), and others negatively.

Different surveys may be given to different organizational groups (such as Board members or activity leaders).

Sample Topics and Questions.

1. **Safety Mission And Vision**
   a. My organization's safety vision statement and aspirational end state are clear and consistently communicated.
   b. There is a good balance between safety and other organizational priorities.
   c. I don't know what our risk management mission statement says.

2. **Leadership Support**
   a. The words and actions of management with regards to safety are consistent.
   b. My organization's CEO and leadership team effectively build enthusiasm for and understanding of my organization's safety vision statement.
   c. My supervisor overlooks safety problems that happen over and over.
3. **Inclusion and Ownership**
   a. I am asked about safety improvement ideas.
   b. My ideas are valued and taken into consideration.
   c. If I don't act, I would feel responsible if something happened.
   d. My voice matters.
4. **Policies, Procedures, Structures and Systems**
   a. People follow safety policies and procedures when doing so is the safest course of action.
   b. Incidents and near misses are reported when they occur.
   c. Performance assessments and incentives for the organization's leadership include safety culture metrics and performance.
   d. The organisation strikes a balance between following the rules and thinking for one's self.
5. **Systems Thinking**
   a. We think about the interrelationships between different risks and other organizational elements.
   b. When an incident occurs, we look for root causes.
   c. If a mistake is made, we don't automatically blame the person, but examine our culture and practices.
6. **Sufficient Resources**
   a. I have enough time to get my job done.
   b. Staff have the risk management training they need.
   a. The equipment I have is suitable for good safety management.
   b. Staff receive education and review opportunities in safety culture.
   c. When time, money or other resources are tight, safety is never compromised.
7. **Culture of Questioning**
   a. I feel free to question the decisions or actions of those with more authority.
   b. I think about unexpected risks and how to adapt to them.
   c. Leaders are open to hearing new ideas about risk management.
   d. If I speak out, something will be done.
8. **Collaboration**
   a. Staff work together up and down the organizational hierarchy and across departments on safety issues.
   b. My department is in a silo and does not work closely with others on safety concerns.
   c. Different areas of the organization compete for safety-related resources and hoard information and other resources.
9. **Communication**
   a. I am given information about incidents and their follow-up.
   b. My organization has a program for recognition and celebration when individuals or teams excel at key safety behaviors and culture metrics.
   c. My supervisor recognizes others when they see a job done according to established safety procedures.
   d. Staff will freely speak up if they see a safety issue.
10. **Continuous Improvement**
    a. After we make changes to improve safety, we evaluate their effectiveness.
    b. The organization completes and reviews culture of safety surveys every 12 to 18 months and sees evidence of improvement.
    c. The organization makes continuous efforts to improve risk management.
    d. Incidents are used as learning tools to improve risk management.
11. **Just Culture**
    a. Speaking up about safety won't threaten my job.
    b. Individuals are not punished for raising safety issues or confronting supervisors about unsafe practices.
    c. Staff feel like their mistakes are held against them.
12. **Overall Appraisal of Safety Culture**
    a. The prevention of the most serious risks is a priority shared by all.
    b. Management provides a work climate that promotes safety.
    c. People here take safety seriously.
    d. I feel safe here.

5.4.   JUST CULTURE

Just culture is a concept related to systems thinking focused on addressing the underlying structure that led to an incident rather than blaming the person directly involved.

Most incidents are not simply the result of individual errors, but are caused by flawed systems that increase the probability of risk and loss. A just culture acknowledges this fact. In just culture, individuals aren't penalized for making human mistakes. This systems approach fosters an atmosphere in which people feel valued, trusted and respected. It increases the probability that incidents will be reported promptly, fully and accurately. And it therefore enables the organization to learn from incidents, prevent their reoccurrence, and improve its management of risks.

Just culture doesn't mean that anyone can do anything without negative consequences. Individual accountability is maintained, but discipline is linked to inappropriate behavior, rather than harm.

- **Human mistakes:** treated as a learning opportunity for the organization and its staff. Coaching, training and similar support may be provided to persons involved.
- **Gross negligence (willful misconduct), reckless behavior:** disciplinary action applied to perpetrator. Also treated as a learning opportunity.

In this construction, inappropriate behavior may be subject to discipline, even if no harm is caused. No discipline may be enacted, even if harm (due to a human mistake) has occurred.

When an adverse event occurs, the focus is on what went wrong, not who caused the problem. The emphasis is on uncovering and responding to the root causes of the incident.

Fostering just culture in an organization involves an organizational change management process that can be embedded into a larger process of establishing a culture of safety.

5.5. SOURCES OF ADDITIONAL SUPPORT

A great deal of information is available to support initiatives fostering a culture of safety.

1. **Health and safety agencies.** Government agencies concerned with occupational safety and health often provide extensive written information and other forms of support for organizations seeking to sustain an appropriate safety culture.
2. **Consultants.** Private organizations can perform safety culture project management, oversee surveys, and provide other support.
3. **Industry groups.** Outdoor industry groups and industrial safety associations of various types provide research, publications, conferences, accreditation, standards, or inspections. These resources can support good risk management in general or provide support specific to safety culture.

Regulations, standards and audit schemes developed by government authorities, working in concert with outdoor industry representatives, can provide essential support for a culture of safety. So too can national and international accreditation schemes and incident tracking databases. Outdoor programs, particularly those which are larger or have access to sufficient resources, enhance safety culture industry-wide when they advocate for and support such larger-scale risk management systems.

An Observation on Conservative Safety Culture

Just as people mature and may become less risk-seeking over time, organizations—and their approach to risks—evolve as well.

Organizations that exhibit a culture of being conservative with regards to risks, thoughtful, and deliberative—verging on boring—are among those who do the best in outdoor program risk management. These are sometimes long-standing institutions (some over 100 years old) with well-established clientele, a reputation for quality, and significant financial resources. They may depend on their history and reputation for sustaining their business. They often have a lot to lose if things go wrong.

This is in marked contrast to organizations with an ethic of 'move fast and break things' found in certain industries and in some startups and highly entrepreneurial organizations.

Managing Change

People resist change. This occurs even when the change is clearly desirable. Those leading efforts to change organizational safety culture should be aware of challenges in managing change.

Power. Power over our environment is a fundamental psychological need. It drives babies to cry, billionaires to over-accumulate wealth, and big countries to invade little ones. When change threatens to reduce the power of a person or a department, resistance can be vicious. Taking away money to invest in safety and imposing safety policies can elicit this resistance, just as shifting the balance of money and unearned privilege influences change efforts around civil rights, environmental sustainability, and socioeconomic equity.

In order to effectively manage complex change, then, every element in the change management process must be managed with deftness and skill. Simply sending out a questionnaire about safety culture will not suffice. A commitment from the top for searching, long-term change efforts is essential, as are dedicated resources. For any but the smallest organizations, obtaining the guidance of those deeply experienced and skilled in leading long-term organizational change management efforts may be essential.

Deflecting Responsibility. A leader may loudly proclaim a strong commitment to changing organizational culture, and appoint an internal or external consulting team to lead a change process. The team may find that the source of the deficient safety culture is actually the leader themselves. The leader may resist being identified as a source of problems. In this classic dynamic, cognitive dissonance, power imbalances, and other obstacles inhibit meaningful change.

Managing Complexity. Some safety culture assessments result in a long list of issues, which leads to a corrective plan composed of numerous disparate actions. Failure to take a systemic approach to developing an integrated, coherent plan can doom a change management effort. Likewise, trying to address all issues simultaneously may be less effective than employing a sequential, phased approach to incrementally improving the culture of safety.

————

Change management in the corporate environment—or anywhere else, from addressing nationalist politics to improving one's diet—is a complex subject. Shifting an organizational culture takes time. Change efforts are generally measured in years of continued focus and investment. Many resources beyond the introduction provided here are available and will be useful, particularly in the context of larger organizations, in effectively improving the culture of safety.

Characteristics of Safety Culture

1. **Leadership From the Top**
   a. Culture starts at the top—CEO and Board. They are responsible for generating support at all levels of the organization, for all aspects of safety culture development.
   b. Support must be sufficiently resilient to survive the departure of a CEO or other top leadership.
2. **Inclusion.**
   a. Everyone is involved in improving the safety culture.
   b. All persons are invited to contribute ideas.
   c. Staff at all levels participate in risk management reviews, safety discussions, incident reporting, and safety culture surveys.
   d. Information is widely shared. Incident report data, safety memos and risk management review reports travel through all levels of the organization.
   e. Every person knows they have a responsibility for safety, and feels a sense of ownership for risk management.
3. **Suffusion.**
   a. Safety permeates the organization, in every part and corner.
   b. Safety is not the responsibility of the risk manager, but everyone has a role, including those in marketing, logistics and other non-program areas.
   c. All members of the organization can articulate the vision for safety and how it relates to their individual work.
4. **Culture of Questioning.**
   a. Staff recognize risks are never completely eliminated and no risk management system is perfect.
   b. Staff are vigilant about identifying new risks and finding ways to better manage risks.
   c. It is acceptable to question those in authority when there are urgent safety concerns.
   d. Formal authority defers to greater expertise.
5. **Collaboration.**
   a. Staff work together up and down the organizational hierarchy and across departments.
6. **Effective Communication.**
   a. Upper management listens carefully and respectfully to all voices.
   b. Staff at all levels communicate in both directions (speaking and listening) about safety.
   c. Cultural attributes like unwillingness to admit ignorance, admit mistakes, or ask for help are effectively discouraged.
7. **Just Culture.**
   a. Individuals are not punished for raising safety issues or confronting supervisors about unsafe practices.

Chapter Summary

1. A culture of safety is an important element of good outdoor program risk management.

2. Culture is an integrated pattern of behavior based on shared beliefs and values.

3. Behaviors are visible elements of culture; beliefs and values are not directly visible.

4. Safety culture is the influence of organizational culture on safety and the extent to which safety is emphasized over competing goals.

5. A good safety culture leads to fewer losses, enhances employee well-being and performance, and supports sustained organizational success.

6. Safety culture has unique characteristics in outdoor adventure programs, since such programs are based on taking risks.

7. Organizations have multiple safety cultures in different areas of the organization.

8. Fostering an appropriate safety culture involves influencing the values and beliefs that affect safety-related behavior.

9. Influencing values and beliefs begins with sustained articulation of values and their justification from top leadership.

10. Expectations for behaviors—found in policies, procedures, operating systems and structures—must be established.

11. A balance should be maintained between rules-based safety, emphasizing following procedures, and managed safety, emphasizing judgment and adaptation.

12. Systems thinking should be encouraged.

13. Sufficient resources—time, attention, funding, equipment and staff—must be available.

14. Undesired behaviors should be discouraged, and desired behaviors systematically encouraged.

15. Continuous improvement efforts should be made.

16. Surveys are one method for assessing safety culture, and require expertise to be administered well.

17. Just culture, looking for underlying incident causes rather than unfairly blaming persons, supports appropriate safety culture.

18. Additional support for enhancing safety culture is available from various sources.

19. Shifting the culture of safety is a change management process, which is inherently challenging.

20. Characteristics of safety culture include: leadership from the top, inclusion, suffusion, culture of questioning, collaboration, effective communication, and just culture.

ACTIVITIES AND PROGRAM AREAS

CHAPTER 6

LEARNING OBJECTIVES
1. Activity selection to meet program goals with lowest risk
2. Risk assessment before conducting activities
3. Activity-related authorizations
4. Adhering to general and specific industry standards for activities
5. Policies and procedures for program activities
6. Policies and procedures for hazardous conditions
7. Dynamic risk assessment during activities
8. Post-activity risk assessment, including debriefs and reporting

6.1. INTRODUCTION

The outdoor activities your organization conducts, and the locations in which they are held, are at the heart of your program. They are an essential part of what makes your organization effective. They do, however, have risks.

The risks associated with your activities and program areas interact with risks connected with other areas of program operations, such as staff, participants, transportation, and equipment. For example, a normally low-risk activity becomes more hazardous if staff are inappropriately trained for it or if suitable equipment is not available. Activity- and location-related risks should therefore be considered in conjunction with those other risks, which are addressed in separate chapters.

Some risks related to activities and locations are inherent to those program elements. Traveling in avalanche terrain, for example, brings with it the inherent risk of being caught in an avalanche (Figure 6.1).

Fig. 6.1. Travel in avalanche terrain brings with it inherent risks.

It is possible, however, to reduce some of the inherent and other risks associated with activities and activity sites. Principal factors involved in reducing these risks include choosing activities and program areas with the lowest risks; conducting risk assessments before, during, and after activities, and meeting related standards. We'll expand on these ideas below.

Although 'activities' primarily refers to outdoor experiences such as hiking, climbing, boating, and the like, for the purposes of program risk management, we also include traveling to and from activity sites, unstructured or rest times, and any other time when the organization has a safety responsibility for participants.

6.2. ACTIVITY AND PROGRAM AREA SELECTION

Each activity and program site your organization uses should be specifically selected to help meet established program objectives and the mission of your enterprise. As a general rule, the lowest-risk activities and activity areas that meet organizational objectives should be chosen.

Risks should not be taken for their own sake. They should not be sought out because they pose interesting challenges for field staff. Activities and areas that come with higher risks should not be used just because they are exciting and therefore easier to sell to paying participants.

Cave diving, hang gliding and BASE jumping are generally more hazardous than well-conducted institutionally run single-pitch belayed rock climbing. They may be fun, compelling for activity leaders, or easy to sell at an attractive price. But if different activities can meet your educational, recreational, therapeutic or other objectives with lower risk, a case can be made for skipping higher-risk pursuits for those less likely to lead to harm.

Similarly, program areas that require the least amount of travel to reach, and pose the lowest level of inherent risks such as extreme weather, strong currents, high altitude, delay in accessing medical care, or political instability, should be given preference over others, providing programmatic outcomes can be adequately met.

6.2.1. Assessing Need for Physical Risk, Perceived or Real

A saying at a long-established outdoor program known for challenging, multi-week wilderness expeditions is that any of their adventure courses could be conducted "under a kitchen table." The implication is that meeting the education, recreational or other human development objectives of an outdoor program generally doesn't require highly adventurous activities with high actual risk. At times high perceived physical risk (such as beginning a rappel/abseil down a cliff) can be useful. However, high perceived physical risk is not universally essential.

Sometimes programmatically useful risks can be psychological or emotional, such as might occur during candid group discussions with a skilled facilitator. Yet the rewards of taking these risks can be just as great as from rewards from taking real or perceived physical risks. In addition, while the out-of-doors can strip away some distractions and permit openness to growthful conversations, this does not need to occur in a remote wilderness or involve higher-risk activities like alpine mountaineering.

If activities with higher actual physical risks are involved, then staff, equipment, participant screening and training, emergency procedures, and other parameters should be suitable to address the heightened risks. Participants (and their parents/guardians if participants are minors) should give informed consent.

Tallship sailing is an outdoor activity that provides profound community-based and personal growth opportunities, as the metaphors of pulling together and being in the same boat come alive. The actual risks of well-run institutional tallship sailing (Figure 6.2), however, are comparatively small.

Figure 6.2. Tall-ship sailing brings powerful benefits, often with relatively fewer risks.

Similarly, low ropes challenge course activities skillfully led by an experienced and capable facilitator can be profoundly powerful, but present low actual risk.

6.2.2. Initial Risk Assessment

Risk assessment is an essential tool in managing safety in activities, activity areas and elsewhere. Chapter 2, Approaches to Risk Management, discusses aspects of risk assessment.

When conducting activity- and program area-related risk assessments, it is important to at the same time incorporate an assessment of other factors that can impact activity-related safety outcomes. These factors include equipment, participant populations, staff, and others. This is because some risks only appear due a mismatch between program elements such as activity location and trained staff, and may not be evident if elements are considered in isolation.

Before offering an outdoor activity such as skiing, sailing, or backpacking to potential participants, a risk assessment specific to that activity and the locations in which it is to be held should be conducted. It is often useful to document this initial assessment in a New Element Readiness Assessment or similar format.

Policies and procedures should be developed in response to the findings of the risk assessments. These policies and procedures should be incorporated into field manuals, emergency plans, or other documents as needed. Staff should carry out the policies and procedures as appropriate.

Figure 6.3. Bamboo raft trips bring both adventure and risk.

Special Program Areas. In program areas with cultural, economic, or sociopolitical contexts that are significantly different from those with which participants or staff are familiar, additional risk management procedures may apply.

These contexts may be within the same country that participants or staff are from. For example, participants of a country's dominant ethnic group coming from an affluent city predominately populated by the country's dominant ethnic group might participate in a program situated in an isolated rural region populated by historically or currently marginalized native/indigenous peoples, within the same country.

These considerations can also apply when moving between countries. They are often thought of when moving from countries considered high-income to either a low-resource area of a middle-income country or a low-income country (as defined by the World Bank or similar entity). But they can equally apply in many other situations, for instance when moving between high-income countries with different principal religions and legal systems, for instance Canada and the United Arab Emirates.

Activity-Specific and Area-Specific Topics. Risk assessment areas specific to activities and program areas include:

In Any Location.

Figure 6.4. Environmental hazards vary per location.

1. Environmental considerations such as:
    a. Typhoons, volcanoes, avalanches, tsunamis, rip tides, earthquakes, wildfires, floods, ice, overexposure to sun, darkness, steep or uneven terrain, and landslides
    b. Hazardous animals, plants, microbes and other organisms such as venomous creatures, potentially hazardous large animals, and toxic or allergenic plant material
    c. Reduced visibility
    d. Extremes of temperature and atmospheric pressure (e.g. diving, high altitude)
    e. Hazardous weather conditions such as storms, precipitation, lightning, and high winds
    f. Presence of air, water, ground or other pollution or contamination
    g. Toxic and poisonous substances
    h. Disease, such as malaria, typhus, encephalitis, hepatitis, dengue, rabies, hepatitis, or Zika, including vaccinations and documentation of vaccination
2. Needs for special training, clothing, language interpretation and translation
3. Access to sufficient and uncontaminated food and water
4. Availability of medical supplies, medical care, and methods to access emergency and transportation or evacuation services
5. Specific procedures for requesting emergency services (such as search and rescue, park dispatch, or military assistance with technical rescue)
6. People-related hazards, for example persons who are intoxicated, criminal, predatory, or insufficiently trained

7. Socio-cultural hazards, such as armed conflict, organized crime, political instability, corrupt authorities, or cultural norms or legal precedent that providing bystander first aid is an admission of guilt

8. Hazards of the built environment and infrastructure, for instance:

   a. Accommodations or other facilities that pose unacceptable risks due to problems such as security or reliability of personnel

   b. Structures not compliant with home region building codes or standards (such as regarding earthquake resistance, smoke/carbon monoxide detectors or alarms, emergency exits, fire suppression systems, or general safety of, for example, electrical systems, heaters, balconies, or elevators)

   c. Roads not up to home region safety standards (such as regarding construction, maintenance, guardrails, shoulders or signage)

   d. Vehicles not compliant with home region standards such as presence of seatbelts, availability of trained drivers, or adherence to safe driving practices or vehicle maintenance schedules

   e. Accommodations or other business entities lacking liability insurance, security, or adequately trained staff

   f. Regional and national infrastructure—for example, telecommunications, transportation, medical response, or electrical grid—vulnerable in large-scale emergencies (such as pandemic, terrorism, or natural disaster)

The organization and participants should both be clear on which part holds responsibility for management of which risks. While the program is generally responsible for the bulk of risk management, participants may be responsible for items such as soliciting advice from a travel medicine clinic, obtaining appropriate vaccinations, acquiring passport and visas, or determining which medical supplies for personal use are appropriate to bring.

For International Settings. When crossing significant political borders, the organization should consider:

1. Planning for repatriation services
2. International insurance coverage
3. Contacting or registering with the relevant embassy, consulate, or national government agency dealing with international travel. The government agency can then provide up-to-date information and facilitate assistance in times of need.

4. Contacting national or global health and disease control agencies for medical information in the international destination
5. Legal restrictions, such as regulations pertaining to possession or use of alcohol or other drugs; possession, transportation, and administration of medications; employment; age of sexual consent; possession and transport of souvenirs and specimens; international border crossing with minors; legal liability norms, and motor vehicle operations.

Figure 6.5. Medical evacuation from the Himalayas for international adventurers involves special insurance and other considerations.

6.3. NEW ELEMENT READINESS ASSESSMENTS

Before an organization provides a significant new activity type—such as adding a sea kayaking element to a previously all-terrestrial program—a risk management plan specific to the proposed activity should be developed and approved. Similarly, before a significant new program area—for instance, a country in which the organization has never previously provided programming—is opened up, an acceptable plan should generated.

A New Element Readiness Assessment is typically not needed if the new activity or program area is essentially identical to one already in place. For example, offering activities in a new watershed or district of a national park would typically not require a formal New Element Readiness Assessment if the hazards, risks, local conditions, emergency procedures and other parameters are the same as for the same activities already being conducted in the adjacent watershed or district of the same park.

(New Element Readiness Assessments should also be created and approved for working with new participant population types that would require modifications to risk management systems. Relevant populations might include those with significant disabilities, behavioral management needs, or medical conditions.)

The assessment is normally developed by program staff, and submitted to higher leadership, such as the Risk Management Committee or program executive team, to be reviewed for approval.

The assessment should explain how the new program helps the organization meet its programmatic objectives, identify relevant risks, and propose an approach for managing each risk.

Topics in the New Element Readiness Assessment may include:

- **Brief description of the new program element.** What are the proposed new activities, participant populations, or activity locations? How do they fit into what the organization currently provides?
- **Goals and history.** How does the proposed new element further the aims of the organization? Has it been tried in the past, and with what results?
- **Screening of and preparation of participants.** Are there medical, behavioral, therapeutic, disability-related, or other considerations to address?
- **Special hazards posed by participant population.** Do at-risk youth or others bring heightened risks?
- **Staffing.** What new staff or qualifications are required, and how will they be obtained?
- **Activities.** What are the new activities? What are their principal risks, and how will those risks be managed?
- **Equipment.** What is needed; how will it be acquired and managed, and how will persons be trained in its use and care?
- **Transportation.** New routes, vehicles, transportation modes, contractors and other parameters should be addressed.
- **Subcontracting.** If subcontracting is required, suitability of potential subcontractors should be assessed.
- **Hazards of the new element environment.** If a new environment is to be used, hazardous conditions should be addressed.
- **Emergency procedures.** Accessing medical care or law enforcement, search, rescue, evacuation, and other emergency procedures should be outlined.
- **Emergency communications.** How will emergency services and program administrators be accessible? How are two-way communications assured?

Figure 6.6. Safety management should be assessed when subcontracting with outdoor providers.

6.4. AUTHORIZATION

In some circumstances, permits, licenses or other authorizations are needed before conducting activities or using certain areas. This can take the form of government approval to provide outdoor adventure experiences, as in the case of the UK's Adventure Activities Licensing Authority. It can be specific to a particular activity, such as state-level laws in the US regarding portable climbing structures. Or, it can apply to an activity in a specific geographical location, such as a permit for commercial use in a certain national park.

The process of obtaining authorizations such commercial use permits sometimes requires awareness of certain safety risks, and commitment to implementing risk management measures, in order to receive authorization. Possession of required permissions also reduces business risks such as the possibility of receiving fines or other penalties.

Organizations should comply with the terms and conditions of all authorizations.

6.5. CONDUCTING ACTIVITIES

6.5.1. Adherence to Industry Standards

Activities should be conducted in accordance with industry standards for the activity. Policies and procedures should not only reflect the hazards encountered during risk assessments and those associated with hazardous conditions, but also the established practices for the particular activity type. Activity leaders should have the capacities needed to ensure these standards are met.

Detailed explanations of standards for every possible outdoor activity are not enumerated here. These standards may be available through guides published by industry associations (such as challenge course, mountaineering, sailing, or tree climbing groups). For example, a collaborative of outdoor groups in Australia publishes Good Practice Guides through the Australian Adventure Activity Standard project. The New Zealand government and outdoor industry have developed Activity Safety Guidelines. Mountain Training, a consortium in the UK, publishes national guidelines for climbing in the UK and Ireland.

Consensus standards are also published by standards-setting institutions. For example, the ISO publishes the standard ISO 13289 Recreational diving services – Requirements for the conduct of snorkeling excursions.

Training courses can also provide access to standards, and standards may be available otherwise as well. Following is an abridged sampling of standards to serve as examples.

General Activity Standards. Certain standards generally

Figure 6.7. Bicycling programs should adhere to established good practice standards.

apply across all or many outdoor activities. A partial list of examples includes:

1. Participants receive appropriate training and preparation for program activities, areas, and conditions. This includes safety briefings before activities commence.
2. Participants are appropriately supervised during activities. This includes managing mixed-gender groups especially overnight and when unaccompanied.
3. Procedures are in place to manage risks relevant to terrain and travel conditions such as steep routes, loose footing, rockfall, high winds, waves, currents and tides.
4. The pacing of activities is appropriate, for instance to help ensure groups stay together when needed, ensure belayers keep up with climbers, and minimize

the risk of exhaustion or overuse injuries.
5. Emergency procedures to deal with lost or alone persons, injury, illness, and other safety issues are in place, and staff have the capacities to enact them.
6. Training and conditions necessary for activity leaders and participants to understand and use specialized communication systems and commands where needed are in place, for instance in climbing, abseiling/rappelling, whitewater boating, sailing, or caving.
7. Operations in diminished conditions are adjusted, postponed, or terminated as appropriate in order to manage risks to acceptable levels.

Activity-Specific Standards. In addition to general standards applicable across the outdoor industry, standards particular to sailing, caving, river tracing, tree climbing and other outdoor activities should generally be followed.

Staff to Participant Ratios. One category of activity-specific standards concerns the proportion of activity leaders to participants. The relative numbers of qualified staff to participants should be established and documented. Figure 6.8 gives an example of potential ratios to consider for trained activity leaders and physically capable participants. Note that in remote environments a minimum of two trained activity leaders per group is typical.

Responsible persons (described in Chapter 9, Participants) such as school group chaperones may be not included as a participant (or activity leaders) in leader-to-participant ratios if they are competent to manage their own safety. This could apply, for example, if the responsible person is supervising youth in the safe zone/waiting area at a ropes challenge course at a residential facility. However, the responsible person would be included as a participant for ratio purposes if they would be dependent on activity leader for their safety. An example could be when whitewater canoeing.

- Backpacking (overnight or longer): one leader to eight or fewer participants;
- Mountaineering: one leader to six or fewer participants in Class 3 or 4 terrain; one leader to four or fewer participants in Class 5 terrain;
- Winter camping: one leader to six or fewer participants;
- Top-rope rock climbing: one leader to six or fewer participants;
- Multi-pitch rock or ice climbing, Class 5 terrain: one

leader to three or fewer participants;

- Glacier travel, snow-covered glaciers: one leader to three or fewer participants;
- Flat water paddling: one leader to six or fewer participants in Class I or II water;
- Whitewater paddling: one leader to four or fewer participants in water rated Class III or greater;
- Sea kayaking: one leader to six or fewer participants;
- Rafting: one leader per one or two boats in water rated Class III or less; one leader per boat in water rated Class IV or greater.

In addition to ratios, standards exist for numerous

Figure 6.8. Example ratios of trained, qualified activity leaders to physically capable participants.

different outdoor activities. Figure 6.9 provides a limited sampling of standards topics applicable to specific outdoor activities.

- Land travel: crossing water appropriately.
- Climbing: working near edges. Assessment of participant readiness before lead climbing.
- Backpacking: lead/sweep systems. Pack fitting, adjusting, and weights. How close to other group members to travel.
- Swimming: swim tests. PFD use. Currents and tides. Water temperatures. Buddy systems. Swim area boundaries.
- Boating: availability and appropriate use of PFDs. Staff and participant training in PFD use. Presence of appropriate watercraft flotation.
- Solo instruction: emergency response, including if solo activity leader is incapacitated.
- Unaccompanied activity: training and skills required before unaccompanied travel. Route suitability. Contacting activity leaders and emergency resources.
- Service projects: participant training and supervision regarding use of sharp objects, power tools, dangerous chemicals and other potentially hazardous items.

6.5.2. Dynamic Risk Assessment

Figure 6.9. Partial selection of standards topics for outdoor activities.

During the entire time that staff are responsible for participants, risk should be continuously assessed by activity leaders and any other responsible parties such as site managers, vehicle operators, or on-site course directors.

This includes all times from participant arrival to

participant departure (not just while program activity sessions are in progress), unless provisions are made for time unsupervised by staff. In cases of unsupervised time, participants and staff should be clear who is responsible for managing risks, for instance adult chaperones during school trips, or adult participants themselves during a corporate team-building outing.

With continuous staff risk assessment, adjustments such as modification, postponement or activity termination can then be made promptly as conditions change, for example due to the onset of inclement weather. Risks related to activities, participants, staff, equipment, activity locations, and transportation, including all the areas described in the initial risk assessment section, should be assessed.

Figure 6.10. Dogsledding programs have dynamic risks including weather, dog behavior, and crossing frozen water bodies.

6.6. POLICIES AND PROCEDURES

Activity-specific policies and procedures should be created—and updated as needed—based on risk assessments.

6.6.1. For Program Activities

Policies and procedures should cover the principal program activities such as climbing, boating, caving, bicycling, independent travel, stream crossing, and so on. They should also cover the campcraft and other activities that are a normal part of outdoor experiences such as cooking, cleaning, waste management, hygiene (including outdoor handwashing, Figure 6.11), water disinfection, proper lifting technique, and sleeping warm.

Figure 6.11. Handwashing is an important activity from a risk management perspective.

An example of policies and procedures for bouldering (climbing large rocks without safety ropes) is provided below. Policy and procedure sets for more complex or hazardous activities would generally be larger than what is seen in this example.

Bouldering

Bouldering is a type of rock climbing traditionally done on the sides of large boulders. The climber develops strength and judgment without climbing very high or using much gear. Because there is no rope protecting the climber from falling, the technique of spotting (see the Initiatives and Spotting section) is employed to help prevent injury from any falls or jumps off the rock. Field staff are allowed to supervise a bouldering activity without the presence of a climbing site manager. Bouldering is an excellent energy release and can be used as an educational activity on a variety of levels.

Policies

1. Staff must have properly been trained to supervise and inspect a bouldering area.
2. The bouldering area must be evaluated and comply with the Evaluating Climbing Site section found within this manual.
3. All climbers must have at least one spotter working with them during a climb.

Procedures

1. The ratio of staff to participants is 1:6.
2. Helmets must be worn for bouldering done above knee height.
3. No bouldering shall be conducted traveling higher than the shoulder height of the spotter.
4. Staff shall insure that weather and terrain are appropriate for participant's level of comfort and

skill. If necessary, adjust route or postpone bouldering until weather conditions improve.

Guidelines

1. Select an area that allows for adequate supervision as well as climbing and hiking routes appropriate for the participant's ability level.
2. Familiarize yourself with the bouldering area. It may be possible to offer visual instruction of climbing techniques and movement on rock, while simultaneously inspecting the routes.
3. Instruct participants on spotting techniques.
4. Instruct participants on climbing techniques. This could include three points of contact, keeping the 'butt out,' smearing/stemming/chimneying, and foot and hand placement.
5. Allow participants to begin activity if they understand and accept the responsibilities of climbing safe and spotting. Offer evaluation of climbing and spotting techniques.
6. Debrief the activity as appropriate.
7. Be careful on wet or loose rock; consider bouldering elsewhere.

Note that general policies, emergency medical procedures, participant management, supervision, site management, safety briefings, spotting, helmet use, incident management and other areas that could pertain to bouldering risk management are covered in other sections of the field manual from which this excerpt was taken.

6.6.2. For Hazardous Conditions in Program Areas

Policies and procedures should be established and used for addressing hazards encountered in program areas, such as any listed in the Initial Risk Assessment topics above, including environmental hazards and hazards of the built environment.

If outdoor leaders decide to continue activities of any sort in hazardous conditions, that decision should be defensible.

Outdoor travel during adverse weather should be considered an activity in itself rather than simply a means of keeping to the planned itinerary. Activity leaders should insure that participants are physically and psychologically ready for such travel and that clothing, equipment, and contingency plans are adequate for the activity. This approach applies when experiencing adverse weather even if not traveling.

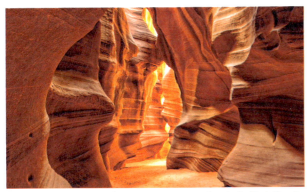

Figure 6.12. Hazards of desert canyon travel include flash flood and rockfall.

6.6.3. Implementation

Staff should verifiably be trained in all relevant policies and procedures. (Chapter 7, Staff, provides an example of check-off documents that can be used for verification.) They should have ready access them while in the field, for example in the form of a paper or electronic field manual. Staff and participants should be willing and able to implement the policies and procedures as required.

6.7. POST-ACTIVITY REVIEW

Following the activity, and at the end of the day, it can be useful to debrief the experience. This provides, among other purposes, an opportunity to identify safety issues. At the end of the entire outdoor program and following the departure of participants, staff have another opportunity to review. A written analysis of successes and opportunities for improvement, including risk management issues, can be made at this time. A standardized form with questions or topics to address may be helpful.

During these reviews, significant incidents should be discussed, and risks related to activities, participants, staff, equipment, activity locations, safety culture, subcontractors and transportation should be assessed.

Issues brought up during these post-activity reviews should then be addressed and resolved by program managers. In order for that to occur, a management system for accountability and follow-up should be put in place to ensure issues raised during post-activity review are not neglected.

Incident reporting and incident reviews are covered in following chapters.

Chapter Summary

1. Risks associated with outdoor activities may be able to be reduced.

2. The outdoor activities with the lowest risks that still meet organizational objectives should be selected.

3. Risks should not be taken for their own sake.

4. Activity-related risks should be assessed before deciding to conduct an activity.

5. Permits, licenses and other required authorizations should be obtained.

6. Industry standards related to outdoor activities should be adhered to.

7. Policies and procedures to address activity-related risks should be developed.

8. Policies and procedures should cover all program activities, locations, and experiences, as well as hazardous conditions.

9. Conditions should be such that staff and participants follow these policies and procedures.

10. Risks should be assessed during activities, with appropriate adjustments made.

11. Following activities, risks should be reviewed through debriefs, reviews and reporting.

CHAPTER 7

STAFF

LEARNING OBJECTIVES
1. Importance of staff in risk management
2. The Human Resources Management process
3. Establishing staff capacity requirements
4. Brain development and risk management
5. Hiring to meet required capacities
6. Staff training
7. Supervising and supporting staff
8. Risk management and the organizational chart
9. Additional resources
10. Systemic issues in staff-related risk management
11. How human factors lead to accidents

7.1. INTRODUCTION

Staff are a critical element in managing risks in outdoor programs. Hiring the right people—and training and supporting them well—is one of the business activities that will have the most impact on an organization, out of any action taken. It's also challenging to get right.

This chapter focuses on activity leaders (such as instructors, guides, facilitators, camp counselors, and trip leaders). However, the same principles apply to managers and to anyone within or connected to the organization who has a safety role. This includes, but is not limited to, lead and assistant activity leaders, logistics staff, managers, members of the Risk Management Committee, Board members, interns and fellows, observers, Responsible Persons such as chaperones, and volunteers.

We'll begin by discussing the human resources (HR) management function in the outdoor program context. This process is simply the application of good personnel management principles, applied to outdoor organizations.

We'll next briefly discuss safety-related positions within the context of the organizational hierarchy, mention sources of additional information about human resources management, and offer a brief note about systems issues in outdoor program HR.

We'll end with an introduction to cognitive limitations such as cognitive bias and cognitive shortcuts (heuristics) that increase outdoor program risk.

7.2. THE HUMAN RESOURCES MANAGEMENT PROCESS IN THE OUTDOOR PROGRAM CONTEXT

7.2.1. Overview

Steps in the Human Resources Management (HRM) process can be summarized as follows:

1. Establish required staff capacities
2. Hire staff to meet baseline capacities
3. Train staff to meet unmet capacities
4. Supervise and support staff to maintain capacities

Our discussion of the HRM process will focus on elements specific to outdoor programs. Best practices for interviewing, reference checking, supervision, evaluation, and other general HR practices are available elsewhere and are not extensively covered here.

7.2.2. Establish Required Capacities for Staff

Before hiring, it's necessary to determine what are the desired capacities for staff 1) to be initially hired, and 2) following training, to work with participants in the field. There are multiple models through which to frame these capacities, each with its benefits and drawbacks. We'll look at four domains of required capacities: knowledge, skills, abilities, and attitudes or values. Descriptions of the latter four terms follow:

Ability: a capacity (to do something), often with an inherited or innate component in addition to a learned component; like dexterity, or ability to distinguish red from green.

In the outdoor context: the ability to lift a canoe out of the water during a canoe-over-canoe rescue.

Skill: a learned competence, developed over time with training and practice. Skill development may also require certain abilities, like able hand-eye coordination in becoming a skilled race-car driver. Skills include time management, surgery, and parenting. (Skill is sometimes used interchangeably with ability, but they are differentiated here.)

In the outdoor context: rescuing an abseiler whose rappel device has jammed; effectively facilitating a group discussion about safety.

Value: how much something is prized/held in regard; preference for action/outcome, view of right and wrong. Attitude: thinking or feeling with respect to favor or disfavor. Although these terms are slightly different, we use them interchangeably here.

In the outdoor context: Taking seriously the safety of outdoor program participants.

The desired capacities in the four domains of knowledge, skills, abilities, and attitudes/values should be clearly documented in published job postings and written job descriptions. They should hold up as adequate under scrutiny. If an employee fails, will your language be seen as contributing to the failure?

In the job descriptions, roles and responsibilities for safety must be clear. Some organizations use a Single Point of Accountability or Person In Charge structure to formalize this responsibility.

Figure 7.1. Staff must have the capacity to handle substantial risks.

Staff Operate Below Limits of Competence. Required capacities for any given position should be such that the individual is operating at a level below their own skill and ability. That is, the activity (such as whitewater boating) at its most difficult should not be a challenge for the activity leader. For instance, a boater who is able to paddle class IV whitewater should only lead trips on class III or lower whitewater. This ensures a margin of safety. Although activity leaders may personally want a challenging high adventure experience, leading a commercial trip with others is not the place for it.

Operating at the limits of one's competence increases the probability of an incident occurring. It also reduces the cognitive capacities of the individual to respond if something does go wrong: research shows that individuals under stress—or being occupied by multiple tasks, which is often also the case in emergencies—have impaired decision-making and tend to make riskier decisions.

Knowledge, Skills, Abilities and Attitudes for Activity Leaders. Desired capacities for activity leaders can be broken down as described below. Hiring managers should then determine which of these capacities must be met in order for a person to be hired, and which are required (following the completion of staff training) before the activity leader is eligible to lead outdoor programs.

Figure 7.2. Facilitation skills are important in preventing risky behaviors.

1. **Technical skills**. These apply to the relevant outdoor activities, such as kayaking, climbing, or sailing.
2. **Interpersonal and leadership skills**. These include critically important skills in communication, judgment, and decision-making. (See Human Factors in Accident Causation, below.) Facilitation and group management skills are included here.
3. **Activity area competence**. This refers to the ability to appropriately manage risk in leading activities in the activity areas used the program. In many cases this is developed during the staff training process.
4. **Emergency management**. This includes the capacity to fulfill relevant responsibilities in the organization's Emergency Management Plan (ERP), following training in the ERP.
5. **Specialized criteria**. Specific qualifications or status here may include a commercial driver's license, a captain's license (for sailing programs), ability to pass drug test (legally required for some maritime positions), and the authorization to legally work for the organization.
6. **Essential functions**. These capacities, described in Chapter 18, Medical Screening, apply to activity leaders as well as participants.
7. **Attitudes**. Conservative safety judgment is an example of a potentially desired value or attitude. This could be addressed in a job description qualification such as 'proven ability to provide conservative risk management supervision.'

Criminal History. A potential activity leader's criminal history can provide some, although limited, guidance on the individual's capacities, particularly when the organization works with minors or vulnerable adults. A criminal history does not necessary preclude an individual from working in an outdoor program. A person with a minor infraction for possession 10 years ago of a drug with low abuse potential, for instance, may in some situations and legal contexts be eligible for hire. However, a criminal conviction for sexual abuse of a minor would generally prohibit a person from working with children.

Figure 7.3. In some jurisdictions, fingerprints or other biometrics are used in assessing criminal history.

If a criminal history leads to an employment restriction, the restriction should be relevant to the offence. For instance, an employee convicted of driving under the influence (of alcohol) could be prohibited from driving, but might be eligible to hold other responsibilities.

Risk and the Developing Brain

What causes risky behavior? Advances in brain imaging technology have led to a theory about how uneven brain development influences risk-taking.

The brain was once thought to have completed maturation in childhood. But functional Magnetic Resonance Imaging shows that the brain continues to develop into the mid 20's. Up until this time, changes in brain structure and function, hormones, and neurotransmitters such as dopamine increase the desire to engage in risky behaviors.

The limbic system of the brain contains the amygdala, and seeks thrills and rewards risk-taking behavior. Research show that this system develops relatively rapidly, typically peaking at around 19 years of age.

The prefrontal cortex (PFC) is the region of the brain that regulates and moderates risk by controlling impulses and promoting thoughtful behavior. The PFC is generally not fully developed, however, until a person reaches their early to mid 20's.

The brain of a young adult, then, is somewhat like an alpine skier who loves to zoom down the slope but has not yet learned techniques to stop. The imbalance in the brain's risk-seeking and cognitive control mechanisms can increase the likelihood of accidents and other incidents.

Until an outdoor leader reaches the mid 20's, their likelihood of risky behaviors may be increased. Although more mature adults are also sensitive to rewards, they have a more fully developed cognitive control mechanism that inhibits risky behaviors.

Changing knowledge, beliefs and attitudes are not highly effective in influencing the neurobiological chemistry affecting risk-taking. Therefore, some outdoor programs may chose to hire outdoor leaders at a minimum age of 24 (or at least 21), in order to avoid the hazards of employing younger persons whose capacities for self-regulation, planning, and weighing risk and reward are still developing. That can be a useful approach even in lower-risk outdoor environments like residential summer camps, but is especially important for higher-risk situations such as remote wilderness, international travel, and extreme environments.

Research on brain science is ongoing, so expect theories on brain development to evolve. One competing theory posits that risk-taking in young persons is a simply a result of the natural desire to explore and learn about the world, without the benefit of the accumulated wisdom that adults have. This leads to risks being taken that more experienced adults would be unlikely to take. With this theory, however, the benefits of hiring older and more experienced outdoor leaders remain.

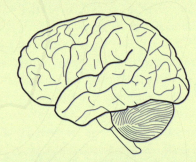

Figure 7.4. The differing timeframes of the development of the amygdala and the prefrontal cortex in the brain lead to increased risk-taking until the mid-20's.

7.2.3. Hire to Meet Baseline Capacities

Once we've established the capacities we need in activity leaders, the hiring process can begin. We now seek to hire staff (or engage volunteers) meeting or exceeding the minimum qualifications necessary to be brought on to the organization, knowing that additional training will be necessary before the new staff are ready to work with participants.

It's important to be able to verify that staff indeed meet these minimum hiring requirements. Determining what is considered to be adequate evidence of meeting requirements depends on the jurisdiction, the activities, participant populations, and the organization's standards (if, for example, they exceed the legal minimums or industry standards).

Evidence of Capacities. Examples of evidence for activity leaders include, but are not limited to:

Qualifications, Certificates, Awards. A document or similar evidence establishing that a person meets certain criteria, particularly regarding technical skills, is

known in different parts of the world as a qualification, a certificate, or an award. In this context, these words mean essentially the same thing; certificates (also known as awards) are examples of qualifications.

Established qualifications, if present for a certain topic (such as mountaineering or canoeing), may be established either by government entities or outdoor industry associations. Examples of government-established qualifications include those from the UK, New Zealand, and Iceland.

In the UK, the Health and Safety Executive publication L77 ("Guidance from the Licensing Authority on the Adventure Activities Licensing Regulations 2004") gives detailed information regarding technical competence qualifications for a variety of outdoor activities at various hazard levels. These apply to commercial outdoor adventure organizations regulated under the Activity Centres (Young Persons' Safety) Act 1995. The document lists, for example, evidence of legally required technical competence for group leaders for foot trekking, as in Figure 7.5 below:

Trekking – On Foot	
Hazard Level	**Group Instructor/Leader**
Moorland country – winter	Mountain Instructor Certificate from Mountain Leader Training UK or British Association of Mountain Guides Carnet holder or Aspirant Guide or Winter Mountain Leader or International Mountain Leader Mountain Leader for rolling terrain where crampons and ice axe are not needed by group members.

Figure 7.5. Required qualifications for certain commercial foot trekking on wintertime moorlands in the UK.

In New Zealand, the WorkSafe New Zealand Safety Audit Standard for Adventure Activities states that staff must have competence for their assigned tasks, using nationally recognized qualifications where relevant. Examples of qualifications include those from the New Zealand Outdoor Instructors Association and those from Skills Active Aotearoa, listed on the New Zealand Qualifications Framework of the New Zealand Qualifications Authority.

In Iceland, the Icelandic Tourist Board Ferðamálastofa, an authority under the Ministry of Industries and Innovation, is working in collaboration with the outdoor adventure industry to establish legal requirements for adventure guide leaders.

Outdoor industry associations, such as National Governing Bodies or peak bodies, have established qualifications for activity leaders. These standards are typically voluntary, and often activity-specific and country-specific. The standards may be published by standards-setting organizations.

For instance, in Australia, knowledge and skills recommended for outdoor activity leaders are noted in Good Practice Guides (GPGs) from the Australian Adventure Activities Standard project. The GPGs refer to competency units such as 'Select, set up and maintain a bike.' Those competency units comprise skills sets such as 'Mountain Bike Guide (Intermediate Environment).' Those skills sets lead to qualifications such as 'Certificate III in Outdoor Recreation' from the Sport, Fitness and Recreation Training Package of the Australian government's training initiative. The 2015 version of the package includes units for climbing, kayaking, bushwalking and many other outdoor activities as well as managerial topics within its more than 8,400 pages.

The Association for Experiential Education requires that program personnel of adventure programs accredited by the association have at least 16 hours of wilderness first aid training when transport to definitive care is an hour or more, and at least wilderness first responder training (typically at least 70 hours) when transport is four or more hours.

Figure 7.6. A variety of qualifications is available to demonstrate staff have appropriate technical skills.

Outdoor Adventure Leader Registration. Evidence of appropriate capacities may be suggested by registration of an activity leader in an appropriate outdoor adventure leader registry, where available. The Outdoor Council of Australia's National Outdoor Leader Registration Scheme is an example.

Prior Experience. Particularly when a qualification is not available (for example for an unusual outdoor activity), or when hands-on experience is useful in addition to training, prior experience can provide useful evidence of capability.

This is only the case, however, when the experience is of high-quality program operations, so care should be taken when evaluating prior experience. For example, the New Zealand rafting industry in the 1990's was criticized for having low standards of safety and training, and resistance to making improvements despite multiple deaths. (Standards have since improved.)

References. Thorough and deliberate checking of professional references (generally three or more) of prospective staff is valuable in assessing a candidate's proven capacities. Not a formality, these reference checks should be conducted in a diligent and searching manner, both to root out potential deception in application materials and to provide a fuller picture of an applicant's strengths and growth areas.

Interviews. A well-developed standardized employment interview process, conducted in accordance with professional practice, is a requirement for adequately assessing potential future safety performance.

Risk to the business is minimized when interviews and other elements of the hiring process are conducted in accordance with applicable non-discrimination requirements. Interview questions and casual chatting before and after interviews should therefore be careful to avoid direct or indirect questions around characteristics protected by law in the jurisdiction, which may include marital status, religious faith, or many others.

Figure 7.7. In jurisdictions with categories of protected classes of individuals, care must be taken to conform to anti-discrimination laws.

Specialized Assessments. Criminal history, results of drug tests, relevant medical history (such as medical restrictions on strenuous activity), and documenting establishing legal authorization to work can be assessed as appropriate.

Verifiability. The organization must be able to verify it has conducted an appropriate assessment of the candidate's suitability for the position. Evidence may include, but is not limited to, an applicant's criminal history record, drug test results, medical health history form, professional resume or curriculum vitae, outdoor resume listing outdoor activity history, cover letter, application form if applicable, references or a record that references were checked and found to be satisfactory, interview notes or records noting a successful interview, motor vehicle operation records, and copies of relevant outdoor industry certifications. These materials should be kept securely on file.

For managers, the same principle applies. Certifications, diplomas and degrees, and job history provided in application materials should be verified to avoid misrepresentation or fraud.

7.2.4. Train to Meet Work-Ready Capacities

A staff person new to the organization, no matter how great the previous experience, needs additional training in order to manage risks unique to your outdoor program context. This training should verifiably indicate that the staff person has the capability to execute their professional responsibilities.

Figure 7.8. Training in an organization's specific safety systems and equipment should happen before working with participants.

Activity Leader Training. Before leading activities, program staff should receive demonstrably adequate training in several topics, such as:

1. **Activities and Program Areas.** This includes the hazards and risks of the activities and the areas in which they are held, and their management, including emergency procedures. It also includes technical skills training and hands-on experience if needed. This training should not be a formality; rushing through orientation to an outdoor program's activity areas has been cited as a contributing factor to outdoor program fatalities (see Chapter 23, Seeing Systems). Check-off documents (see Figure 7.10 below) filled out by a qualified person describing required competencies and documenting their attainment can help ensure that the necessary capabilities are in place.

2. **Equipment.** This includes gear and supplies used for activities and emergency response.

3. **Participant Populations.** Training topics may include supervision, behavior management, medical condition management, and procedures for special populations such as persons with disabilities or a history of behavior problems.

4. **Cognitive and Interpersonal Skills.** Although managers aim to hire individuals who already possess these skills, additional training in topics such as judgment, decision-making, and communication, particularly in emergencies, can be useful. (See Human Factors in Accident Causation, below.)

5. **Emergency Management.** Training in the organization's safety systems and Emergency Response Plan should include exposure to written emergency plans (to which staff should always have ready access), and experiential training through disaster drills. Realistic, hands-on training is essential; simply reading documents is insufficient. Going through past incident reports and reviews is also useful.

6. **Specialized Training and Qualifications.** This may include successfully completing motor vehicle operator training, orientation to legal requirements such as reporting disclosure of child abuse, or a review of the organization's medical protocols and authorization to provide medical care.

Figure 7.9. Cave rescues can be highly complex, and require special emergency management training.

The organization should be able to provide reasonable evidence that staff have been suitably trained in the appropriate topics. Evidence should generally include:

- A record of required training topics, along with detailed content, outlines or lesson plans
- Verification of attendance, such as sign-in sheets at trainings
- Verification that trainees have the appropriate knowledge, abilities, skills, and values. This can include:
    - o Check-off documents
    - o Observation of performance during disaster drill
    - o Signed documents attesting to having read required readings such as safety reports, Emergency Response Plan, and Risk Management Plan
    - o Written and practical driver test forms
    - o Assistant leader evaluations and any other performance evaluation documents

Activity Checkoff: Canoeing Instruction

Employee Name_____   Date   Supervisor Initials

☐ Has read and understood the canoeing, swimming and PFD
sections of the Outdoor Education part of the Field Manual
and the Field Risk Mgt. Manual   ___/___/___   _____

☐ Understands outcomes of canoeing courses   ___/___/___   _____

☐ Understands policies, procedures and guidelines for canoeing ___/___/___   _____

☐ Understands course format & progression   ___/___/___   _____

☐ Can conduct safety briefing, including whistle and paddle signals ___/___/___   _____

☐ Understands how to teach and evaluate use of canoeing
program equipment (e.g. canoe, paddle, PFD, rocket box, throw
rope), including paddle strokes and techniques   ___/___/___   _____

☐ Can properly inspect equipment (e.g. canoe, paddle, PFD, rocket
box, throw rope, skiff) and knows when to do so   ___/___/___   _____

☐ Understands care of gear   ___/___/___   _____

☐ Can appropriately frame/brief and debrief the activity   ___/___/___   _____

☐ Understands and can conduct basic rescues such as canoe-
over-canoe rescue   ___/___/___   _____

☐ Can evaluate weather conditions and take appropriate action;
knows when to get off the water   ___/___/___   _____

☐ Demonstrates an understanding of winds, currents, waves
and hydrology, and how they affect canoeing   ___/___/___   _____

☐ Understands and can use emergency telecom equipment   ___/___/___   _____

☐ Can teach basics of local area natural history and ecology   ___/___/___   _____

☐ Can teach proper loading, unloading, carrying and tying
up of canoes   ___/___/___   _____

☐ Understands swimming policies, procedures and systems   ___/___/___   _____

☐ Understands lead/sweep system and awareness of skiff purpose ___/___/___   _____

Comments: _____

_____

_____   _____
Program Director signature   Date

I have read and understood the canoeing, swimming and PFD sections of the Field Manual and the Field Risk
Management Manual. I certify that I have all the competencies and capabilities described above.

_____   _____
Field Staff person signature   Date

Figure 7.10. A check-off document helps verify activity leaders are capable of appropriately conducting activities.

Administrator Training. A similar process applies to training of program managers. A verifiable record of appropriate training should provide evidence of trainee competence in areas such as:

1. Understanding and applying the organization's risk management philosophy, methodology, and Risk Management Plan
2. Appropriately conducting the administrative components of the organization's Emergency Response Plan
3. Managing media relations during crisis
4. Use of the medical screening system (for medical screeners)
5. Managing workplace safety issues (see Chapter 12, Business Administration)
6. Administrative leadership of safety reviews, incident reviews, staff training, and business administration systems

Office and Administrative Training. All employees and volunteers who may use the organization's facilities should be able to manage office-oriented risks. This includes the ability to identify emergency exits, use fire extinguishers and first aid kits, and participate in emergency response such as evacuation from the office. A new employee orientation checkoff form covering these topics and kept in each employee's file may help ensure orientation to these subjects occurs.

Figure 7.11. Documentation of training should be kept in personnel files.

Culture. As all training and similar activities occur, it's appropriate to pay explicit attention to how the words and actions of trainers and authority figures establish corporate culture. Messages that overtly or implicitly convey a culture of conservative risk management are beneficial as new team members absorb organizational norms.

Curriculum Design in Training. To be effective, trainings should be well-designed. Summaries of three principles of curriculum design are briefly outlined here.

Structure. Well-designed curricula have three principal components:

- **Goals.** These are the explicit learning objectives of the training.
- **Lesson Plans.** These are the detailed descriptions for each discrete learning activity, targeted to meet the goals.
- **Assessments.** These are tools that show whether students successfully met the goals, after completing the learning activities.

Methodology. Risk management trainings in outdoor programming are often most effective when they employ the following educational methodologies:

- **Experiential learning.** Direct experience followed by focused reflection.
- **Scaffolding, or constructivism.** Learning builds upon and relates to previous knowledge.
- **Progression through learning domains.** Learning proceeds through a sequence of learning domains (such as Bloom's taxonomy), moving through knowledge to application and synthesis and beyond.

Alignment. All aspects of the organization's risk management systems and risk management training infrastructure are closely and intentionally aligned.

- **Risk Management systems.** The organization's risk management infrastructure (including risk management philosophy, mission, policies and procedures, Risk Management Plan, Emergency Response Plan) are organized and documented.
- **Training Plan.** A Training Plan exists for the organization, and covers
  - o What should be covered (all risk management topics and information in the risk management systems in the previous bullet point)
  - o Who should be trained (broken down by categories such as activity leaders, vehicle operators, various layers of management, etc.)
  - o When training should occur (for example, before working with participants)
  - o How often training should occur or be refreshed (for instance, annually) for each topic for each audience.

- **Lesson Plans.** Lesson plans (or "learning activities") for risk management trainings, and their associated syllabi, are aligned with the training plan (bullet point two), which is aligned to completely cover the relevant topics of the risk management systems (bullet point one).
- **Assessments.** Evaluation instruments are matched to each learning activity in the risk management training system.

Figure 7.12. Risk management information in the employee handbook and other materials should be incorporated into the risk management training plan.

7.2.5. Sustain Capacities, and the Performance They Engender

A fantastic staff team has been hired and trained, and is running outstanding outdoor programs. Clients are thrilled. How to sustain excellence?

Activity Leaders. Staff in the field maximize risk management performance when they work within an established supervision structure that provides guidance, coaching, recognition and discipline. Formalized evaluation systems encourage good performance; evaluation tools can include direct observation; written evaluations by supervisors, supervisees, and peers; and indirect evaluation instruments such as incident reports, post-program debrief forms, land manager feedback, and season-end exit interviews. These and other documents such as commendations and reprimands should be kept on file.

A just culture environment (see Chapter 5, Culture) also supports good risk management.

Professional development and advancement opportunities maximize staff engagement and retention, and ease the often chronic problem of high staff turnover in outdoor programs.

Ongoing training, as part of the organization's established Training Plan, should keep staff apprised of recent incidents and learning from them, and any changes in policies, procedures or practices.

The outdoor program will benefit from having a system that reminds staff to renew expiring certifications (such as first aid certificates) prior to their expiration, and otherwise ensures required qualifications stay current.

Particularly with busy seasons and extended outdoor expeditions, time should be built in for staff recuperation and rest.

Clear written criteria should be developed and followed for promotion of staff. Documentary evidence should be kept showing that staff have met advancement criteria.

Activity Checkoff: Canoeing Instruction

This evaluation is to be used as a learning opportunity for the activity leader in regards to their professional performance in the areas listed below. Keep answers concise and neatly written. Staff must fill out narrative and numerical sections. Please comment on positives as well as improvement areas. Use the back of this sheet if necessary.

Activity Leader Name:_____   Program Dates:___/___ to ___/___/___

Organization:_____   Location:_____

Scale: 1=Unacceptable 2= Needs Improvement 3=Satisfactory 4=Above Average 5=Exceptional

Leadership ability	
Enthusiasm and attitude	
Planning and organization	
Preparation	
Teaching ability (e.g. accurate and clear)	
Communication and interpersonal skills	
Interaction with students and chaperones	
Technical skills as they related to this course	
Safety	
Acting as an organizational representative	
Ability to cope with stressful situations	
Flexibility during course	

Greatest Strengths:

Specific improvement areas:

Evaluator Name, Title:_____

I have read and understood this evaluation. Activity Leader signature: _____

Figure 7.13. Sample activity leader evaluation for school group outdoor program.

Managers. For administrators and other staff, the same principles apply. For instance, any staff person who might be involved in responding to a crisis should go through annual training and practice in the program's Emergency Response Plan.

Retention. Keeping high-performing staff, who are expert in the organization's programs and safety systems, is an important business objective. Approaches to this complex topic include:

- Establishing and tracking retention goals, and developing strategies to meet objectives
- Surveying staff on engagement and retention topics
- Maximizing compensation, professional development, and other benefits to the extent possible
- Advancing staff through the organizational hierarchy, as possible, to sustain high engagement
- Maintaining a positive and supportive organizational culture
- Addressing systemic barriers to retention in the industry, such as financial constraints

Figure 7.14. Opportunities to climb the corporate ladder help retain outdoor professionals.

7.3. POSITIONS

Risk management, to some degree, should be in the job description and performance evaluation criteria of every staff person. Larger organizations should have full-time safety personnel, such as a Vice President of Safety or a department devoted to risk management. In outdoor programs of any size, one top program administrator should officially serve as the organization's Risk Management Officer, and execute the responsibilities for overseeing safety management.

To maintain effective emergency response and risk transfer, adherence should be made to applicable requirements regarding distinguishing employees from independent contractors.

The role of Responsible Persons such as school group chaperones is discussed in Chapter 9, Participants. Staff to participant ratios are addressed in Chapter 6, Activities and Program Areas.

7.4. SOURCES OF ADDITIONAL INFORMATION

The SupportAdventure project of the New Zealand outdoor industry, funded by the New Zealand government, has resources on safety-related staff matters. Additional guidance is available in the Education Outside the Classroom resources of the New Zealand Ministry of Education.

The Australian Adventure Activities Standard provides guidance on training and assessing outdoor leaders, among other topics.

The UK's Health and Safety Executive publication L77 ("Guidance from the Licensing Authority on the Adventure Activities Licensing Regulations 2004") provides information on ratios, qualifications, and safety advisors, among other matters.

Government agencies addressing workplace matters provide general HR management resources.

Human Resources Management associations (such as the Society for Human Resource Management) offer literature, consultant services, conferences, and other support to their members and the public.

7.5. SYSTEMS ISSUES

Systemic issues in the outdoor industry affect human resources management and safety performance. These complex problems are not resolvable by any individual outdoor program, but by working together, progress can be made.

Issues include pay rates, employee retention, sustainability of work schedules, minimal training requirements, widely adopted safety standards, cultural expectations, and financial concerns.

Chapter 23, Seeing Systems, also considers this topic.

Figure 7.15. Outdoor leader training requirements compared to those in other occupations is a systemic issue.

7.6. HUMAN FACTORS IN ACCIDENT CAUSATION

Human error plays a major role in causing accidents. This is the case in outdoor programming as well as other industries such as aviation and health care. Often, multiple factors are involved, including human error, equipment failure, and environmental conditions. Many times, however, analyses show that the accident could have been prevented if the human error was not made.

The human factors are typically not deficits in technical skills, but problems with cognitive and interpersonal skills. Cognitive skills include decision-making and problem-solving. Interpersonal skills include communications, managing group dynamics, and leadership (Figure 7.16).

Factors Leading to Human Error

Figure 7.16. Elements of human error causation.

The aviation industry has recognized the significant role human error plays in major accidents like airplane crashes, and has developed an approach called Crew Resource Management (CRM) in response. Aviation staff receive CRM training in topics including communications, situational awareness, developing contingency plans,

awareness of fatigue, problem-solving, decision-making, and teamwork.

A number of elements in this book address some of these human factors. Debriefing, just culture and a culture where supervisees can question the decisions of supervisors are ways to reduce human error.

Let's look more closely at the cognitive skills aspect of human error, and how these limitations in thinking affect judgment and decisions. Elements here include two cognitive limitations: cognitive shortcuts and cognitive biases.

Managing Cognitive Limitations

Cognitive Bias and Cognitive Shortcuts

The human brain is immensely capable, but it has limitations. Two of these limitations are cognitive bias and cognitive shortcuts (Figure 7.17).

Cognitive biases are systematic errors in thinking that lead to poor decisions. These include faulty thought processing regarding factors such as attention, memory, and attribution. Cognitive biases arise out of deep-rooted psychological traits: a psychological desire to view ourselves positively, a reluctance to change beliefs, and our tendency to be influenced by others.

Dozens of cognitive biases have been described. There is no universal list or classification of these biases.

Cognitive shortcuts are assumptions, or generalizations about the way things are, that are often but not always true. Because the world is complex and presents a sometimes overwhelming amount of information to process, with too many possible decisions to contemplate, these mental shortcuts help us arrive at decisions quickly and efficiently. But although they are often useful, these assumptions, also called "heuristics," cause problems when they turn out to be not accurate. The role of heuristics in making poor judgments was popularized by researcher Daniel Kahneman, who won the Nobel Prize in Economic Sciences for this work. Cognitive shortcuts can sometimes lead to cognitive biases.

Cognitive biases and cognitive shortcuts are sometimes confused with logical fallacies, but they are different. Cognitive limitations have to do with weaknesses in our default patterns of thinking. Logical fallacies, for example circular reasoning, are errors of reason in a logical argument.

CONFIRMATION BIAS

Confirmation bias describes the tendency to give precedence to information that reinforces what one believes or wants to be true, and to discount information that contradicts it. We see what we want to see.

Examples: Our group skied on this avalanche terrain yesterday without a problem, so despite a change in the weather it's likely to be fine today. The whitewater rapids have higher water than we are used to, but another paddling group made it through, so we can try it too.

GROUPTHINK, OR BANDWAGON BIAS

Groupthink occurs when individuals suppress their concerns due to reluctance to take a position contrary to others in the group. This can easily occur when leaders or socially dominant group members are opinionated and forceful. Social conformity outweighs realistically considering risks.

Example: Some group members are exhausted, and I think we should camp here rather than push on through the dark. But others want to continue, so I won't say anything.

NORMALCY BIAS

The normalcy bias refers to people's tendency to fail to adequately prepare for or decisively respond to a disaster or other incident. Individuals deny that something could happen or is happening.

Examples: An organization might not plan for a rare disaster like earthquake, wildfire or flood in a program area, figuring it'll probably never happen, and things will remain normal. And when an official evacuation order arrives, individuals may be in a state of denial and fail to evacuate, until it's too late.

ILLUSION OF CONTROL

When individuals believe they can control uncontrollable events, they may underestimate the risk of incidents. They may also continue to pursue a failing strategy.

Example: I can predict avalanches by analyzing the snowpack and conditions.

ANCHORING

Individuals tend to rely too much on the earliest information received, and compare all new information to that reference point. This is why an item for sale looks more attractive when the regular price is listed.

Example: A participant on a wilderness trip complains of abdominal pain, but it's only from eating too much dinner. Days later they again complain of abdominal pain. It's dismissed as over-eating, but it actually was dangerous internal bleeding.

SUNK COST

This is the tendency to consider past investments that no longer have an impact on the future. It might be unsafe to continue to the mountain peak, but the client paid a lot of money for the trip and saved up their vacation time, so they want to continue.

Example: After days of travel, we're almost to the mountain top; let's push past our turn-around time just a couple hours to reach the peak.

OPTIMISM BIAS (OVERCONFIDENCE BIAS)

Research shows people tend to overestimate their own capabilities. Optimism bias is the mistaken belief one will be more fortunate and successful than one actually will be.

Examples: Despite the increasing winds, I think I can guide the kayaking group through the long open-water crossing without incident. There's a thunder and lightning storm approaching, but we still have time to hike up over the ridge and get back down to safety before it arrives.

NORMALIZATION OF DEVIANCE

In 1986, the US Space Shuttle Challenger exploded, killing all aboard. The shuttle's o-rings were known to be defective, but they hadn't ruptured in earlier flights. So the faulty components were eventually considered not a risk—until they catastrophically failed. This is normalization of deviance.

Example: We keep putting underqualified activity leaders in the field, but nothing serious ever happens, so we won't do anything about it.

Figure 7.17. Examples of cognitive limitations.

Treatment

Cognitive limitations are built into how human brains function. There's no way to eliminate them that's known to be effective. There are ideas about how to mitigate their impact, but research demonstrating the effectiveness of these ideas is lacking. Nevertheless, some approaches to consider include:

1. **Education.** Understanding more about the weaknesses in human thinking processes may help, although it appears to have limited effectiveness. Case studies and role-playing with structured group discussions may be useful, research suggests. Disseminating "lessons learned" and narratives of previous incidents may reduce optimism bias.

2. **Rules.** This avoids having to make high-consequence decisions in stressful situations like emergencies, when thinking is compromised. Rules provide structure to replace emotion and intuition in conducting outdoor activities and managing emergencies. Examples include:
    a. Operating policies, procedures and guidelines
    b. Mandatory use of checklists (for instance, before driving a vehicle)
    c. Algorithms or decision trees, for example regarding decision-making about medical evacuations
    d. Decision points such as pre-established turn-around times in mountaineering

3. **Social norms marketing** principles (see Chapter 5, Culture) to counteract groupthink

4. **Group dynamics management** to diminish confirmation bias, groupthink, and sunk cost bias:
    a. In groups, obtain the opinions of members before the leader provides an opinion.
    b. Solicit anonymous opinions.
    c. Establish a "devil's advocate" or "red team" entity that takes a contrary position and attempts to find weaknesses in the established plan.
    d. Conduct pre-mortems (see Chapter 23, Seeing Systems). Even just asking one's self, "would I like explaining to my boss how we got into this situation?" may help.

5. **Unbiased external viewpoints.** External risk management reviews can counteract a group's cognitive limitations like groupthink and confirmation bias, particularly when they are truly independent and not subject to conflict of interest. Risk Management Committee members who are psychologically independent of the organization can also help.

Chapter Summary

1. Staff are an essential part of an organization's risk management system.

2. Human resources management involves determining required staff capacities, hiring and training staff to meet those capacities, and providing support and supervision.

3. Capacities include knowledge, skills, abilities, and attitudes/values.

4. Activity leaders should operate well under the limits of their technical competence.

5. Specific capacities include technical skills, interpersonal skills, activity area competence, emergency management, and appropriate attitudes.

6. Criminal history can help inform hiring decisions.

7. Because the self-control part of the brain develops after the risk-seeking part, risk-taking behavior only declines in the mid-20's age range.

8. Qualifications and prior experience can indicate staff capacities.

9. Staff training should verifiably cover all necessary risk management topics.

10. Training should be well-designed and aligned with risk management infrastructure.

11. A variety of approaches support supervision and retention of staff.

12. Every staff person has a risk management responsibility, and should be clear on what it is.

13. Additional information on human resource management is available.

14. Systemic issues affect staff-related risk management.

15. Cognitive and interpersonal skill deficits affect risk management.

16. Cognitive limitations include cognitive biases and cognitive shortcuts (heuristics).

CHAPTER 8

EQUIPMENT

LEARNING OBJECTIVES

1. Select gear appropriately, taking into account standards, laws, and your program's unique circumstances
2. Purchase genuine equipment and document appropriately
3. Use equipment appropriately, paying attention to special hazards, continuous telecom capacity, and documentation of use
4. Maintain and clean gear to applicable standards and document as required
5. Repair equipment in the field and at central facility per original equipment manufacturer instructions and best practices, documenting as needed
6. Inspect equipment at appropriate intervals by qualified persons against relevant criteria
7. Locate gear to be suitably available and store in appropriately secure and suitable environments
8. Permanently retire equipment and supplies per appropriate schedule and document accordingly
9. Attend to and comply with gear recall notices
10. Control equipment inventory using appropriate security, incentives, and tracking systems
11. Document gear history from selection and purchase through retirement or disposal
12. Ensure program staff have the resources and capacities necessary to manage gear adequately and use personal gear appropriately
13. Ensure administrators provide the resources and culture suitable for responsible equipment management
14. Responsibly loan program equipment to staff
15. Ensure participants bring appropriate equipment and clothing and are suitably trained in gear use
16. Appropriately access, inspect and use third-party equipment
17. Address equipment safety issues in the administrative and managerial contexts

8.1. INTRODUCTION

Equipment comprises essential physical tools of the outdoor program leader. Quality outdoor gear can make the difference between a positive outdoor experience and an unsuccessful trip. This applies to not just avoiding a malfunctioning carabiner that doesn't properly close and jeopardizes a life. It can be about a raincoat that keeps the wearer warm and comfortable. Or it can be about the stove with the perfect simmer setting that helps get those tasty cinnamon buns baked just right. It can be as small as an o-ring on a camping stove or as large as a high ropes Challenge Course or fleet of 15-passenger vans. In all cases, in order to appropriately manage the risks of an outdoor program, equipment should be selected, purchased, maintained, repaired, inspected, located, stored, and retired in a verifiably careful manner in line with accepted industry standards.

8.2. SELECTION

8.2.1. Standards and Legislation

Equipment selected for your outdoor program should be appropriate for the activity areas, environmental conditions, skill and experience of staff and participants, activities, and emergency situations you reasonably anticipate to be part of your outdoor experience.

In addition, equipment, especially life safety items such as climbing gear, should meet relevant standards for safety.

There are dozens of standards-setting bodies. They range from well-known and well-respected organizations to those less so. Some are international in scope; others confine themselves to one country.

Some standards-setting entities cover numerous standards over many industries. For instance, the American National Standards Institute (ANSI) has about 10,000 standards covering everything from challenge courses to software and aerospace. Others are more specific: the Parachute Industry Association sets standards for webbing used in activities such as rock climbing and parachuting.

Standards are generally voluntary, unless they are incorporated into law or regulation by a government authority. That said, it's generally a good idea to adhere to well-developed consensus standards. This is because quality standards represent the end result of a thoughtful and inclusive process of industry specialists coming to agreement on best practices.

Standards and standard-setting groups are always changing, however, so pay attention to standards evolution.

Different "industry" groups in outdoor programming, such as mountaineering and challenge courses, have their own sets of standards which gear should meet. Some standards, for instance for static ropes, apply to both the climbing and challenge course fields.

Standards-setting organizations borrow from and reference each other. They frequently build each others' standards into theirs. The geographic and activity areas of applicability for standards-setting organizations may also overlap. For example, standards of the European Committee for Standardization (CEN) apply to Europe; standards of the International Climbing and Mountaineering Federation/Union Internationale des Associations d'Alpinisme (UIAA) apply to mountaineering, and both address mountaineering in Europe. Similarly, standards of the British Standards Institution (BSI) apply to Britain, so it shares many standards with CEN, which sets Europe-wide standards.

Which standards should I pay attention to? Generally, quality equipment manufacturers will do the work for you by determining to which standards their products should conform. That said, it's a good idea to be aware of the standards-setting entities for your geographical location and industry or activities. This way, you will have a sense of what standards apply to you and purchase equipment that meets those standards.

Sometimes multiple standards may apply to the same piece of equipment. For example, to meet the American National Standard ANSI/ACCT 03-2016 Challenge Courses and Zip line/Canopy tours pertaining to static ropes, any one of the following standards can be met: UIAA 107, NFPA 1983, EN 1891 (Type A), CI 1801, or approval from the manufacturer for belaying a single participant.

To find the relevant standards-setting organizations in your area of the world, check multi-national standards-setting entities such as the International Organization for Standardization (ISO) or CEN. Or check with international industry groups—for example, with mountaineering, the UIAA. Reputable outdoor equipment manufacturers should also list the standards their products meet, and the organizations that set those standards.

You may also see a "CE" mark on some equipment. Personal protective equipment (such as helmets) and certain other items intended to be sold in the European Economic Area (EEA) are required to comply with European safety laws. The "CE" ("Conformité Européenne") mark indicates compliance with the relevant legislation. This mark, shown in Fig. 8.1, may be seen on equipment sold outside the EEA as well.

Fig. 8.1. CE mark indicating conformity with European safety laws.

Figure 8.2, below, lists a sample of standards-setting entities that may be applicable to equipment used by outdoor programs.

ENTITY	DESCRIPTION	EXAMPLE
American National Standards Institute (ANSI)	American organization setting a wide variety of standards across many industries	*ANSI/ACCT 03-2016 Challenge Courses and Zip line/Canopy tours*
CSA Group (formerly Canadian Standards Association)	Canadian organization setting a wide variety of standards across many industries in North America	*Z259.10-18 Full body harnesses*
National Fire Protection Association (NFPA)	US-based standards-setting organization on fire, electrical and related hazards, including ropes, harnesses and webbing	*NFPA 1983 Standard on Life Safety Rope and Equipment for Emergency Services*
European Committee for Standardization (CEN)	European organization setting a wide variety of standards across many industries	*EN (European Norm)1891:1998 Personal protective equipment for the prevention of falls from a height - Low stretch kernmantel ropes*
British Standards Institution (BSI)	British organization setting a wide variety of standards across many industries	*BS EN 1891:1998 Personal protective equipment for the prevention of falls from a height. Low stretch kernmantel ropes*
International Climbing and Mountaineering Federation/Union Internationale des Associations d'Alpinisme (UIAA)	Climbing and mountaineering group setting internationally recognized standards for climbing and mountaineering equipment	*UIAA 121 Carabiners (connectors, karabiners)*
Cordage Institute	International association setting standards for ropes	*CI 1801 Low Stretch/Static Kernmantle Life Safety Rope*

Fig 8.2. Sample standards-setting entities applicable to outdoor equipment.

Figure 8.3. Ice Axe with CE and UIAA markings.

8.2.2. First Aid

What comprises appropriate contents of a first aid kit is a common question. There is, however, no single answer. Variables that influence kit contents include:

1. The nature of the activities
2. Location
3. Environmental conditions
4. Anticipated hazards
5. Nature of participant group
6. Level of medical training of leaders
7. Legal and regulatory restrictions

Sample first aid kit inventories exist in many wilderness first aid reference books. Suppliers of outdoor first aid kits also provide a variety of suggested kit contents.

Preventing accidents from occurring in the first place, coupled with calm and sensible incident management—even from unskilled medical practitioners—is often more valuable than the contents of any first aid kit. That said, principles of medical kit organization follow:

1. Kit contents range from comfort care to live-saving. At a minimum, bring the latter. This includes medication for life-threatening allergy (anaphylaxis) and gloves and mask for conducting CPR.
2. Avoid bringing first aid items you don't know how to use.
3. Consider bringing items with multiple purposes; be prepared to improvise.
4. Bring a reference book, electronic resource, or telecommunications device for accessing detailed medical knowledge.
5. Consider generic medications over brand-name equivalents; the same efficacy is provided at a reduced cost.

Legal and regulatory restrictions refer primarily to medications. The use of certain medication such as injectable epinephrine is restricted in certain US states, for example. Some countries in regions such as the Middle East and Africa have very stringent regulations on certain prescription and even over-the-counter medications, and violations can bring imprisonment and other penalties. Additional information on international restrictions may be available from federal agencies that deal with international relations or health, international travel consultants, and embassy and consulate resources.

8.2.3. Low-Resource Environments

In low-resource environments such as low-income countries and certain areas of middle-income countries, equipment normally available in high-income countries may not be present. Availability should be researched beforehand, and the appropriate accommodations made.

For instance, vehicles with seat belts, which might be required by an organization's safety policies, may be unavailable in some parts of the world. A group on an international program staying at a hotel for a night before venturing into a remote area might find the hotel lacking smoke detectors—and so might choose to bring and temporarily install their own. Groups might decide to bring syringes, medications, and other medical supplies during programs in low-resource communities where patients admitted to a hospital are expected to bring their own medication.

8.3. PURCHASING

8.3.1. Counterfeit goods

Counterfeit outdoor gear should never be purchased and used. There are significant safety problems with counterfeit equipment. For example:

- Counterfeit carabiners sold as genuine Petzl equipment had a breaking strength of 13 kilonewtons (kN); the required strength is 20 kN.
- Down jackets sold as genuine Canada Goose products did not contain sanitized down but instead "feather mulch" which might contain bacteria and mold that could lead to dangerous infectious disease in the wearer.
- Those same down jackets, due to lower insulating quality, could increase the chance of frostbite or life-threatening hypothermia.

When purchasing equipment, beware of online marketplaces with third-party sellers of goods at discount or too-good-to-be-true prices. Purchase only through the manufacturer's network of official distributors and authorized retailers. Many manufacturers provide information on legitimate sales channels through a "store locator" or similar feature on their official website.

Detecting counterfeits. Counterfeit equipment may show poor quality work or inferior materials. Logos and other similar identifying information may not match the authentic original. Misspellings may be present. Figure 8.4 gives an example.

Figure 8.4. Counterfeit Petzl knife with prominent misspelling of brand name.

Some counterfeits are extremely difficult to distinguish from genuine items. If in doubt, take the item out of service and contact the manufacturer of the authentic merchandise.

8.3.2. Documentation

Keep thorough and accurate records of purchases. Record the date of purchase, which for some items like climbing ropes, helmets and harnesses can be important in determining retirement schedules.

Document the source of purchase, so that evidence of acquisition from a reputable source can be available.

8.4. USE

8.4.1. Special Hazards

Some outdoor equipment can be hazardous if used improperly. An appropriate standard is to use all equipment in accordance with manufacturer's recommendations, unless in the unlikely situation that doing so would clearly increase risk. This means that activity leaders should either have access to the manufacturer's written use guides or access to that information in another format. In addition to official use recommendations, it can be valuable to include tips and best practice guidelines in a field manual to which activity leaders refer, the contents of which they have demonstrably read and agreed to abide by.

For medications carried in first aid kits, it is useful to carry in the kit information outlining the description, indications, contraindications, dosage, route of administration, precautions, side effects, and drug interactions of each medication. For inhaled, injected, or other drugs with a more complex method of administration, that should be described as well. Figure 8.5 gives examples.

Medication & Dosage	Indications, Contraindications, Dosing, Precautions, Site Effects
DIPHENHYDRAMINE HCl 25-30 mg Every 4-6 hours	Anti-histamine. Provides relief of respiratory allergy symptoms and colds. Relieves itching of allergic skin reactions, seasickness and treats insomnia. Used to assist in anaphylaxis and stings/bites. Side effects are drowsiness, nausea, dry mouth and excitability. Do not give to 12 year olds or under unless under a physician's orders.
EPINEPHRINE (vial & needles) 0.3 mg	For severe allergic reactions to bites, stings, food, and other allergies. Read and become familiar with instructions before use if needed. Evacuate patient and administer anti-histamine before or following injection. Use epinephrine at first sign of systemic allergic reaction (per protocol).
ALBUTEROL (Inhaler)	For asthmatic reactions, when subject's personal inhaler is unavailable. Read instructions before using. Shake the inhaler; breathe out fully through the mouth; while breathing in deeply and slowly through the mouth, fully depress the top of the metal canister; hold your breath as long as possible.

Figure 8.5. Examples of information accompanying first aid kit medications.

In addition to providing usage information, in some cases, prescription medications should be accompanied by the prescription document, and sometimes a signed letter from a physician as well.

Portable backpacking stoves (figure 8.6) are an example of outdoor equipment that can pose notable hazards during use. Older-model camp stoves that pressurize fuel by locating the fuel tank next to the burner can be prone to over-pressurization, leading to unexpected bursts of flame from the filler cap pressure relief valve. When cooking for big groups, large pots balanced on backpacking stoves can tip over if not carefully supported and balanced; this can lead to scalding and other injury.

Figure 8.6. Moderately-sized pot on camping stove. Large pots make stoves unstable unless they are secured by rocks or other means.

8.4.2. Telecommunications

Outdoor groups should consider adhering to a standard of instantaneous communications from any location at any time, back to their operations base or emergency rescue services. It may be expected that outdoor program leaders be able to reach emergency services immediately or within two hours, if the telecom technology to do so is available and not prohibitively expensive.
(If this will not be the case, informed consent from participants and their guardians should generally be obtained.)

Technology for these telecommunications continues to evolve, and includes satellite phones, mobile phones, radios of various frequency ranges, and satellite-based emergency locator/messaging devices.

Activity leaders—and participants, if activity leaders could potentially be incapacitated—should understand proper procedures and protocol for the use of the telecommunications equipment available. For VHF radios, this could include knowing how to:

1. Assemble and disassemble
2. Turn on and off
3. Perform radio checks at the proper time and to the proper entities
4. Select appropriate radio frequencies that are legal to use
5. Obtain reception
6. Manage for channel noise (squelch)
7. Use clear, professional, succinct messages and standard radio communications protocol to appropriately transmit and receive messages
8. Avoid overexposure to radio frequency radiation

8.4.3. Documentation

Equipment use should be documented when records of this information can be important for establishing accountability, scheduling maintenance, or related reasons. For instance, each use of an organization's motor vehicle should be recorded in the vehicle's use log (see Chapter 11, Transportation.) This helps organizations ensure vehicles are used only for business purposes, determine who may have been operating the vehicle when damage occurred, and conduct regular maintenance based on distance driven in a timely manner.

Many organizations that use ropes for belaying, rappelling/abseiling, rescue training, or other technical/vertical operations where life safety ropes are employed record each use of a rope, with notes recording any unusual conditions or usage.

Although not all outdoor programs have a practice of maintaining rope logs, a number of rope manufacturers recommend or provide usage logs. It's generally a good idea to follow manufacturer recommendations where they're available. Use of rope logs can make it more likely that pre-use and post-use inspections get done (since inspections are recorded in the log), provide evidence that those inspections were actually conducted, and be useful for logging cumulative use or wear that can lead to earlier rope retirement. Rope log formats vary; figure 8.7 shows sample text for a typical rope log.

Rope Log

Rope Name: _____   Type (static/dynamic): _____

Primary Use: _____   Length: _____

Color/Description: _____   Date of Purchase: _____

Diameter: _____

INSTRUCTIONS

An entry should be made in this book every time the rope is used. It is imperative to the integrity of this official record to thoroughly inspect this rope both before and after each use period. Record: dates checked out, site manager initials, number of days used (any part of a day counts as a whole), and the climbing site or use location. Record rope condition in the "remarks" section and any other important information regarding its use during each period. If it is necessary to shorten this rope due to wear, re-measure the rope, mark the cut end, then record the date and new length in the appropriate space on the cover of this book. Use the designated section this book to record rope washing information. Also see the Field Manual for other essential information.

Date(s)	Site Manager	Number of Days Used	Climbing Site/Area	Usage (Normal / Extraordinary)	Inspected before use (initial)	Inspected after use (initial)	Remarks (e.g. hard use over sharp edge, significant falls)

CLIMBING ROPE WASH INSTRUCTIONS & RECORD

1. Wash this rope with clean, cold water in a front-loading washing machine (or, second choice, in a mesh bag in a top-loading spindle-agitator washing machine).
2. Use mild soap; do not use detergent or bleach.
3. Allow to air dry (out of direct sunlight) before storing.

Date washed: _____   Date washed: _____

Brand of soap used: _____   Brand of soap used: _____

Date washed: _____   Date washed: _____

Brand of soap used: _____   Brand of soap used: _____

Figure 8.7.
Example Rope Log.

8.5. MAINTENANCE

8.5.1. Maintenance Standards

Maintenance on outdoor equipment should be done to the original equipment manufacturer's standards. If those standards are unavailable or insufficient for your situation, comply with written industry association standards. For instance, the UIAA, in conjunction with the British Mountaineering Council, has published inspection, maintenance and retirement guidance for carabiners, harnesses, helmets, ropes and other climbing and mountaineering equipment.

In the absence of written standards by an authoritative body, unwritten industry best practices should be employed. These can be established through information-gathering from well-respected and experienced individuals working in the same outdoor specialty areas as those in which your program is involved. Qualified inspectors, safety reviewers, and senior colleagues in your network can help define these expectations.

An example of climbing rope maintenance guidelines follows. This list is not exhaustive. Similar maintenance guidelines should be established and used for helmets, harnesses, cord, webbing, hardware, and other safety equipment. Note that different products, manufacturers and industry groups may have differing guidelines.

1. Never store the rope above 80 degrees Celsius, or permit the rope to overheat, for example by rapid rappelling/abseiling.
2. Keep the rope away from chemicals, including acids or alkalis—which may cause invisible rope damage—and engine exhaust fumes. Keep rope away from potentially dangerous common items such as batteries, products that contain benzene, phenol (pine oil cleaners), carbon tetrachloride, formaldehyde, and gasoline or other petroleum distillates.
3. Do not expose the rope to significant electrical conductivity.
4. Do not store the rope in direct contact with cement or concrete, which can expose the rope to damaging acids.
5. Keep the rope away from UV exposure when possible; sunlight and other UV exposure can shorten rope life.
6. Do not step on the rope.
7. Store the rope in a cool, dry, dark area.
8. Keep the rope out of the dirt with a rope bag and/or tarp or similar items.
9. Wash dirty ropes by hand, in a front-loading washing machine, or manufacturer-approved rope washing device in clear cold to lukewarm (< 30 degrees C) water with a non-detergent soap designed for delicate fabrics. A synthetic bristle brush may be used. Do not use bleaching agents or a high pressure water sprayer.
10. Rinse rope with fresh water after use in a salty environment (e.g. near the ocean); let dry.
11. Use only disinfectants that will not damage the rope. To disinfect, soak rope for 10 minutes in a mix of 60 ml non-concentrated household bleach (~5-6 percent sodium hypochlorite) and 4 l tap water. Thoroughly rinse and let air dry (not in a commercial dryer).
12. Dry wet ropes in a cool place with good air circulation out of direct sunlight.
13. If a rope is cut, treat the new ends to prevent fraying and maintain original end markings.
14. Avoid abrading the rope or exposing to humidity, which can shorten rope life.
15. Store the rope for a maximum of five years before use.
16. Periodically assess rope length, as ropes tend to shrink with use.
17. The maximum life of the rope is 10 years. This is reduced, potentially to immediate retirement, if:
    a. The rope has held a major fall or load
    b. Inspection indicates nontrivial damage
    c. The sheath is significantly worn
    d. The rope has been in contact with damaging chemicals or environments
    e. The rope has been subject to frequent or heavy use
18. Retire ropes of unknown history or which are unusable due to changes in law, regulation, or standards, or incompatibility with other gear.
19. Inspect the rope before and after each use. Rope should be dry when being inspected. Look at each centimeter of rope for damage such as cuts, burns, fraying, fuzziness, bulges or narrow areas, and signs of chemical damage such as discolored, fused, stiff or brittle fibers. Feel the entire length of the rope with bare hands for hard or stiff spots; bulges or narrow areas; soft/mushy areas; melted, glazed or glossy areas from heat damage, or other signs of damage. Bend rope in small loops or bights to check for consistent curved shapes. Assess for chemical odors. Ensure markings and terminations are in good condition. Document inspection results and take action as appropriate.

20. Conduct an annual inspection of each rope, using criteria as above. Document results and take action as appropriate.
21. On retirement, destroy or discard the rope such that it cannot be used again as a lifeline.

Maintenance information, customized for your particular equipment and circumstances, should be published and made accessible to appropriate personnel.

8.5.2. Cleaning

Most outdoor gear such as tents and backpacks should be cleaned in accordance to brief written guidance from equipment management staff. Figure 8.9 in section 8.7 on gear inspection gives example instructions. However, some items require careful disinfection in order to reduce to possibility of disease transmission, and in some cases, to comply with applicable laws or regulations.

Non-disposable medical supplies such as scissors and forceps that may have been contaminated by blood or other bodily fluids should be carefully disinfected, for example by use of an appropriate disinfectant solution.

Reusable containers used for temporary storage of human waste on river trips, caving expeditions, or other outdoor experiences should similarly be sterilized in accordance with a written procedure outlining personal protective equipment use, disinfectants employed, and cleaning and storage procedures.

Kitchen utensils should also be cleaned and sanitized to prevent the transmission of illness. Local food handling ordinances or regulations often require disinfection using approved germicidal solutions, and should be consulted in the development of kitchenware cleaning procedures.

8.5.3. Documentation

Document in writing the maintenance expectations you aim to meet. Maintain detailed records of equipment maintenance and its congruency with those expectations.

Something as straightforward as wiping down dirty sleeping pads generally doesn't need to be recorded, but care of life safety equipment such as ropes, cord, webbing, carabiners, helmets and harnesses should be documented. Care of items with significant potential safety impact such as vehicles and medical supplies should also be documented.

8.6. REPAIR

Outdoor equipment needing repair should be mended following original equipment manufacturer (OEM) instructions, if available. For repairs of non-life safety equipment such as tarps or stuff sacks, basic sewing and patching practices are generally sufficient.

Larger outdoor programs often have staff focused on gear repair and supplied with heavy-duty sewing machines and other specialized equipment. Field staff may also have repair duties; it's common for a repair kit to be carried by groups on extended expeditions to facilitate field repairs. Written procedures for how and when to use the contents should be included in the repair kit to ensure best practices are followed. Figure 8.8 shows a sample field repair kit inventory. Repair kits should be customized for the equipment, staff skills, environments and activities of each outdoor program.

Contents for Field Repair Kit

1. Sewing awl
2. Needles (3 or 4) and thread in cardboard
3. 3 meters parachute cord
4. Large square of taffeta (tent material)
5. Small roll of taffeta tape
6. Tube of seam sealer
7. Small roll of duct tape (wrapped around pen)
8. 4 different-sized buckles
9. 6 safety pins
10. 1 zipper
11. 1 clevis pin with ring (for backpacks)
12. 4 shade tarp wingnuts
13. Pliers or multitool
14. All purpose oil for stove parts and metal
15. O-rings for large basecamp stove
16. One stove repair kit (from OEM) for each type of backpacking stove

Figure 8.8. Example field repair kit inventory.

Having equipment in good repair reduces the risk of safety incidents due to deficiencies in gear. Although a small tear in a sleeping bag liner is unlikely to be more than an inconvenience, a satellite phone, camp stove or SCUBA tank that fails when you most need it can have a significant impact.

Repairs of safety-critical items should be documented, just as with recording maintenance of those items.

For some equipment, such as seriously damaged climbing rope, there is no repair. The damaged portion should be cut out and destroyed or permanently discarded.

8.7. INSPECTION

Proper inspection of outdoor equipment is essential to minimizing risks associated with inadequate gear.

8.7.1. When to Inspect

Equipment inspection generally falls into six timeframes:
1) At Acquisition
2) Before Use
3) During Use
4) After Use
5) At Regular Intervals (regardless of use status)
6) As Part of Comprehensive Safety Reviews

Inspection at Acquisition. Newly acquired or installed equipment should undergo an acceptance inspection on receipt or completion of installation or major modification. Only on successful completion of this inspection should the item be declared ready for use.

Inspection Before Use. Gear should be inspected for suitability prior to each use. When a field staff person accesses or is issued gear by logistics personnel, a thorough inspection of equipment should be made. For example, ropes should be in good condition (see rope inspection criteria in Maintenance Standards, above). Cooking items should be clean and functional. Stoves should be briefly tested. First aid kits should be inventoried. Tarps, tents, and raingear should be examined for holes or rips. Radios, phones, and other battery-powered devices should be tested for functioning. Every item should be evaluated before each use to ensure it is likely to function as intended when needed.

When a youth participant on a multi-week wilderness expedition went missing, rescue personnel were dispatched deep into the wilderness to search for the missing child. One rescue team brought a VHF radio to communicate with search and rescue coordinators, but on arrival at the search site, the radio did not work. The rescuers had neglected to do a radio test before departing to check the batteries, which were dead. Leaving the wilderness, acquiring batteries, and returning to the search site would take days.

For safety-critical items like climbing gear, motor vehicles and emergency medical supplies, results of inspections should be documented—on a rope log, pre-drive vehicle checklist, first aid kit inventory form, or otherwise.

Inspection During Use. Staff should consistently scan gear during use to help ensure it continues to be in suitable condition. A site manager for a climbing or challenge course site should regularly observe equipment as it's being used so any issues can be identified promptly, and that sticky carabiner a participant is struggling with can be replaced right away. A sea kayak trip leader should observe the condition of boats, paddles, PFDs, bilge pumps and other equipment during launch, while on the water, and at the end of the day back at camp.

Inspection After Use. Prior to handing in gear to be stored away, field staff and logistics personnel should carefully assess equipment. Items needing attention should be cleaned, repaired, destroyed, or discarded as appropriate. A written checklist outlining criteria that must be met prior to check-in for each item of equipment can provide useful guidance for field staff. Items not meeting requirements are returned to activity leaders for further cleaning, repair or other remedy before being accepted by logistics staff. Figure 8.9 provides a partial example of such an instruction sheet.

Post-activity gear inspection checklist [partial]			
Item	Requirements	Approved by logistics staff for return	Rejected for return. Note deficiency to be corrected
First Aid Kit	Inventory completed and signed by field staff. Contents clean and dry. Kit bag/box intact and in good condition.		
Stove fuel bottles	No leaks or holes. Lid gasket present and in good condition. Empty of fuel.		
Camp stove	Test burn successful. Fuel depressurized. All components, including bushings and o-rings, intact. Pump gasket oiled if dry.		
Cookware	Cleaned with hot soapy water, rinsed and sanitized.		
PFDs	Buckles, straps intact. Fabric in good condition. Rips sewed (not patched) and shown to logistics staff.		

Figure 8.9. Instruction sheet (partial) for gear check-in inspection standards.

Inspection at Regular Intervals. Safety-critical items should be inspected on a regular basis, with results recorded and appropriate action (such as maintenance, repair or retirement) taken, regardless of whether or not they have been used. These inspections are in addition to pre-use and after-use inspections. For example:

- Some rope manufacturers recommend that climbing ropes be inspected annually. Inspections may also be recommended more frequently, for instance quarterly, if heavily used, as well as after any episode of "exceptional use."
- Motor vehicles should be inspected regularly per OEM recommendations.
- The American National Standard ANSI/ACCT 03-2016 Challenge Courses and Zip line/Canopy tours requires a professional inspection by a qualified person at least annually. This is often done by an external specialist. Some organizations may add to this regime a quarterly inspection done internally by a competent employee.

Inspection as Part of Comprehensive Safety Reviews. Comprehensive risk management reviews, as described in Chapter 19, Risk Management Reviews, assess the entire organization from a safety perspective. Equipment, along with staffing, activities, locations, emergency plans, and other factors are evaluated at this time. One or more years may normally elapse between these risk management reviews, which will evaluate not only equipment but the results of the other, more frequent equipment inspections described above.

8.7.2. Inspector Qualifications

The knowledge and skill of the inspector should be adequate for the nature of the inspection conducted. Requirements will vary depending on the item being inspected and the type of inspection.

For instance, a person conducting an annual challenge course inspection should be a trained and experienced professional meeting rigorous requirements, for example the Qualified Inspector requirements as outlined in the Qualified Course Professional guidelines of the Association for Challenge Course Technology.

In some cases, for example with certain challenge courses, zip lines, or portable climbing structures, government regulations may require specific inspector qualifications.

A pre-use inspection of helmets and harnesses before a day of rock climbing requires a lower level of knowledge and ability. That person should have some familiarity with rock climbing and climbing equipment, understand the relevant inspection criteria and be oriented to their use, and have a reliable source to consult with if there are any questions.

In case of an accident, expect that your inspection criteria, documented inspection results (or lack thereof), and inspection criteria will be scrutinized. Any weaknesses or omissions, no matter how tiny, may be raised as evidence of your program's negligence. In one near-drowning case in which a participant was trapped underwater for approximately 20 minutes while on a whitewater swimming adventure, the qualifications of those who inspected the rapids and supervised the activity were investigated very deeply, to the extent that the course syllabi of the training classes the activity leaders had taken years ago in college were retrieved from the college's deep storage in order to assess field staff qualifications.

For safety-critical inspections, it is important to be able to provide evidence that inspectors of safety-critical equipment are appropriately qualified. Resumes, experience logs or portfolios, and other documentation should be kept current and on file. The documentation should meet or exceed requirements established in job descriptions, written industry guidelines, or relevant laws or regulations.

8.7.3. Depth of Inspection

Inspections will vary in their intensity of analysis. For instance, using a high ropes challenge course as an example:

- A pre-use high ropes challenge course inspection may be conducted from the ground, using binoculars or the naked eye, taking several minutes to walk the course and look for hazards such as damaged elements, dangerous overhanging tree limbs, or missing equipment. A quick report checking boxes with brief narrative is generated.
- A quarterly internal inspection by a challenge course program management employee could involve climbing every element, visually inspecting each component of each element at close range, and performing hands-on evaluation of equipment function. A detailed report is written.
- An annual external inspection by a professional inspector qualified under published national standards could involve a close-range visual and physical inspection of each element, inspection of the condition of the environment surrounding each element, and an assessment of the strength of elements and structures regarding resistance to live and dead loads for each type of material. A comprehensive written report is issued, documenting the condition of each element, a pass/fail grade for

each element, an enumeration of concerns warranting continued observation, and an evaluation of each piece of life safety system equipment, including a pass/fail grade for each piece.

8.7.4. Inspection Criteria

What are the standards against which equipment is measured? Authoritative standards for equipment inspection can be established by a number of entities. These are listed below, using PFDs as an example item to be inspected.

1. **Government.** Relevant laws and regulations must be met. For example, coast guard or other maritime agency officials in some countries may set and enforce regulations regarding sailing programs operating in marine environments. In the US, the United States Coast Guard sets requirements for minimum buoyancy, methods of storage, and type of PFD required. In the UK, Adventure Activities Licensing Authority guidance outlines requirements for the type, size and number of buoyancy aids.
2. **Manufacturer.** Manufacturers may provide information on assessment criteria for inspection of their products. For example, a PFD manufacturer may give guidance on checking for adequate buoyancy of their products.
3. **Installer.** Organizations placing large installations such as artificial climbing walls, canopy tours, or ziplines may provide criteria for inspecting their products. (This is not applicable in our PFD example.)
4. **Industry Groups.** The Personal Flotation Device Manufacturer's Association provides PFD inspection criteria, covering how to check belts and tie tapes, appropriate storage, and observation for waterlogging, mildew odor, fading and shrinkage.
5. **Standards-setting Organizations.** ISO standard 12402-5:2006 sets safety requirements, including performance standards, for PFDs.

As with establishing standards for equipment maintenance, in the absence of sufficient written guidance from authoritative officials or organizations, seek information from reliable, experienced colleagues in your outdoor specialty areas. Continue to scan for the most authoritative guidance available.

Figure 8.10. Outdoor Gear. The right gear, properly inspected and in good condition, reduces the risk of incidents.

8.8. AVAILABILITY, LOCATION AND STORAGE

8.8.1. Availability

Equipment should be strategically located to ensure it is accessible when needed. A first aid kit should be immediately available at all times when people are present. A technical rescue kit may need to be staged high up in a challenge course so it is promptly available for rescuing participants in trouble. Emergency medical and evacuation gear might be stashed at the base of a remote climbing site or below major whitewater rapids. Avalanche beacons/transceivers (figure 8.11) must be on each person and switched on when travelling through avalanche terrain, and shovels and avalanche probes accessible to each person.

Figure 8.11. Avalanche beacon (transceiver), shovel and probe.

On multi-day expeditions, caches of supplies placed in advance—with land manager permission—may be needed. During periodic food resupplies, an accompanying assortment of gear for re-stocking lost or damaged inventory can be useful.

A contingency plan for damage to or loss of critical equipment and clothing should be in place.

> *During a three-week mountaineering expedition, a tiny bushing came off a camp stove, but the trip leader who noticed this failed to notify her instructing partner. The next day the second leader pressurized and lit the stove, which due to the missing component promptly spewed flaming fuel over the nearby vegetation. In an alpine area with little material for smothering the fire, the leader stripped off his new high-end parka and covered the burning stove and plants with it, extinguishing the fire but destroying his rain jacket. Fortunately, within a week the group met a resupply vehicle at a remote mountain road and the trip leader was able to obtain a new jacket.*

Figure 8.12. Outdoor gear storage.

Locating and storing outdoor gear properly maximizes useful life and helps ensure optimal performance. When conditions are not optimal, extra precautions should be taken to help ensure safety.

Humidity is the enemy of much outdoor gear. Nylon ropes and textile products like tents and backpacks can be damaged by mold and mildew brought on by humid conditions. Moisture in maritime environments can combine with salt spray to cause chloride stress corrosion cracking (figure 8.13), leading to corrosion in climbing anchors within a year of installation. This can reduce anchor strength dramatically—from the minimum of 22 kN to between one to five kN—and increase the risk of catastrophic anchor failure.

Figure 8.13. Chloride stress corrosion cracking on nut, hanger and ring on Cayman Brac island in the Caribbean.

The need to store climbing ropes away from exposed cement or concrete to avoid damage from acid leaching was mentioned earlier, along with other rope storage requirements.

Equipment should be secured in a locked and secure facility when not in use. This helps prevent theft, unauthorized use, and intentional or inadvertent damage. Figure 8.12 shows a lockable outdoor equipment room at an outdoor program in China where gear is organized (if not overly tidy).

Figure 8.14. Locking and labeled flammables storage container.

Flammables and Combustibles. In a basecamp or headquarters environment, flammable and combustible liquids such as stove and lantern fuel should be stored in a suitable locked enclosure (such as a grounded metal safety cabinet designed for flammable liquids) and protected from extreme heat.

When the liquids move against something else—such sloshing in a container being transported, or flowing through a hose while being poured from a storage tank into a camping stove fuel bottle—static electricity can build up. If the charge discharges, it may cause a spark that ignites the flammable liquid, resulting in a fire or explosion.

Factors that affect the risk of fire or explosion include the type of solvent and its flash point, the vapor concentration of the liquid in the air, the conductivity of the containers, and air pressure.

To reduce risks, metal or other electrically conductive dispensing and receiving containers should be securely electrically bonded, for example with a special metal bonding strap. Fuel drums in storage and dispensing areas should be electrically grounded. Non-conductive containers generally do not need to be bonded or grounded, although precautions should be taken when filling these containers to reduce static charge. Occupational safety and fire protection authorities can provide additional detail.

Flammables should also be stored in containers clearly labeled as to their contents. Some stove fuel containers for field use may look similar to drinking water bottles, so labeling is important to avoid accidental fuel ingestion.

Medication. Some over-the-counter and prescription medications can be dangerous if taken improperly. Accidental or intentional overdose of the common pain-reliever acetaminophen (paracetamol, APAP), for instance, can be fatal. The psychoactive medication methylphenidate, taken to manage attention deficit, can be addictive and has a high potential to be abused with serious and potentially fatal effects.

Close management of potentially hazardous medications is important, especially with populations at high risk of improper use. Direct physical control over inventory 24 hours a day by responsible adults (along with release of medication only in amounts needed, logging each administration of medication, and oral or other inspection to ensure medications are actually taken) are among the methods to reduce potential for abuse.

8.9. RETIREMENT

8.9.1. When to Retire Gear

Outdoor equipment should be retired from service according to a pre-determined schedule. These retirement schedules should be documented. Staff responsible for equipment should be advised of these schedules, and their training in retirement policies should be documented as well.

Retirement schedules for safety-critical gear, just as with standards for maintenance and inspection, can come from a variety of sources. Legal directives, manufacturer and installer guidance, industry group recommendations, and published consensus standards can be consulted.

Retirement often depends on a variety of factors, including the type and frequency of usage, environmental conditions, and extraordinary stresses to which the gear may have been exposed.

Although life-safety equipment made with plastic or textiles, such as climbing ropes and helmets (with fabric straps), generally have a maximum life of ten years, a rope used weekly could be retired in a year or less, even if no damage is evident.

Equipment that has significant damage, has been subjected to a major stress, or does not function properly (and cannot be suitably repaired) should be retired.

Metal equipment such as carabiners may not have a manufacturer-established retirement date. However, excessive wear, nicks, cracks, deformity, corrosion, loss of function, or misalignment are cause for retirement.

With some less safety-critical items, such as foam sleeping pads or plastic kitchen spice containers, retirement can be on the basis of common sense, aesthetics, and general judgments about functionality.

8.9.2. How to Retire Gear

Retirement is forever. This means retired gear should not be permitted to come back into service. Gear slated for retirement should be stored away from usable equipment so it's not inadvertently picked up and brought back into service. It should be permanently marked as retired. For example, a retired climbing rope could be draped over a sawhorse and repeatedly spray-painted with fluorescent orange spray paint. From there, it could be cut into small pieces suitable for non-technical group games, or permanently discarded.

Document gear retirement in rope logs or elsewhere. This helps ensure gear is not accidently re-used and can help prove in case of accident that you followed proper procedures.

8.9.3. Retiring Medications

A special note is deserved regarding the retirement of medications, which often come with an expiration date from the manufacturer. The conservative institutional approach is to automatically discard all medications past their expiration date. Industry and government testing shows, however, that not all medications lose effectiveness or become harmful at or near their expiration date. In some cases, the government has extended expiration dates, for example in the case of drug shortage.

If an organization chooses to stock medication past its expiration date, it should do this on a case-by-case basis for each medication. Most medications exposed to extreme conditions (such as heat or humidity) should not be kept past their expiration date. And reliable evidence from an authoritative source supporting drug efficacy past the expiration date should be available to back up a program's choice do extend an expiration date. Cost should never be a factor for an outdoor program making this decision.

8.10. RECALLS

Outdoor equipment is occasionally recalled due to unexpected malfunction. Recall notices should be complied with promptly and completely, with gear retired, repaired, or otherwise handled according to the recall notice.

Stay attentive to outdoor industry news in order to be advised of recalls. Information on recalls is available through manufacturer websites, various industry outlets such as blogs and other social media, and government consumer agencies (in the U.S., the Consumer Product Safety Commission).

8.11. INVENTORY CONTROL

Do we have enough gear for that big group next month? Is it time to order new helmets and harnesses? Are the recently-returned first aid kits restocked and ready to go back into the field? Good inventory control helps you answer these questions and keep the right supplies in the right amounts at the right places and times.

8.11.1. Security

Part of inventory control is security. Gear should not be normally be accessible by anyone not specifically authorized to have access. It should by default be behind locked doors. At a base facility before an expedition, gear issued to a field group should be kept secure in a separate locked space accessible to activity leaders for that field group only. Inventory lists should track the flow of every item.

8.11.2. Financial Charges

If equipment goes missing due to the negligence of activity leaders or participants, charging responsible individuals for wholesale replacement costs can be an inducement to keeping good track of remaining items. Explaining this policy and providing price sheets in advance helps make this approach effective.

8.11.3. Inventory Systems

Strict adherence to procedures and attention to detail are useful traits in logistics staff and those who work directly with them. Explicit gear check-in and check-out procedures with fully completed inventory forms are essential for good inventory management. Some items, such as the contents of first aid kits, are notorious for challenges in maintaining appropriate inventory. Here, close compliance with a well-developed system is greatly useful.

A reliable system might begin with activity leaders being issued a first aid kit along with inventory sheet. Leaders document that the proper amount of each item is in their kit. They also record that no medications are past their expiration date. Then they sign and date the form in the "initial check-out" area, and provide a copy (electronic, paper, or otherwise) to logistics staff. A copy stays with the leaders and their kit.

At the end of the outdoor program, leaders are provided with a restock supply with which to replenish their first aid kits, or submit an inventory of missing items and receive the needed replacements. Leaders then document that the proper amount of each item (including unexpired medication) is in the kit, sign and date the form in the "final check-in" area, and provide the full kit and documentation to logistics staff.

If the following users identify any deficiencies in the kit contents, accountability can be traced to the appropriate activity leaders.

8.12. RECORD-KEEPING

Keeping detailed, accurate, comprehensive records provides multiple benefits, including:

1. Helping ensure tasks are performed correctly, by providing written guidance regarding work to be performed, each element of which is then "checked off" as done
2. Encouraging individuals to perform tasks fully, by requiring persons to assert in writing they have done so
3. Providing evidence to supervisors, arbiters and in a court of law that work has been done as specified, thereby defending against negligence or other charges

Multiple elements combine to make for quality equipment management: purchase, use, maintenance, repair, inspection, availability, location, storage, retirement, recall, and inventory control. Documentation of effective performance of each element contributes to effective outdoor programming where risks are well managed.

8.13. STAFF CONSIDERATIONS

The most brightly gleaming ice axe and lightest late-model canoe paddle do not achieve their full potential without outdoor staff who know how to properly care for and use them, supported by a workplace culture that values respect for tools of the trade. Equipment managers, activity leaders, and administrators all have important roles in ensuring that outdoor gear use reduces rather than increases risks.

8.13.1. Equipment Managers

Logistics staff in charge of gear need sufficient time and resources allocated to management of outdoor equipment. This includes an adequate budget and a clean, dry, code-compliant, secure, humidity- and temperature-controlled facility in which to store, clean, repair, issue and de-issue gear.

Without knowledge of the newest research on anchor alloy effects on stress corrosion cracking, your climbing or caving program may be taking unnecessary risk. Logisticians need access to the most current gear management standards and industry norms. This can come through conferences, networking, manufacturer-provided training, or other sources.

When considering desirable characteristics of equipment management personnel, having detail-oriented and systematic-minded staff can help ensure successful management of gear inventory.

8.13.2. Activity Leaders

Training. A trip leader for next week's backpacking experience just injured her ankle and has to drop out. Should we replace her with that brand-new hire or the senior staff who's an experienced boater but who has never led a backpacking trip?

Staff leading outdoor activities require the necessary training in order to do their job well. That rapidly-promoted intern or climbing specialist who jumps in at the last moment to fill a staffing hole on a backpacking trip may not be able to help a novice participant adjust their backpack hipbelt and various straps for a comfortable fit. The result can be miserably sore shoulders or worse.

Field staff should have ample training in the fitting, adjustment, field repair, and proper use of safety-critical outdoor gear including PFDs, harnesses, helmets, backpacks, stoves, footwear, raingear, emergency response resources, and more. Training prior to use is also required for telecommunications devices, power tools used on service projects or elsewhere, and much other specialized equipment.

In some cases, government requirements for training, certification or licensure may need to be met. For instance, persons providing commercial food service may need to be trained food handlers knowledgeable in how and when to use food safety equipment such as gloves, sanitizers, animal-proof containers, and cooling mechanisms, certified by the relevant government agency or its approved contractor. Crewmember training on safety equipment may be required by coast guard or other government regulation in some marine sailing settings. In some jurisdictions, the law requires certain training of zipline and canopy tour employees.

An array of industry associations and manufacturer groups provide training, or accredit or certify other entities that provide trainings. Examples include the American Canoe Association, British Canoeing, Association for Challenge Course Technology, Global Organization of Tree Climbers, member federations of the UIAA, and many others.

In the absence of external training certification, or to complement it, many organizations systematically train activity leaders on use and care of their particular gear. To help ensure that training happens and can be verified, it can be useful to keep detailed training syllabi on record and use certificates, checkoffs or other mechanisms to document successful completion of specific trainings. Figure 8.15 gives an example of such a training checkoff, which might be required before an activity leader is permitted to lead a program requiring specialized gear.

Activity Checkoff: Rappel Station Operation

Employee Name_____   Date   Supervisor Initials

☐ Has read and understood the Rock Climbing Manual, the Technical & Vertical Activities section of the Outdoor Education section of the Field Manual, and the Field Risk Mgt. Manual   ____/____/____   _____

☐ Understands outcomes of rock climbing program and rappelling component   ____/____/____   _____

☐ Understands policies, procedures and guidelines for rock climbing program and rappelling, and general technical & vertical activities   ____/____/____   _____

☐ Understands rappel station format & progression   ____/____/____   _____

☐ Can inspect rappel station for appropriateness of setup, including inspection of rappel and belay anchors and load-releasing hitch   ____/____/____   _____

☐ Can tie, untie, retie and evaluate a load-releasing hitch such as the munter-mule-overhand   ____/____/____   _____

☐ Understands and can tie and check appropriate knots and carabiner clipping in techniques   ____/____/____   _____

☐ Can clip in participant to rappel and belay ropes   ____/____/____   _____

☐ Can belay and manage others in standard belay system, including roles & positions, commands, and belay technique   ____/____/____   _____

☐ Can explain rappel body position and how to avoid having tems caught in belay device   ____/____/____   _____

☐ Understands how to lock off the belay if needed to lower the rappel rope with load-releasing hitch   ____/____/____   _____

☐ Can demonstrate multiple methods for releasing a jammed belay device such as simple hauls and use of load-releasing hitch   ____/____/____   _____

☐ Understands organizational rappelling system   ____/____/____   _____

☐ Can properly inspect equipment (e.g. belay devices, webbing, ropes, harnesses, helmets, carabiners, cord, shoes) and knows when to do so   ____/____/____   _____

☐ Understands care of gear   ____/____/____   _____

☐ Can appropriately frame/brief and debrief the activity   ____/____/____   _____

☐ Can appropriately encourage a rappeller over the edge, and coach them through challenges encountered on rappel   ____/____/____   _____

☐ Has previously sent someone off the rappel set up in standard institutional format four times   ____/____/____   _____

Comments_____

_____   _____
Program Director signature   **Date**

I have read and understood the Rock Climbing Manual and the Technical & Vertical Activities section of the Outdoor Education section of the Field Manual and the Field Risk Management Manual. I certify that I have all the competencies and capabilities described above.

_____   _____
Field Staff person signature   **Date**

Figure 8.15. Staff checkoff required before leading rappelling. Gear-specific requirements are highlighted.

Continuing education is important for activity leaders, as new technologies, standards, and equipment regularly appear. Conferences, industry-sponsored workshops, and various media are sources of this ongoing training.

Teaching. Knowing how to work with outdoor equipment is only part of the picture. Outdoor leaders must be able to effectively teach participants about gear to help ensure its safe and appropriate use.

Safety briefings are one method for teaching proper equipment use and care. These are most consistent when an established set of topics is consistently covered. In some critical instances, such as a safety briefing of novice sea kayakers about to embark on a challenging sea kayak itinerary, trip leaders may document through a checkbox or other means for each topic that they have covered all topics in their briefing, including use of paddling equipment and safety materials like paddle floats and marine radios. The document may be signed or otherwise certified, and securely kept in long-term storage.

Figure 8.16 gives an example of a challenge course safety briefing that covers gear-related topics. A briefing your program uses should be customized for your particular situation.

Challenge Course Safety Briefing for Participants

Instructions for facilitator: each one of these sections is to be covered in detail before the start of the course day. It is your responsibility to ensure that all participants understand and follow these safety procedures. All points must be covered.

1. **Be Aware of your Environment:**
   a. The grounds of the course are uneven; roots and rocks do exist, so watch your step.
   b. Watch for deadfall; dead branches and other debris have been known to fall. To avoid injury on course, have participants wear helmets in all designated areas, i.e. under or within 6 meters of the high elements.
   c. Always be alert and aware of others. If anyone sees someone doing something unsafe, speak up and say, *"STOP!"* At this point the facilitator will address the situation and make appropriate changes.
   d. It can be hot and sunny; be sure to use sunscreen and drink plenty of fluids. Eat enough for the activity. In chilly weather, dress in warm layers for comfort and safety; in warm weather take steps to stay cool.

2. **Clothing and Other Considerations:**
   a. *Shoes:* All shoes must be closed-toed and tied.
   b. *Hair:* All long hair must be tied back and put under one's helmet or clothing.
   c. *Jewelry:* No dangling earrings or hoops. Hoops have been known to get hooked on clothes, other participant's fingers, and elsewhere. No dangling necklaces or other objects such as scarves are to be worn around the neck. All watches are to be taken off and left with your personal belongings or given to the designated adult leader. Rings are strongly discouraged; they can cause blisters and may inhibit performance.
   d. *Clothing:* Shorts are discouraged due to the abrasive nature of the environment. No skirts are allowed. Baggy pants are discouraged due to the possibility of snagging on safety equipment or challenge course elements. Avoid large belt buckles on the course. Remove or snug up loose clothing that could get caught.
   e. *Valuables:* Please leave all valuables in a safe place, or with the designated adult leader. No electronic devices (excluding cameras) are allowed on course.
   f. *Other objects:* No pens or other sharp objects are to be held in one's pocket.

3. **Food and Objects in Mouth:**
   a. No gum or similar substances should be chewed while going through the course.
   b. No foreign objects such as toothpicks shall be placed in the mouth when on the course.
   c. Food is to be eaten during designated times. Make sure to be clear with the participants as to when these times will be.

4. **Technique:**
   a. Ensure that a staff person checks your harness, helmet and hardware before belaying or climbing.

5. **Equipment Care:**
   a. Do not drop metal objects such as carabiners or belay devices. If you do, tell a staff person immediately.
   b. Lay helmets right side up; place all gear on tarps rather than the ground.
   c. Have no food or insect repellent come in contact with harnesses, ropes, webbing or other gear.
   d. Do not step on rope, webbing, or other soft articles. Dirt ground into the material will weaken the item.

Figure 8.16. Example safety briefing for high ropes challenge course. Instruction on participant items as well as challenge course equipment is covered.

The use of a "belay school" is a well-established method for instructing novices in the appropriate use of vertical equipment. Belay school often involves a visual demonstration of climber-tie in, belay device attachment, climbing or rappelling/abseiling commands, and belay technique, conducted on flat ground. Learners then take a position along a rope stretched on the ground and practice attaching and feeding rope through a belay device. Finally, the learner begins belaying a climber with a backup belayer; while the climber is still less than a meter off the ground, the belayer is guided to practice braking technique under direct supervision.

Similarly, teaching cleaning and hygiene techniques in the outdoors helps prevent serious communicable diseases. Participants may require instruction on how to wash and sanitize dishes in the outdoors. They may need to learn new procedures for handwashing and prevention of infections in the genitourinary tract. Using camping equipment to clean dishes, hands and crotch in the absence of running water or shower requires conscientious education.

> Multiple participants in one outdoor program traveling in a low-income country contracted Hepatitis A, a serious and potentially fatal disease, by eating contaminated food prepared by a local villager. Hepatitis A, which is passed by fecal-oral transmission, can often be prevented by ensuring that food handlers practice good handwashing technique after using the toilet.

Outdoor activity leaders should also teach participants to inform them if important safety equipment appears damaged. For instance, a ripped PFD should be brought to a leader's attention so it can be repaired or replaced before use.

Use of Personal Gear. It should generally be acceptable for staff to supply their own technical gear, such as helmets and harnesses, providing that the equipment is competently inspected and found to be in good condition.

8.13.3. Inspectors

Inspectors of life-safety equipment or complex installations and associated equipment, for example challenge courses and mobile climbing walls, should be suitably qualified, as discussed earlier in this chapter.

8.13.4. Administrators

Administrative leadership has a responsibility to ensure that the personnel, financial, intellectual and physical resources applied to equipment management are sufficient to meet standards and reasonably prevent loss, including illness, injury, property damage and death.

In addition, executives play an essential role in establishing a culture of respectful care of program equipment. Culture-setting begins at the top. By supporting policies and practices that encourage pride in showing outstanding stewardship of the tools that allow us to experience the outdoors safely and enjoyably, organizational leadership motivates others to take care of the gear that in turn takes care of them.

One wilderness canoe tripping program uses wooden canoes covered by canvas to traverse long distances across remote lakes and down wild rivers. These delicate craft require attentive care; one scrape against a sharp rock lurking just underwater can tear a great hole through the hull days from civilization. Trip leaders carefully lift the boat in and out of the water each travel day, careful to never grind the hull against the rocky shore. On occasion trip leaders use the overturned boat to roll out dough in preparation for baking. The organization is famed for the respectful attention it pays to its craft, and is noted for its admonition that the hull of its boats never touches "anything but water, air, and bread dough."

8.13.5. Lending Gear to Staff

Providing staff access to outdoor gear that they may not already have can enable outdoor leaders to gain valuable experience in outdoor activities that improves their leadership skills. Borrowing an organization's sea kayak that's not otherwise being used for a few days is an inexpensive way to support this professional development.

Organizations might freely provide backpacks, canoes, or similar gear to off-duty staff at no cost. It might be prudent, however, to prohibit loaning critical life-safety equipment such as climbing, mountaineering, or related technical gear (for instance, ropes or a climbing rack), as closely monitoring the use of this gear and minimizing wear and potential for damage are of vital importance.

8.14. PARTICIPANT CONSIDERATIONS

8.14.1. Equipment Lists

Equipment brought by participants on outdoor programs should be suited for the environment and activities that participants experience. A gear list provided by the organization can provide an essential guide for what to bring and not to bring.

The list should include the types and amount of clothing items, including equipment for rain, heat, cold, sun, insects, or other expected conditions. Footwear and necessary camping equipment should be included. Instructions on what type, quality, brands or other characteristics (such as fabric type, backpack capacity, or sleeping bag temperature rating) are suitable should be listed. Information about breaking in footwear and bringing properly sized packs or other items should be provided. In addition, directions on what not to bring: for example, drugs, alcohol, electronics, or makeup—is important.

If participants are bringing important prescription medications or supplies such as prescription eyewear, it's useful for twice the expected quantity to be carried, in case some medications or supplies inadvertently are left back at camp, dropped overboard, or otherwise become unavailable.

Figure 8.17 provides an example of an equipment list for outdoor program participants. Any list should be customized for the activities, locations, and participant population types specific to the program.

Clothing & Equipment Checklist: Winter Snowshoe Expedition Programs

Quantity	ITEM/DESCRIPTION
	FOOTWEAR
3-4 pr.	Wool or synthetic hiking socks
2 pr.	Liner Socks: For extra protection and warmth
1 pr.	Waterproof, Insulated Boots: Over the ankle boot. Insulated to keep feet warm and dry in slush and snow
1 pr.	Sneakers or Running Shoes: For in-camp use
1 pr.	Gaiters: For snow protection
	UPPER BODY CLOTHING
1	Heavy Weight Synthetic Underwear Top: For evening and nighttime warmth
1	Medium or Heavy Weight Synthetic Underwear Top: Insulation layer for hiking
1	Synthetic or Wool Sweater, Pullover or Jacket: For cold evenings; pile, wool, down or fleece
1	Additional Sweater, Pullover or Jacket: For extra insurance against cold. Down jackets are the definitive item; a fleece jacket or wool sweater may also suffice.
1	Rain Jacket: Should fit comfortably over all layers; must be absolutely 100% waterproof
2	T-shirts: Synthetic preferred
	LOWER BODY CLOTHING
1	Heavy Weight Synthetic Underwear Bottoms: For evening and nighttime warmth
1	Medium or Heavy Weight Synthetic Underwear Bottoms: Insulation layer for hiking
1	Synthetic Long Pants: Nylon pants or warm-ups
1	Fleece or Wool Long Pants: For night-time warmth
1	Rain pants: Should fit comfortably over all layers and be absolutely100 percent waterproof
	Underwear: One pair per every other day
	HAND AND HEAD COVERINGS
1	Hat: Wool or synthetic fabric for cold nights and sleeping
1	Baseball Cap or Broad-brimmed Hat: for sun protection
1 pr.	Sunglasses
1	Bandanna
1 pr.	Mittens: Dual-layer--wool or heavy synthetic inner liner, waterproof outer liner
1 pr.	Synthetic liner gloves (for triple layering mitten/glove system)

☐	1	Large Capacity Backpack*: Approx. 75-80 l. For all your clothes, sleeping bag and some group gear
☐	1	Sleeping Bag: Mummy type, rated to -18° C or lower. Synthetic or down, not cotton.
☐	1	Sleeping Bag Liner: Nylon or similar fabric for warmth and cleanliness
☐	1	Insulating sleeping pad: Closed-cell foam or inflatable
☐	1	Ground sheet: Typically polyethylene plastic, at least 2 m x 1 m
☐	1 ea.	Toothbrush and Paste
☐	1	Lip Balm: Should have SPF 15 or greater
☐	1	Sunscreen: With SPF of at least 15
☐	1	Flashlight: (Headlamp style preferred) with new batteries, extra batteries and extra bulb
☐	1	Journal or Notebook
☐	2	Pencils
☐	6	Large Plastic Bags: Approx 125 liters, 1.2 mil thickness, for waterproofing packs and stuff sacks
☐	1 ea.	Mug with Lid, Plate/Bowl Combo, Spoon and Fork: Durable plastic style plate/bowl combo works well.
☐	4	1 Liter Water Bottles: Please bring only high quality bottles which will not leak or rupture.
☐		Essential prescription medications

OPTIONAL ITEMS:

☐	1 pr.	Extra glasses
☐	1	Packable Camp Chair
☐	1	Camera with extra film and batteries
☐	1 pr.	Down booties: for toasty toes in camp
☐	1	Down jacket: for extra security against the cold

NOTES:

*Be sure the backpack is fitted to size. If the backpack is too large or does not fit properly, it may lead to an uncomfortable experience.

Break boots in prior to backpacking by wearing around the house, school or work for a week or more, or by taking several short hikes. Many backpacking/mountaineering shops rent and sell some of the items on this list. If you are unable to find suitable gear, please contact us; we have equipment to rent at a reasonable cost. Do not bring: drugs (excluding medications prescribed to you), alcohol, weapons, or electronics.

Why not cotton? Cotton fabrics soak up body perspiration and hold it next to your skin. Once cotton gets wet, it stays wet, and can chill the wearer. Synthetic fabrics—for example, polypropylene and polyester fabrics—wick moisture away from the skin, keeping the wearer warmer and dryer. Inquire at your local outdoor retailer for further details.

Clothing items are designed to be layered. This allows multiple, less bulky individual clothes items to be added or removed, helping control body temperature at a comfortable level despite changes in activity level, environment and weather conditions.

This list is extensive by design. Weather in our course areas is extremely variable so it is possible that not all items will be needed on every course. *However*, an otherwise well-planned outdoor program can suffer from participants having inadequate clothing and equipment, or unnecessary items. If you have any questions about this list contact us and we will be happy to advise you. We're looking forward to an educational and fun time to be had by all!

Figure 8.17. Sample participant equipment list. Specific brand names are omitted in this example but can be included to provide more detailed recommendations.

8.14.2. Preventing Bringing of Inappropriate Items

With populations that have a higher than normal probability of bringing inappropriate items such as drugs on an outdoor experience, it can help ensure everyone's safety to go through participants' gear to ensure only the correct items are carried.

This can take a variety of forms. A typical method has participants, on arrival, repack their equipment from their travel luggage into the pack they'll use on the outdoor program, item by item, as each piece of equipment is listed by a trip leader. Anything not called is to be left in the original luggage.

A more intensive version involves participants handing over each item (such as a pair of pants or hat) to a trip leader, one by one, as a roster is read out. The trip leader inspects each item, checks for hidden contraband, and packs the equipment in a bag. The bag is then brought on the program, and anything else is placed elsewhere. In some cases the participant, who changed into swim clothes before the gear inspection, immediately takes a swim test, so that remaining stashed contraband may be wetted and made unusable.

8.14.3. Participant Technical Gear

Participants may be discouraged from bringing their own life-safety gear such as helmets and harnesses. If such gear is permitted, the organization should have a system for assessing the suitability of the equipment.

8.14.4. In Case of Missing or Inadequate Gear

It's useful for organizations to have on hand a collection of extra clothing, footwear and other items, in case the items participants bring are found to be inadequate.

8.14.5. Training

Participants should be appropriately trained in the use of equipment (figure 8.18). This applies not just to specialized technical equipment such as sailing, climbing or mountaineering equipment, but also for potentially dangerous equipment used in activities like service projects, for example chainsaws, axes and other power tools and sharp or pointed implements.

Figure 8.18. Participants being trained in self-belay technique at high ropes challenge course.

Instruction should also be provided regarding everyday items such as water disinfection materials, general camping equipment, and cleaning supplies. For instance, proper cleaning and disinfection of kitchen utensils without a dishwasher or running water requires instruction in the use of washing bins and drying systems to prevent the spread of foodborne illness. It is not too much to have a written lesson plan to which activity leaders refer in instructing participants assisting

in food preparation and cleanup how to do so in a safe and hygienic manner. Similarly, if a water-based or other program uses containers to deposit and carry solid human waste prior to disposal at journey's end, any person setting up, using, or cleaning the system must be trained in the appropriate operating procedures.

Participants should also be given appropriate information on when certain items should or should not be used. For example, participants should know when close-toed shoes are required, when open-toed footwear is acceptable, and when it is okay to be barefoot.

8.15. THIRD-PARTY EQUIPMENT

8.15.1. Rental and Similar Use

Outdoor programs may decide to rent or otherwise temporarily gain access to equipment owned by others. This might be the case with renting vehicles for transportation, renting a facility such as a high ropes Challenge Course, or renting relatively expensive but rarely-used equipment such as watercraft for an organization that runs few water-based programs.

In these situations it is prudent to thoroughly and carefully inspect the equipment before approving it for service. Equipment quality along with maintenance and repair history should be examined. Although renting a vehicle from a well-reputed global-scale rental agency is generally low-risk, first-time use of a third party's ropes course should only follow a successful and detailed on-site inspection of the course elements, and a review of safety plans and incidents.

8.15.2. Emergency and Rescue Caches, and Other External Resources

At times outdoor programs may need to access emergency medical or evacuation supplies placed by search and rescue groups or other agencies. These gear caches are sometimes placed near climbing sites, expedition basecamps, major whitewater rapids, or other high-risk locations.

Program leaders should know the location of and how to access these supplies. Staff should keep in mind that equipment may or may not be present when needed, and it may not be in good condition.

Land managers, park rangers, search and rescue teams, and emergency medical services may also have equipment that can be brought to your location to assist in case of emergency. It is useful to know what types of equipment these groups may be able to provide, how to request it, how long it might take to arrive, and other factors that can be useful in times of need.

Low-Resource Environments. **Extra** caution should be taken when relying on equipment to be provided by others in low-resource environments. These environments include low-income countries, areas of middle-income countries, and regions that may be subject to natural disasters such as earthquakes or typhoons that can damage transportation, medical, security, communications, and other infrastructure.

In these situations, vehicle transportation, medical supplies, rescue equipment and other items may be of limited availability or dubious quality. In some situations it may be prudent to do on-site inspections of equipment and facilities (such as hospital departments) to verify what might realistically be available in time of need, and to develop contingency plans with this information in mind.

8.16. ADMINISTRATIVE AND MANAGERIAL CONTEXTS

Although the focus of this text is risk management in the outdoor context, a brief mention of safety in the office and administrative environment can be made. Risks present in offices, staff and participant housing, gear storage areas and other facilities should be considered. This includes engineering controls, reporting requirements, and many other occupational safety and health concerns, along with zoning and building codes. Specific examples include safe lifting, fire control, ergonomics involving computer workstations, and repetitive stress injuries, among others.

Occupational safety and health and other government agencies can provide direction and support for addressing these topics.

Chapter Summary

1. Programs should obtain the necessary equipment and verifiably manage it to appropriate industry and legal standards.
2. Gear should be selected to meet program needs and per safety standards.
3. Avoid counterfeit equipment and document important equipment purchases.
4. Follow procedures to minimize loss from potentially hazardous equipment.
5. Consider a practice of uninterrupted telecom connectivity and ensure staff know how to use telecom devices.
6. Document gear use, especially use of life-safety equipment.
7. Maintain and clean equipment to manufacturer's or other suitable standards, and document maintenance of safety-critical equipment.
8. Repair equipment in the field or at base facility per manufacturer recommendations or best practices; document safety-critical gear repairs.
9. Qualified persons should inspect equipment on acquisition; before, during, and after use; at regular intervals, and as part of periodic safety reviews. Depth of inspection should be appropriate to the inspection type. Inspect for compliance with legal, manufacturer, installer, and industry specifications.
10. Ensure equipment is available when needed. Store gear in an appropriate climate and with necessary security. Store flammables to prevent ingestion or ignition.
11. Retire gear according to a schedule determined by legal, manufacturer, or other relevant guidelines. Ensure retired gear is not inappropriately re-used.
12. Stay attentive to and comply with recall notices.
13. Control inventory through secure storage, use of incentives, and tracking and accountability systems.
14. Logistics staff need appropriate facilities, budget, training, and continuing education to properly manage gear. Activity leaders likewise require sufficient verified training, licensure or certification, time, teaching skills, and other resources for suitable gear care. Administrators must provide needed resources and maintain a culture supportive of good equipment management.
15. Activity leaders generally may use their own technical equipment if it passes inspection.
16. Loan of life-safety equipment to staff for personal use should be restricted or prohibited.
17. Participants should be provided with a gear list and related guidance. Structures should be in place to prevent participants from bringing inappropriate items. Participants should avoid bringing and using their own technical gear, unless inspected and approved. Participants should receive suitable gear use training.
18. Third-party equipment should be inspected before use; this may sometimes include reviewing insurance, safety plans and incident history.
19. Program staff should know how to take advantage of cached and external emergency equipment and be careful about depending on access to it. In low-resource environments, emergency equipment may be unavailable or in unsuitable condition.
20. Occupational safety and health standards should be addressed in the office, gear warehouse and related non-outdoor environments.

CHAPTER 9

PARTICIPANTS

LEARNING OBJECTIVES

1. The important role participants play in both causing and preventing incidents
2. How participant psychology contributes to taking risks
3. Anticipating that participants will commit unsafe acts
4. Risk-related connections between participants, equipment, staff, activities, areas and elsewhere
5. Medical and psychological participant screening
6. Ensuring organizations are prepared to serve particular enrollee population types
7. Providing preparatory information and verifying appropriate responses
8. Educating participants on risks and their management during the program
9. Appropriate participant supervision
10. Working with responsible persons and special participant populations
11. Post-program assessment and risk management

9.1.   INTRODUCTION

Participants and their behavior are fundamental to successful risk management of any outdoor program. Many incidents are directly related to participants and the actions they take, for example as a result of failure of staff to adequately supervise participants, or failure of participants to appropriately follow instructions.

Many participant-related risks can be minimized by proper participant selection and initial screening, suitable preparation by enrollees before programs commence, appropriate participant education and supervision during the program, and effective assessment and follow-up after program completion.

9.1.1.   Dynamics that Increase Risky Participant Behavior

An understanding of participant psychology can assist in anticipating and preventing safety problems related to participants. A sample of these potential dynamics is highlighted below.

Ignorance and Experimentation. Participants do not know what trained and experienced outdoor program staff know (and may take for granted as common knowledge) about outdoor risks. As a result of their relatively lesser knowledge, you should expect that participants may experiment with taking inappropriate risks. Participants might ask themselves, "What if I don't use the toilet outdoors for a week?" or "What would happen if I jump out of the boat right now?" or "Will it be a bad thing if I don't put on my rain gear on this cold and rainy day?"

It was well into a wilderness semester experience, and the group was on a multi-week paddling expedition deep in the backcountry. As a group arrived at their lake-side campsite and set up camp, one college-age participant dove head-first into the shallow lake. He smashed his head into a large rock just under the surface. Although he survived without serious injury, the trip leader filling out the incident report recorded that the participant stated that he dove into the shallow water due to "a monumental lack of judgment."

Pushing Boundaries. Outdoor leaders and program managers should anticipate that participants will push, and sometimes exceed, the boundaries of appropriate behavior. This behavior is well-recognized in teens, and understood to be part of normal human development towards adulthood. However, it occurs in adults as well. Grown-up individuals who find themselves under the supervision of an outdoor leader may enjoy not having to play the part of the responsible party—boss, parent, or the like—for once. They may regress to a less responsible approach to their own behavior.

Unrealistic Expectations of Leaders. In some cultural contexts, particularly those lacking a value system of taking responsibility for one's actions, participants may expect outdoor leaders to at all times prevent them from doing unsafe things, or to invariably save them if they attempt an unsafe act. This may be an unreasonable and unrealistic expectation, but it still can occur. Participants with this attitude may be reckless, for example backing up to the edge of the crumbly cliff for the perfect selfie, or eating samples of a poisonous plant found along the trail.

Prudent Staff Response. How to manage participants who choose to commit unsafe acts? A perspective that may help reduce the impact of poor participant judgment is to anticipate that participants will do unwise and unsafe things. If it is dangerous, and ill-advised, the prudent outdoor professional anticipates that nevertheless, sooner or later, some participant will try it.

With this in mind, outdoor program staff may be better equipped to prevent incidents from occurring, and to minimize the impacts when incidents occur.

9.1.2. Participant Interconnections with a Greater Risk Management System

Risk management of participants is deeply connected to and influenced by risk management systems related to staff, equipment, activities, transportation, activity areas, culture, and more. For example, participant safety is affected by good equipment management (Figure 9.1), for instance through proper inspection of participant-brought equipment, and securing potential hazardous items like medications and flammables. Due to this network of interlocking influences, all aspects of risk management covered in this text combine to influence participant safety and well-being.

Figure 9.1. Proper equipment management affects participant safety.

9.1.3. Defining 'Participant'

The term 'participant' used in this chapter and throughout the text refers to those program enrollees for whom the outdoor experience is purposely designed. It also refers to responsible persons such as school group chaperones, language interpreters, or others associated with the outdoor activities. Further information is under the term 'Participant' in the Glossary.

9.2. PRIOR TO THE OUTDOOR EXPERIENCE

Good risk management begins well before the outdoor experience commences. Potential participants must be screened to see if they are a good match for the program. Would-be participants must receive and process a variety of information, and a risk transfer procedure should take place.

9.2.1. Assessing Suitability of Individual Participants

Each person who wishes to participate in an outdoor experience should be assessed to see if the capacities of the prospective participant suitably match the requirements of the program. This assessment includes an individual medical screening, which should incorporate an appropriate psychological and behavioral assessment. Enrollees must be able to perform the essential functions required of all participants. Chapter 18, Medical Screening, covers these topics in detail.

9.2.2. Matching Participant Population Type to Organizational Competencies

Outdoor programs can serve a variety of participant population types, from typically well-adjusted youth to older adults, children with psychiatric or behavioral issues or criminal histories, groups of different ethnicities, groups with specific medical profiles (such as diabetes), recent refugees, persons with any of various physical or mental disabilities, and many others.

Many outdoor organizations tend to specialize in serving a small number of population types. Outdoor programs can at times make efforts to expand the types of participants they serve, however, in order to increase their programmatic impact, take advantage of a business opportunity, improve financial performance, or achieve other objectives. Yet when an organization reaches beyond the participant demographic they are experienced with, both benefits and risks can follow.

When considering providing services to a new type of participant group, it's important to first assess whether or not the organization is suitably prepared to be successful with the new parameters and needs that come with a different participant population (Figure 9.2). An organization should assess whether or not it has suitably trained staff, a thorough awareness of the needs of the new participant type, and a well-developed curriculum that meets the unique needs of the new demographic group.

It can be tempting for program managers with budget responsibility to take on new paying customers, even if the organization may not yet be optimally prepared to serve them. Prudent leaders should beware of "participant creep" where the scope of populations served slowly grows beyond the core competencies of the organization, leading to increased risk of programmatic and safety-related failures. Entrepreneurialism must be balanced with risk management. This is sometimes easier said than done.

A sign of failure to match an organization's skill set to participant demographics is mass evacuations of entire groups from outdoor activities or environments due to activity leaders feeling unprepared to successfully manage their groups. This can be especially likely to occur when outdoor organizations that typically serve normative (generally well-behaved) youth begin offering programs to at-risk youth with a history of behavior problems.

Figure 9.2. Participants should be well-matched to the outdoor activities.

If the participant population you're going to be working with is new and different from what you're set up for, a New Element Readiness Assessment should be completed before engaging with the new population. (See Chapter 6, Activities and Program Areas, for Assessment details.) This tool can help organizations successfully prepare to work with new populations with distinct risk management and programmatic needs.

It was week three of an alpine mountaineering expedition. One of the two trip leaders had left the group to head out to a resupply point. The trip had been physically and mentally strenuous for everyone. At a campsite far from any trail and about 15 kilometers from the nearest road, tucked between a snowfield and a steep talus field of large, unstable boulders, one participant snapped. He was a homeless youth, plucked off the street by a youth services program and given a scholarship to participate in the wilderness adventure. But the stresses of group living, trusting others, and technical mountaineering had been too much. He stole a map and compass from the group, threw on his backpack, stated he was "going home," and disappeared into the talus field, his helmetless head bobbing up and down as he jumped from rock to rock, receding down the trackless mountain landscape. He was moving too fast for the group to catch up with him. The remaining participants and trip leaders never saw him again.

The lone staff person with the group managed to radio a government dispatch center, which contacted the program's headquarters. Basecamp staff fanned out to trailheads around the wilderness area, and eventually intercepted the fleeing participant, who was unharmed, and arranged for his transportation back to the city from where he came.

Could this incident have been prevented? The program was accustomed to working with affluent, well-behaving teens. Compared to programs that specialize in working with at-risk youth, the organization provided minimal training, curriculum, or support structures specifically designed to help at-risk youth succeed in a challenging new environment. The failure here was less the participant's precipitous departure from the expedition than the organization's failure to build the systems and competences needed for participants like him to succeed.

9.2.3. Participant Preparation

When deciding whether or not to sign up for an outdoor experience, and prior to the program's commencement, it's important for participants to appropriately prepare for their experience. This involves receiving and responding to pre-event information, and completing a risk transfer process.

Information to Participants. Participants (and their parents or guardians, as appropriate) should receive information on a variety of subjects prior to the start of the program. They should complete the preparations outlined in this introductory information. Topics may include:

1. **Program objectives, activities, locations, hazards and risks.** Participants need to have this information in order to give informed consent for their participation (Figure 9.3). (See Participant Risk Transfer, below.)
2. **Training and conditioning requirements.** Participants should receive information and follow recommendations regarding physical fitness training and other requirements to be completed prior to attending the outdoor program. Information should include potential negative consequences of insufficient training and conditioning such as injury or early departure.
3. **Conduct expectations.** Participants should be advised of requirements regarding appropriate behavior, including drug and alcohol use, harassment, and abuse. Consequences of failing to meet behavioral standards, such as limits to participation or expulsion, should be explained. In some cases, a behavior contract describing expected and prohibited behavior, discipline structures, and consequences for misbehavior should be read, signed and returned by the participant prior to joining the program.
4. **Required, recommended, and prohibited equipment and supplies.** This may take the form of a written equipment list, and include outdoor gear, clothing and footwear. Preparation guidance, for example around breaking in boots, properly fitting packs, and where and how to acquire suitable gear, may be supplied.
5. **Required and recommended skills.** Examples include level of climbing ability, whitewater boating experience, or foreign language fluency.
6. **Required documents.** Primarily in situations involving international travel, this includes passports, visas, proof of vaccination, and related documents.
7. **Medical preparation.** Especially for travel to international locations or destinations with health

risks participants may not be familiar with, this includes information about vaccinations and preventive or other medications to be carried. Information should be provided on where the necessary items may be obtained and how to access additional information.

Figure 9.3. Participants must understand the risks in order to give informed consent.

Verification. In addition to providing information, program staff should verify compliance with critical requirements. In some settings, for example with youth or novices preparing for a wilderness adventure, it is important for program coordinators from the sending institution (if applicable) or program staff to do a thorough, in-person check of participant equipment, clothing and footwear well prior to the program. Ensuring that documents necessary for international travel are present and in order is another example.

Participant Risk Transfer. Participants should complete indemnification, release of liability, assumption of risk (informed consent) and other agreements required by the outdoor program. These should be signed by appropriate parties and returned to the organization prior to participation. (See Chapter 13, Risk Transfer, for additional information.)

9.3. DURING THE OUTDOOR EXPERIENCE

9.3.1. Education

The outdoor program is responsible for ensuring that participants have the knowledge, skills and attitudes necessary to recognize and appropriately respond to risks encountered during their outdoor experience. Risks can involve:

1. The participant themself
2. Other participants and staff involved in the

outdoor program

3. Bystanders and others who may be involved
4. Risks related to equipment, environmental hazards, inter-cultural contexts, hygiene, or activities

Figure 9.4. Training in proper spotting technique is required when bouldering.

Participants should understand what behavior is expected of them. They should understand, agree to follow, and be able to follow relevant policies and procedures. They should be encouraged to communicate safety concerns to staff. And they should understand and be prepared for their role in incident response. For example, in the event staff are not present or are incapacitated, participants should be suitably trained in first aid and organizational emergency response plan activation, including procedures for evacuation and requesting external assistance.

Technical skills training, for example in whitewater boating or belaying, is an important part of activity-related participant education.

Safety briefings are an important element in educating participants about risks and how to manage them. Participants should take part in pre-defined safety briefings at the beginning of the program, before each activity, and at other times as needed. Briefings should cover applicable risks and their management.

The organization should be able to convincingly demonstrate that participants received appropriate training. Tools to support this aim include documented training topics, written training materials, evidence that training was conducted, and evidence that participants had the necessary knowledge, skills, and attitudes following training and before commencement of activities.

9.3.2. Supervision, Roles and Management

Participants should be continually assessed to see if their capabilities for managing risks meet the requirements of the activities and environment (Figure 9.5). Assessment should specifically be done:

1. On an ongoing informal basis throughout each day through general observation of participants
2. Before each new activity
3. Before granting of each new privilege or level of independence, such as youth cooking without direct supervision, or outdoor travel unaccompanied by activity leaders
4. As regular formal or informal one-on-one check-ins or casual conversations. An appropriate aim on multi-day programs is for at least one staff person to talk with each participant daily.
5. Group check-ins held about every day, for example, in the form of evening meetings
6. As debriefs after activities

Written procedures and policies should be developed and followed by staff regarding an organization's particular supervision requirements.

Procedures regarding supervision and separation of participants by sex, particularly regarding minors and segregated sleeping areas, should be developed and followed.

Figure 9.5. Supervising groups in flood-prone or other hazardous terrain is important.

Medication Management. Procedures around managing participant use of medication should be developed and followed. Topics may include:

- Whether medications are brought by participants, the organization, or both.
- In what circumstances participants carry their own medications, and when program staff hold them. (For example, participants might carry their own

emergency medications such as epinephrine and inhaled medication for asthma attacks; adult staff with youth participants might carry backup supplies, psychotropics, and medications prone to abuse.)

- Who administers medications: participant (youth or adult) or program staff.

Industry best practices and relevant regulations should be considered when developing medication management procedures for your particular circumstances.

Unaccompanied Time. When participants are unaccompanied, adequate supervision standards should be in place. This could take the form of periodic check-ins with affirmative responses regarding well-being, and from-a-distance observations.

Responsible Persons. We think about those directly involved in an outdoor activity to be activity leaders (lead or assistant), and participants. Another category is the Responsible Person.

This is a person who is able to handle select responsibilities, but generally does not possess the knowledge and skills to lead technical outdoor activities. An example is a parent or teacher chaperone on a school group outdoor trip.

Responsible Persons may supervise participants during specified times within the limits of their competence. This could include supervising participants during a break time or while waiting for an activity to begin. This could also be in the form of an accompanying school teacher managing behavior issues with school pupils on a school outing.

Responsible Persons generally are not permitted to lead technical activities, including leading evacuations or otherwise traveling without a competent activity leader over technical terrain.

How Responsible Persons fit into staff-to-participant ratios is discussed in Chapter 6, Activities and Program Areas.

Special Populations. Appropriate procedures for special populations such as participants in outdoor behavioral healthcare programs or persons with disabilities (Figure 9.6) should be in place.

This includes procedures for preventing and responding to psychiatric incidents such as self-harm or suicidal ideation. Procedures for managing violence or other aggressive behavior, including de-escalation, should be in place as needed. Procedures for addressing medical conditions and age-related considerations like risk-seeking teens or older persons with reduced capacities should also be established, if required by the nature of the population being served.

Figure 9.6. Appropriate procedures should be in place for persons with disabilities.

9.4.   AFTER THE OUTDOOR EXPERIENCE

The risk management process continues following the conclusion of the outdoor program. At the end of an outdoor experience, participants should document an evaluation of the program, including risk management aspects of staff, activities, equipment, program areas, and any other relevant subjects (Figure 9.7). Figure 9.8 below provides a sample evaluation form.

In some cases, additional assessments may be useful, for example in the form of a brief oral "exit interview" by program staff of participant group members or group leaders (in the case of intact groups as with school or corporate clients), with relevant details about risk management and other topics noted in writing.

This evaluation information should be provided to program management and appropriate follow-up should be conducted.

If significant incidents have occurred, the organization should follow up with those directly affected, members of the families of those affected, and any sending group (such as a school, religious group, or corporation whose students, members or staff participated in the outdoor experience as a group) as appropriate. Chapter 14, Incident Management, provides details on long-term follow-up.

Figure 9.7. A happy camper.

Evaluation of Program
For completion by leader of intact group

Name:_____Group Name: _____

Program Location: _____ Dates: ___/___ to ___/___/_____ Leader name: _____

Your feedback concerning this event is invaluable in continuing to improve the quality of our outdoor programs. Please take a few moments to answer the questions below with both narrative and numerical feedback. Rate the following on a scale of 1 to 5: 1 = unacceptable, 2 = poor, 3 = fair, 4 = good, 5 = excellent. Thank you!

Quality and timeliness of pre-course information received from us about the course goals, itinerary, equipment requirements and the course location to prepare you for the program	
Quality and timeliness of pre-course information received from your organization about the course goals, itinerary, equipment requirements and the course location to prepare you for the program	
Quality and effectiveness of pre-course student and parent presentation at your school/organization by our administrative staff (if applicable)	
Program area appropriateness towards achieving program goals	
Quality of program structure and organization in effectively supporting program goals	
Quality and effectiveness of curriculum and activities	
Quality and effectiveness of program leadership by the our Program Coordinator	
Effectiveness of our staff in delivering program curriculum	
Sensitivity of our staff to participant concerns	
Quality of group management by our staff	
Level of risk management provided by our staff and operations	
Quality and quantity of food	
Quality and appropriateness of equipment provided	

1. Please describe the most successful aspects of the experience.

2. Please comment on specific areas of the program that need improvement.

3. What was your impression of program staff? Please comment on your instructor's strengths and weaknesses.

4. Do you feel the program goals were successfully achieved? Yes No Explain:

Figure 9.8. Sample program evaluation form completed by participant group coordinator.

Chapter Summary

1. Participants play a fundamental role in both causing and preventing incidents.

2. Ignorance of risks, pushing boundaries, and unrealistic expectations of leaders on the part of participants increase outdoor risk.

3. Staff should anticipate that participants will exercise poor judgment and commit unsafe acts.

4. Participant risk management is interlinked with risks from equipment, activities, staff, transportation, activity areas, culture, and elsewhere.

5. "Participant" indicates the enrollee for whom the program was designed but also certain accompanying Responsible Persons.

6. Risk management begins well before the activity commences.

7. Participants should pass medical and behavioral screening prior to being admitted for participation.

8. The organization should be suitably prepared if it will be working with specialized populations, such as those with particular behavioral, medical, cultural or psychological circumstances.

9. Relevant information should be given to prospective participants prior to the program. This includes information on program goals, activities, locations, risks, training, behavior expectations, equipment, skills, documents, and medical preparation.

10. The organization should verify that the pre-program information has been suitably processed prior to participation.

11. Participants should complete the organization's participant risk transfer process prior to participation.

12. During the program participants should receive education sufficient to appropriately manage program risks.

13. Participants should be appropriately supervised during the program.

14. Assessments of risk management performance should be made by participants after program completion, and follow-up should be done on any recommendations.

CHAPTER 10

SUBCONTRACTORS

LEARNING OBJECTIVES
1. Why subcontractors may be hired
2. Safety risks of employing subcontractors
3. Assessing suitability of potential subcontractors
4. Ongoing assessment of subcontractor performance and suitability

10.1. WHEN SUBCONTRACTORS ARE USED

Subcontractors (a term sometimes used interchangeably with contractors) are used to provide services or goods when access to their offerings saves money, increases convenience, or—most relevant for our purposes—reduces risk.

More specifically, a contractor might have expertise, permits, or equipment that your program does not possess. There might be a program type you offer at such a low volume that it is not cost-effective for your organization to invest in the trained staff, equipment, operating systems and other elements necessary to provide that type of programming to your quality and risk management standards, as compared to obtaining it from a specialist. For instance, if you only offer a scuba diving program around once a year, or run a challenge course (Figure 10.1) program in a certain area only rarely, it may be preferable to use a contractor for those experiences, rather than to invest in your own infrastructure.

Figure 10.1 A contractor's challenge course or climbing wall should be assessed before use, including permits, inspections, standards conformity, safety record, maintenance, staff qualifications, and more.

Additionally, having a contractor provide services such as bus transportation of participants, where there is a significant risk of serious accident occurrence, can shift the risk of incurring such a loss from your program to the contractor.

10.2. RISKS OF SUBCONTRACTOR USE

Subcontractors can face the same financial pressures that any business might face. They may have incentives to minimize expenses, including those related to risk management. This can lead to safety systems don't meet the expectations held by you or your program participants.

However, you might not be aware of a prospective contractor's potentially insufficient risk management systems without conducting a thorough assessment. It is therefore important to do a careful examination of the potential contractor's safety infrastructure to ensure it meets your requirements.

This review should be completed prior to hiring a contractor.

10.3. SUBCONTRACTOR ASSESSMENT

A subcontractor's risk management systems should generally meet the same standards to which the outdoor program holds itself (figure 10.2).

Figure 10.2. Subcontractor systems should meet the same standards that the contracting organization holds. Some contracted transportation services, such as those using these songthaews without seatbelts, common in some areas of Southeast Asia, may not meet an organization's transportation safety standards.

To assess if this is the case, it's useful to ask the prospective subcontractor a series of questions, as in Figure 10.3. A questionnaire to which the potential subcontractor gives written responses may be a suitable format for this.

In order to maximize the probability that answers are provided to questions about normally private information, it may be useful to note that response to these questions is required for compliance with the organization's safety standards or insurer requirements, assuming this is the case. In some cases, reviewing documentation at the prospective subcontractor's location may address reluctance to have proprietary information leave the subcontractor's direct control. It can be helpful to provide clear reassurance that responses will be held in strict confidence.

These inquiries are not intended to be invasive but rather to provide convincing evidence—beyond simple assertions not backed up by documentation—that your risk management requirements will be met.

If the activities the subcontractor is to conduct are outside the area of expertise of the contracting organization, to the extent that an evaluation of the potential subcontractor's risk management system is not able to be made by the contracting organization, a qualified third party should be retained to perform the evaluation.

1. Copies of any authorizations (including permits and licenses), accreditations, and certifications relevant to the activities and areas under consideration
2. Level of experience with the activity and activity area (measured, for example, by length of time)
3. Summary of safety record for last 10 years, including incidents, insurance claims and legal actions

4. Summary of safety review findings
5. Copy of emergency plan
6. Standards for equipment use, care, and management (including selection, inspection, maintenance, repair, storage, and retirement) for the equipment that will be used with the activities under consideration. Safety and emergency response equipment provided.
7. Qualifications for staff, including required experience, skills, training, certifications (medical, technical outdoor skills, licenses, or other) and background check results
8. If providing transportation: transportation safety policies, including vehicles (including management standards in item number six above), licensing, operator testing and training, motor vehicle record checks, vehicle operating procedures
9. List of sub-subcontractors that may be used by the subcontractor, and the above information for each sub-subcontractor

Figure 10.3. Areas of inquiry in considering approval of potential subcontractors.

In some cases, such as when considering the use of a contractor's accommodations or structures such as climbing structure, sailing ship, or challenge course, an on-site inspection is warranted.

Evidence of appropriate insurances should also be provided, as described in Chapter 13, Risk Transfer.

10.4. RISK TRANSFER

Transfer of risk from outdoor program to subcontractor includes appropriate insurance policies, release of liability, and indemnification, among others. These items are discussed in Chapter 13, Risk Transfer.

10.5. ONGOING ASSESSMENT

Assessment of subcontractor suitability should be conducted on an ongoing basis. For instance, it might be required for the questionnaire referenced in section 10.3 to be filled out by the contractor once a year.

Program staff present during activities should continually assess subcontractor performance, and take steps necessary to address any perceived deficiencies.

In addition, a review of subcontractor performance and suitability should be held after each use of a subcontractor. This could be integrated into the post-program written debrief by the activity leaders of the outdoor program, for example.

Chapter Summary

1. Retaining subcontractors can be useful when an organization does not have readily available the services a subcontractor provides at a competitive cost.

2. Retaining subcontractors can transfer risks from an outdoor program to a subcontractor.

3. Subcontractors may not have adequate risk management systems, but this might not be evident without conducting a thorough examination.

4. Such an examination should provide written responses and documents providing clear evidence of satisfactory risk management.

5. Examination topic areas include authorizations, certifications, accreditation, past experience, safety record, safety review findings, emergency plans, equipment, staff, transportation systems, sub-subcontractors, and insurance.

6. A variety of techniques such as standardized questionnaires and on-site document review can ease concerns regarding divulging confidential information.

7. On-site inspections of built structures and other items may be part of the examination.

8. Release of liability, indemnification, and other risk transfer instruments should meet organization requirements.

9. Contractor suitability should be assessed before, during and after contractor use.

CHAPTER 11

TRANSPORTATION

LEARNING OBJECTIVES

1. Transfer transportation risk from your organization to others
2. Assess motor vehicle operator eligibility initially and on an ongoing basis
3. Operator training standards
4. Motor vehicle operation standards
5. Expectations for vehicle occupants
6. Fleet manager and administrator responsibilities
7. Vehicle use policies

11.1.   INTRODUCTION

The two fifteen-passenger vans hummed smoothly down the dark and empty highway. Cacti and spindly desert ocotillo flashed by in the light of the headlights, as the vehicles cruised swiftly along the straight, deserted road. It was close to 5 am, and the travelers had been driving through the night. They were almost home.

The vehicles held a group of college students and their two professors returning from a three-week field course in Baja, Mexico. Atop the van roofs were roofracks brimming with fully loaded backpacks. Sleeping passengers mingled with a boogie board and jumbled camping gear, dusted with beach sand, in the back seats. Eager to return home, the group had decided to drive all day and then through the night to get back to campus as soon as possible. Professors and students took turns at the wheel.

The driver of the van in front could see the headlights of the closely following second van in her rear-view mirror. Suddenly she saw the headlight beams swerve away, then violently swerve back. She watched with horror as the beams, and the vehicle emitting them, rolled over on their side. The vehicle skidded down the highway, leaving behind a trail of shattered glass and blood.

The first van pulled over and the occupants ran back through the blackness of the desert night to give help to the injured,

who were slowly clambering out of the smashed second van. About 15 minutes later, a lone car drove up, and the driver was asked to get help. The nearest town was kilometers away, and the closest hospital over an hour's drive.

An ambulance shuttled the injured students to the hospital, returning several times over multiple hours to pick up more patients and transport them, two at a time. Eventually all were treated and released with no major injuries. But what happened?

After long hours at the wheel in the middle of the night, the driver of the second van, an untrained college student, had allowed the vehicle to drift off the highway and onto the soft gravel shoulder, about 10 centimeters below the level of the road surface. The vehicle operator turned the wheel hard to get back on the road, overcorrecting and causing the van to lurch into the oncoming traffic lane. The driver then quickly turned the steering wheel back, but—top-heavy with metal roofracks piled high with gear—the vehicle lost balance and rolled over onto its side.

Was this accident preventable? What do you think led to the incident? Here are four issues that, if addressed, might have stopped this rollover from occurring:

- *The vehicle was fully loaded. Fifteen-passenger vans have a high center of mass, and the more the passenger compartment is filled with occupants and cargo, the more unstable the vehicle can be.*

- *A roofrack was on the roof top, and heavily loaded.* Roofracks and their contents also raise the center of mass, increasing the likelihood of rollover.
- *Travel was occurring at night.* Night-time driving significantly increases the risk of motor vehicle accident. In this case, driving through the night was not required.
- *The driver was untrained.* The vehicle operator had no training in how to recover from driving onto a road shoulder or other procedures to reduce the risk of van rollover.

In this chapter, you'll learn about procedures and systems to manage transportation risks. They will help prevent accidents like the one described here.

Transportation of people and equipment in outdoor programming presents significant risks. Motor vehicle accidents are a leading cause of fatalities and serious injuries in outdoor organizations. High levels of force are involved—thousands of kilograms of steel traveling at high speed. Some of the hazards cannot easily be eliminated—on a drive to or from a trailhead, put-in, or climbing site, the possibility of encountering distracted or otherwise impaired drivers on the road is inescapable.

11.1.1. Risk Transfer

Some outdoor programs choose to transfer transportation risk to another organization by contracting out participant transportation to a third party. A third party such as a bus company may have full-time professional drivers with extensive experience and training. In case of an accident, the contractor holds much of the responsibility, providing that the contractor was carefully selected after a thorough evaluation of their qualifications.

In other situations, participants may transport themselves (or be transported by parents or guardians).

These approaches do not eliminate the risk of accident when transporting outdoor program staff and gear, however.

Appropriate motor vehicle insurance, addressed in following sections, can be considered a method of risk transfer as well.

11.1.2. Risk Reduction

Risks can be minimized by several approaches.

Vehicle operators should meet strict qualifications and receive ongoing training and testing.

Vehicle operation practices should be established and employed to meet safety standards and reinforce a safety-first culture.

Passenger behavior should be managed to reduce risk.

Fleet manager and administrator practices including preventive maintenance, insurance, documentation, safety culture and travel planning should be established and maintained.

Vehicle selection and use criteria regarding evacuation and personal vehicles and other factors should be met.

Emerging issues such as newly appearing hazards and technologies should be proactively considered by transportation staff.

We will cover these risk reduction approaches in detail throughout this chapter.

Figure 11.1. Appropriately selecting and maintaining vehicles helps manage transportation risks.

11.1.3. Other Resources

Since motor vehicle transportation is not unique to outdoor programs, many resources for transportation management are available. Motor vehicle insurance companies, particularly the insurer covering your vehicles, may have helpful resources. Automobile associations may also have guidance on driving safety. And regional and national transportation agencies (in the U.S., state motor vehicle departments and the federal Department of Transportation) provide regulations and recommendations.

These sources and others can provide guidance, standards and support in developing and sustaining a high-quality, low-risk transportation program.

11.2. STANDARDS

The standards outlined here apply to owned vehicles, rented or leased vehicles, and volunteer or paid staff vehicles when used for company business. In addition to road vehicles, these standards are relevant to all-terrain vehicles, watercraft, aircraft, snowmobiles and other vehicles, as applicable.

11.2.1. Vehicle Operators

The motor vehicle operator is an essential element of transportation safety. Research from the U.S. National Highway Traffic Safety Administration indicates that operator error is a factor in at least 90 percent of serious motor vehicle accidents. It should be made clear to all occupants that, as with ship's captains and airplane pilots, the driver is completely in charge of and responsible for the operation of the vehicle and the safety of passengers.

Operator Eligibility. Holding the status of an approved driver is not automatic. It should be granted only after a thorough assessment of the candidate's skills, performance, and driving history. Driving privileges can be revoked at any time.

Driver approval criteria may include:

1. **Review organization's vehicle manual and agree to abide by its terms.** Figures 11.3, Sample Driver Assessment Form, and 11.5, Driver Record Check Permission, document written agreement. The vehicle manual may contain information, policies and procedures (for example, items included in this chapter) that may help ensure the organization and motor vehicle operators meet safety and other transportation objectives.

2. **Written test.** Reading the organization's vehicle manual and passing a written test on its contents (see Figure 11.2, Sample Written Motor Vehicle Operator Test).

3. **Practical test.** Successfully passing an on-the-road practical test (see test subjects listed in Figure 11.3, Sample Driver Assessment Form).

4. **Acceptable initial driving record.** Proof of satisfactory motor vehicle operating record from the relevant authority (in the U.S, the state motor vehicle department).

5. **Acceptable ongoing driver record.** If available, ongoing satisfactory motor vehicle operating record, based on notifications of driving violations from a motor vehicle department offering Employer Notification Services (ENS) or an analogous program. ENS provides a notification of driving violations to employers of commercial drivers. Approximately 18 U.S. states offer ENS.

6. **Commercial use regulations.** In the US, if federal commercial vehicle use regulations apply to your organization, compliance with U.S. Federal Motor Carrier Safety Administration regulations. Elsewhere, compliance with any analogous laws or regulations.

7. **Age and experience.** As young persons mature and gain experience driving, they become safer drivers. Therefore, some organizations set a minimum age and amount of driving experience. For example, an organization could require drivers to be at least 19 (or for improved safety, 21) years of age and have at least three years' driving experience.

Written Test. The written text should ensure that drivers demonstrate sufficient cognitive knowledge regarding vehicle operations and risk management. In the example test in Figure 11.2, below, at least 80 percent correct is required to pass.

Sample Vehicle Operator Written Test

Name: _____   Date: _____

1.) No one who will be driving a company vehicle shall have any drugs or alcohol in their system _____ hours prior to driving.

2.) What is the organization's policy regarding seatbelts? _____
_____

3.) Vehicles shall be operated _____ or _____ the posted speed limit at all times.

4.) What is the organization's policy regarding use of headlights (day or night)? _____
_____

5.) Drivers shall not operate a motor vehicle for more than ___ hours consecutively, or ___ hours in a day.

6.) The _____ is completely in charge and responsible for the operation of the vehicle and trailer and the safety of the passengers.

7.) When shall a "pre-drive checklist" be filled out? _____

8.) Most accidents are caused by:

a. _____

b. _____

c. _____

9.) When are employees allowed to transport participants in their personal vehicles? _____
_____

10.) Where should you pull over if having mechanical trouble or a breakdown? Why? _____
_____

11.) What should you do if in a vehicle accident? _____
_____
_____
_____

12.) Should you plead guilty or assess or admit fault? _____.

13.) What should you do if the wheels of the vehicle travel off the paved roadway (and onto the shoulder)? _____
_____
_____
_____

14.) What should you NOT do if the wheels of the vehicle travel off the paved roadway? _____
_____

15.) What will minimize understeer problems and will reduce the risk of van rollover? _____
_____

16.) Entering a turn at a _____ speed decreases the negative effects of oversteer and reduces the risk of van rollover.

17.) The load in a 15 passenger van should be _____ and _____ for best stability.

18.) Weighing down the back seat of a van "un-weights" the front of the van; therefore, keep the load on the back seat as _____ as possible.

19.) Allow at least a ___ second gap between you and the vehicle in front of you. In adverse weather allow at least a ___ second gap.

20.) There are blind spots behind any vehicle. What should you do if you cannot get assistance to back up your vehicle?
_____

Figure 11.2. Sample written motor vehicle operator test. A test customized for your organization's unique circumstances may look different from this example.

Practical Test. This test involves the driver candidate driving a representative vehicle through a set of driving conditions and activities that would typically be encountered when driving. The examination also tests emergency procedures. The test is designed to assess the candidate's psychomotor vehicle operation skills.

Figure 11.2 shows a sample Driver Assessment Form that includes practical test components. This completed document, and updated motor vehicle records if available from the relevant motor vehicle authority, should be kept on file for every driver.

Driver Check Off

For (Name of Employee):_____

EMPLOYEE ACKNOWLEDGEMENT

I, _____, have read the "[Name of Company] Vehicle Manual" and understand I am responsible for adhering to the policies, procedures, and guidelines contained within this document. I understand that failure to follow the requirements set forth in the [Name of Company] Vehicle Manual could lead to termination of employment.

_____   _____
Employee Signature   Date

AUTO INSURANCE

Logistics Manager or designate initial and date when this employee has been added as a driver to the auto insurance:_____

DRIVING PRACTICAL ASSESSMENT

The Logistics Manager or designate shall initial blank space after employee has shown competency in each of the following areas:

Driving vehicle
☐ Has read the [Name of Company] Vehicle Manual and signed above stating that he/she has done so.
☐ Completed the pre-drive inspection form
☐ Driving under control in the types of areas the vehicle will be used
☐ Pulling off road safely (e.g. in case of oncoming car or tire blowout)
☐ Reversing vehicle
☐ Emergency braking
☐ General "defensive" & safe driving techniques (adjusts mirror, stays in lane, two hands on wheel, adheres to speed limit, doesn't tailgate, etc.)

Driving vehicle with trailer
☐ Securing to AND removing trailer from vehicle
☐ Completed the pre-drive inspection form
☐ Backing with trailer (reviewed jackknifing)
☐ Turning corner around building (or other obstruction)
☐ Changing lanes with trailer
☐ Driving under control on streets
☐ Driving under control on highway or freeway (if applicable)
☐ Review how to safely load the trailer
☐ Emergency braking

_____   _____
Logistics Manager or designate signature   Date
(sign if shows competency to be a driver)

WRITTEN TEST

Logistics Manager or designate shall initial and date when this employee has completed the written vehicle test. They have answered all of the questions correctly or reviewed the correct answer(s) with the Logistics Manager or designate: _____

MOTOR VEHICLE DEPARMENT PULL LIST

Logistics Manager or designate initial and date when this employee has been added to the Motor Vehicle Dept. Pull List: _____

DMV BACKGROUND CHECK

The Logistics Manager or designate shall review employee driving background check results for approval of driving privileges. [Check box after asking employee verbally; sign bottom when DMV report is officially reviewed]

☐ The employee has met the standards for the [Name of Organization] Motor Vehicle Record check with a status of "clear" or "acceptable" as noted in the [Name of Organization] Vehicle Manual under the Driver Eligibility section in order to be able to drive for [Organization].
☐ The employee does not meet the standards for the [Name of Organization] Motor Vehicle Record check, as they have a status of "borderline" or poor" and they are unable to drive for [Organization].

_____   _____
Logistics Manager or designate signature (after DMV report reviewed)   Date

Figure 11.3. Sample driver assessment form. Specific components may vary by operator activity, equipment used, areas of travel, insurance requirements, jurisdictional requirements, and other factors.

Acceptable Initial Driving Record. A driving record is assessed for acceptability by comparing the record to a set of pre-established criteria. Follow the procedures necessary to obtain the potential driver's record from the local motor vehicle department. In some cases, filling out a special form or obtaining written permission from the driver is required. In some locations, private companies may be hired to run motor vehicle record reports for a fee.

Next, compare the records to a standard such as in figure 11.4, below.

When using the standard in figure 11.4, in order to be granted driving privileges, the applicant's record should be graded as "acceptable" or "clear." A "borderline" or "poor" motor vehicle record results in ineligibility to drive. In addition, a driver should not have a Driving while Under the Influence, Driving While Intoxicated, or similar drug- or alcohol-related offence within the last five years.

Types of Violations

Major Violations	Major Violations
Driving under influence of alcohol/drugs	All other traffic violations (such as speeding) are counted as "Minor"
Failure to stop/report an accident	
Reckless driving/speeding contest	**The following citations are minor but will not be included in the count:**
Driving while impaired	Motor vehicle equipment, load or size requirement
Making a false accident report	Improper/failure to display license plates
Homicide, manslaughter or assault arising out of the use of a vehicle	Failure to sign or display registration
Driving while license is suspended/revoked	Failure to have driver's license in possession (if valid license exists)
Careless driving	
Attempting to elude a police officer	

Motor Vehicle Grading Criteria (Last Three Years)

Number of Minor violations	Number of at-fault accidents			
	0	1	2	3
0	Clear	Acceptable	Borderline	Poor
1	Acceptable	Acceptable	Borderline	Poor
2	Acceptable	Borderline	Poor	Poor
3	Borderline	Poor	Poor	Poor
4	Poor	Poor	Poor	Poor
Any major violation	Poor	Poor	Poor	Poor

Figure 11.4. Sample grading criteria for acceptable motor vehicle record.

Drivers should promptly report any driving violations to their supervisor. In addition, if your organization does not participate in an Employer Notification Services system where driving violations are promptly reported to employers, the motor vehicle record should be obtained at least on an annual basis and compared to grading criteria as above.

Written permission to check motor vehicle records should be obtained from each prospective vehicle operator. Figure 11.5, below, shows a sample form, which also contains a notification clause and other terms.

Driver Program

I, _____ (print name), authorize [Organization] to check my driving record as frequently as it is deemed reasonably necessary. This serves as my authorization to have the organization request my motor vehicle record.

I understand that if I do not maintain a record satisfactory to the organization or its insurance carrier, I may be prohibited from operating company vehicles and/or from driving my own vehicle on company business.

I agree to notify the company of any changes in my driving record, including any violations or accidents, within 24 hours.

I affirm that I have read the organization's Vehicle Manual and agree to abide by its terms.

Due to the potential legal liability created for the company, I hereby acknowledge that violation of the company's transportation policies may result in disciplinary action up to and including termination of my employment/volunteer status.

_____   _____

Signature   Date

Driver's License Number: _____

State of Issue: _____

License Number: _____

Expiration Date: _____

Birth Date: _____

Complete name: _____

Home Address: _____

I do not want to participate in the Driver Program. I will not operate any company vehicles or drive any other vehicle on company business.

_____   _____

Signature   Date

Figure 11.5. Permission to check motor vehicle record.

Commercial Use Regulations. In the U.S., the Department of Transportation's Federal Motor Carrier Safety Administration sets regulations for property-carrying and passenger-carrying drivers. If your business uses a motor vehicle in multiple US states and transports nine or more passengers for compensation, these regulations may apply to you. Other circumstances, such as transport of 16 or more passengers (including the driver) not for compensation, may be regulated under the same rules.

The following policies may help an outdoor program comply with these commercial vehicle regulations:

1. Driver minimum age 21.
2. Driver record background check completed.
3. Driver testing completed.
4. Driver must provide a list to their employer of all motor vehicle traffic violations for which they have been convicted or forfeited bond in the previous 12 months.
5. Driver must have a current medical exam, which must be renewed every 24 months, and may be subject to random drug testing.
6. Vehicles may not transport alcohol across state lines.
7. Hours of service regulations observed.

In some jurisdictions, a special class of driver's license must be obtained when operating certain vehicles in some commercial situations. Operators must obtain the correct driver's license in order to comply with these regulations.

Regulations change over time, so check to ascertain the most current rules.

Your automobile insurance company may have requirements or useful resources regarding driver approvals.

Operator Training. Following their initial training, drivers should go through a driver training session annually. Topics should include key elements of safe driving, applicable regulations, and special equipment or situations particular to your organization.

Figure 11.6. Special training is required before driving heavy loads on steep mountain roads.

Specific subjects to cover may include:
1. Fifteen passenger vans (unique design and handling, risks, history and causes or rollovers)
2. Center of mass, causes of lateral instability, under-steering and over-steering
3. Weigh distribution, loading and unloading
4. Emergency handling
5. Federal commercial driver regulations
6. Review of all topics in organization's vehicle manual

Use of trailers or other special equipment should be covered in additional training and assessment which might include braking, hitching, trailer loading, tongue weight, safety equipment and other topics as deemed necessary by the conditions in which the equipment is operated.

Successful participation in this annual vehicle risk management training should be documented for each participant and kept on file.

Individuals who may not drive but who might assist with activities such as loading or unloading, trailer operations, and vehicle inspections should also receive initial and ongoing training regarding the activities in which they will participate. An annual review of the organization's vehicle manual, with attention to safe lifting, trailer hitching, and the like, may be advisable for these persons.

Motor vehicle operator training is often done in-house by operations staff, but training from private companies (which may even specialize in driver training for outdoor programs) may be available for a fee.

Figure 11.7. Drivers should take and pass practical and written exams prior to being permitted to drive.

Safer Operator Behavior. Driving vehicles for outdoor programs is different from typical personal driving: larger vehicles, heavier loads, different vehicle handling, special equipment like trailers, long travel distances, and remote locations reached by poorly maintained roads over rugged terrain. Vehicle operators need special training and techniques to safely transport people and gear to their final destination.

The probability and severity of a motor vehicle accident or related loss can be reduced by following strategies for safer vehicle operations.

Culture. A strong and continuously reinforced safety culture can contribute to a long record of accident-free transportation. Vehicle operators should be encouraged to operate a vehicle only if they feel fully capable and qualified to do so, including given the conditions (such as inclement weather or other hazards) that may be present. Operators should be encouraged to decline to drive if they feel that due to fatigue, alcohol or other impairments, their performance might not be optimal. Operators should be made to feel comfortable to stop and ask for help if needed. Occupants—including staff, program participants, and anyone else—should be made aware of their responsibilities for transportation safety and encouraged to fulfill them.

Drugs. Vehicle operators must be free of the influence of recreational drugs, alcohol, and medications that could impair judgment, vision, or any other factor necessary for satisfactory vehicle operation performance. In addition to establishing this as policy, some organizations require a minimum time, for example eight or twelve hours or more, between exposure to potentially performance-diminishing substances and vehicle operation. The eight-hour guideline has been established by US federal aviation regulations regarding alcohol consumption by pilots. In some cases, depending body weight and amount of alcohol consumed, after eight hours the blood alcohol content could still exceed the .02 percent blood alcohol (BAC) concentration that US federal regulations set as an upper limit for pilots operating aircraft. (For comparison, the U.S. Federal Motor Carrier Safety Administration sets 0.04% as the maximum allowable BAC for a commercial driver holding a commercial driver's license. A BAC of .08 percent in the US is considered impaired for driving a car. Other national aviation agencies may have different limits than those of the US.) A twelve hour "bottle to throttle" standard is a more conservative approach, although it is possible to be above .04 percent BAC after 12 hours. Studies have shown pilot performance is diminished at a BAC of .025 percent. The U.S. Federal Aviation Administration (FAA) recommends a minimum of 24 hours between alcohol consumption and piloting aircraft. Although the FAA does not regulate driving cars or trucks, their guidance can be used as a reference for setting an outdoor program's motor vehicle operation standards.

For operations not involving standard terrestrial motor vehicles, other regulations may apply. For instance, for sailing operations in U.S. waters, U.S. Coast Guard regulations on drug use and testing described in the Code of Federal Regulations (Titles 33, 46 and 49, as amended) must be followed. In other countries, the relevant regulations must be understood and followed.

Headlights. Vehicle operators should keep the vehicle's headlights on when the vehicle is in use, day and night. In some locations and situations, this is legally required. Studies show that using headlights during the day can reduce the probability of motor vehicle accident occurrence.

Speed Limit. Vehicle operators should not exceed the posted speed limit for their vehicle type. (Automobiles, trucks, and vehicles towing trailers, for instance, may have different speed limits.) Operators should drive even more slowly in diminished conditions such as limited visibility or severe weather.

Loading and Unloading. Loading vehicles appropriately is an essential component of reducing the risk of motor vehicle accident. A properly loaded vehicle is less likely to roll over or injure participants with flying objects.

Vehicles should not be loaded in excess of their capacity. This is sometimes indicated as Gross Vehicle Weight Rating and listed inside the vehicle door jamb. Avoid loading in excess of 75 percent of the weight rating to reduce risks further. In addition, loads should not exceed the Gross Axle Weight Rating, the maximum weight for each axle.

Loads should be placed to keep the center of mass as low as possible. This reduces the probability of a rollover. Load should also be balanced from left to right.

Items should be secured so they do not fly about in case of sudden deceleration, rollover, or other accident. Suitable tie-down supplies (for example, ropes, straps or nets) should be available in each vehicle for this purpose.

In some vehicles, for example some vans, a heavier load over the front axle than the rear axle may improve handling and thereby increase safety. Check with the vehicle manufacturer to see if this is the case for your vehicle.

Hazardous substances should not be transported in the passenger or vehicle operator cabins. Camp stove and lantern fuel and other flammables, for instance, should be transported in a separate trailer, or if lightweight, secured on a roof rack. Care should be taken that containers holding hazardous substances are not heated (for example by sun warming a vehicle compartment), banged, or otherwise affected in ways that might cause contents to leak or react.

In vehicles with a high center of mass, such as certain vans, loading heavy items on top of the vehicle, for example on a roof rack, can significantly increase the risk of rollover. Therefore, heavy items should not be carried on a roof rack with these vehicles.

Vehicles should not carry more occupants than the manufacturer recommends. Fifteen-passenger vans may have superior handling and safety if carrying a maximum of 11 people, with the rearmost seat bench kept empty.

Individuals loading and unloading vehicles should practice safe lifting and carrying practices. Lower back pain is one of the most common causes of workplace injuries and workers' compensation claims. Leaning over and lifting a heavy pack out of a trailer, then turning so to be able to carry the load, is a classic way to cause chronic back injury. When lifting heavy objects, individuals should use best lifting practices, including:

- Use the right number of people to lift
- Bring the load close to your body
- Lift with your legs, not your back
- Keep your head up and back straight
- Bend at the hips
- Shift—don't twist—your body to turn
- Don't drop loads, but let your muscles carry it down.

Hours of Service. Vehicle operators must be well-rested before and while operating a motor vehicle. To this end, vehicle operators should observe hours of service regulations for the areas in which they operate. If operators are subject to the commercial vehicle use regulations of the U.S. Department of Transportation's Federal Motor Carrier Safety Administration (see Commercial use regulations, above), then the rules regarding number of consecutive driving hours, rest breaks, maximum driving hours per week, and other subjects must be followed. The regulations (and analogous regulations in other jurisdictions) may provide a useful reference even for those not required to follow them. For example, it can be a good idea to limit motor vehicle operations to no more than eight consecutive hours or 10 hours in a day.

Hands on Steering Wheel. The vehicle operator should drive with both hands on the steering wheel, and in the proper position.

Use of Phones and Other Electronics. The vehicle operator should not use mobile phones or other potentially distracting electronics while the vehicle is in motion.

Insurance. Vehicle operators should receive necessary information from fleet managers regarding vehicle operation requirements from insurers, and see that compliance occurs.

Pre Drive Checklist. Drivers should thoroughly check the interior and exterior of the vehicle before using it. Exceptions may be made if the vehicle has very recently been used (for example, that same day) or if trips are exceedingly short (for instance, 50 meters from a parking area to a loading dock).

Figure 11.8 gives an example of a checklist that must be completed and signed before using a vehicle. Vehicle condition, presence of necessary items, and function of key components should be examined and found suitable before the vehicle is operated. Checklists will vary depending on vehicle type, expected travel conditions, equipment and accessories carried, and other factors. A fully loaded van taking a long journey on a snowy mountain road hauling a trailer, for example, will require a different inspection regime than driving a passenger vehicle a short distance into town to run errands.

Pre-Drive Vehicle Inspection Checklist

Date(s): _____   Vehicle: _____

Destination: _____   Driver(s): _____

Start Mileage: _____   End Mileage: _____

Purpose/Program: _____

INSTRUCTIONS:

Use the following general checklist to perform an inspection of the vehicle before each trip. If also pulling a trailer, complete trailer checklist. Please be thorough. Advise Logistics staff if something is missing or needs repair/maintenance. Make note of any repairs or maintenance you made before/during/after journey.

UNDER HOOD. Check and circle one:

☐   Oil level (high, adequate, low)

☐   Coolant level (high, adequate, low)

☐   Windshield wiper fluid (high, adequate, low)

☐   Jack

EXTERIOR. Check for:

☐   Adequate tire tread

☐   Hide a key

☐   Damage: _____

EQUIPMENT. Ensure presence of:

☐   Vehicle Manual

☐   Pressure Gauge

☐   Working Flashlight

☐   Flares

☐   First Aid Kit

☐   Jumper Cables

☐   Tire Iron

☐   Fire Extinguisher

☐   Tie-down supplies

☐   Tire chains (winter only)

INTERIOR. Check:

☐   Running/Parking Lights

☐   Headlights

☐   High Beams

☐   Turn Signals (front/back)

☐   Brake Lights

☐   Reverse Lights

☐   Horn

☐   Seats Secure

☐   Damage: _____

TRAILER. Check:

☐   Hitch completely on ball

☐   Hitch lock in down position

☐   Pin (or padlock) on hitch lock

☐   Jack completely pulled up

☐   Both chains secured to vehicle

☐   Blocks removed from tires

☐   Back door completely shut

☐   Brake lights work

☐   Turning lights work

☐   Running lights work

COMMENTS or other concerns:

I (print) _____have completed all parts of the above form: (sign) _____

Figure 11.8. Pre-drive vehicle inspection checklist. These checklists should be filled out for every trip and securely stored after completion.

Vehicle Log. A vehicle log records start and end mileage, date, and name of vehicle operator. Some make a provision for recording maintenance needs or other comments. Figure 11.8, above, gives an example of vehicle log information incorporated into a pre-drive checklist. Vehicle logs can take multiple forms, including paper and electronic. They can be produced in-house (as in this example) or purchased from a commercial supplier of fleet management resources. Fleet managers should retain vehicle log records.

Adverse Conditions. Certain situations can diminish the motor vehicle operating environment from its optimal condition. (See Figure 11.9.)

Adverse Driving Conditions

- Reduced visibility
  - Blind corners, intersections, summits, and curves
  - Darkness
  - Fog
  - Glare
  - Dust
  - Snow, heavy rain, or other precipitation
- Steep grades
- Long downhill slopes, especially when transporting heavy loads
- High winds
- Slippery driving surfaces; dirt roads; roads in poor repair
- Lack of guardrails above drop-offs
- Towing a trailer or other vehicle
- Anticipated or actual presence of children or bicyclists
- Anticipated or actual presence of livestock or other animals
- Heavy traffic
- Roads in low-resource regions of the world not up to international road construction, maintenance and signage standards

Figure 11.9. Examples of adverse driving conditions.

Figure 11.10. Livestock and animals on the road cause injuries, property damage and fatalities every year.

In these circumstances operators should drive at a sufficiently reduced speed to adequately compensate for these hazards.

Since accident rates rise sharply at night, it is best to plan transportation schedules to avoid driving at that time.

When approaching blind curves on narrow or one-lane roads, it's recommended that drivers briefly blow the horn.

For programs that experience extreme adverse conditions—for example, desert sandstorms, security and criminal behavior issues, or snow and ice—expanded protocols may be necessary. For instance, travel in cold and icy areas may require additional standards regarding bringing warm clothing and insulating materials, reducing speed, using studded tires and chains, weighting vehicles to improve handling, increasing stopping space, braking on snow and ice, and managing skidding and sliding, among others.

Braking. Vehicles hauling trailers or carrying heavy loads need additional time for braking. Overly sharp braking can reduce stability. Drivers accustomed to operating personal vehicles may to be reminded of these contrasts.

Operators should allow at least a three-second gap between their vehicle and the vehicle in front of them. In adverse conditions at least a four-second gap should be maintained.

Shoulder Driving. If a vehicle drifts off the paved road surface onto the road shoulder (the strip along the side of the road), it is at high risk for rollover if the proper procedures are not followed. This is especially true if the driver turns the steering wheel sharply to bring the vehicle back onto the road surface.

When the vehicle travels off the pavement onto the shoulder, the operator should hold the steering wheel firmly and let off the gas pedal. The operator should not apply the brakes aggressively or turn sharply. The vehicle should gradually slow to below 40 kph (25 mph). At that time the operator should gradually turn the steering wheel to get back on the road. The operator should proceed with caution when merging with traffic.

This maneuver should be practiced by candidates for driver status, and successful performance of safe recovery from shoulder driving should be demonstrated, before the candidate is eligible to drive.

Backing. Backing vehicles, with or without trailers, is a leading cause of collisions. Vehicles typically used in outdoor programs are longer, higher, and wider than passenger car drivers may be accustomed to operating. Fully loaded vehicles or trailers may obstruct rear vision. Low-hanging branches, deep sand and other obstacles may be present.

For these reasons, backing should be done with care. Successful backing should be demonstrated by would-be drivers before they are approved to drive. When backing, a second person should safely stand behind the vehicle in sight and sound of the driver and give directions. If no backing assistant is available, the driver should inspect the area to be backed into in person before attempting the backing maneuver. Any obstacles or hazards identified should be addressed before backing.

Route Selection. Driving routes that are the safest and most efficient, with the fewest hazardous driving conditions, should be selected.

Fueling. To help ensure that following drivers are not stranded, vehicles should be returned at least half full of fuel.

Breakdowns. If a vehicle experiences mechanical trouble and breakdown, the top priority is protecting the safety of vehicle occupants and passengers in other vehicles. Occupants should get off the roadway, and the vehicle should safely and promptly be situated out of travel lanes.

Detailed procedures in case of breakdown may include:

1. Immediately park the vehicle in a safe place, completely off the roadway. Avoid stopping on the shoulder of freeways. If possible, drive to an off-ramp and pull onto a surface street.
2. If one must continue on the roadway to reach a safe place off the road, turn on the emergency flashers and proceed with caution. Do not hesitate to drive on a flat tire if it is necessary to reach a safe place completely off the roadway. (Drive slowly, since the scraping tire and wheel could cause a fire.)
3. If the driver can't get the vehicle well off the road and in a safe area, have the vehicle towed to a safe place for maintenance or repair (for example, for fixing a flat tire).
4. Use reflectors, high visibility cones, or flares during any mechanical trouble when pulled over to the side of the road, especially at night or in other situations with diminished visibility.

5. All individuals should position themselves in a safe location to avoid being hit by oncoming traffic or being exposed to other hazards. If the vehicle is in a hazardous location, all individuals shall stay away from the immediate area until safety has been established by the police or other traffic authorities.
6. It's wise to contact supervisory staff so that accommodations can be made if the breakdown significantly disrupts planned transportation schedules.

Accidents. Procedures to follow in case of a motor vehicle accident should be known to the driver and accompanying staff before travel, to help ensure that procedures are followed correctly despite the stress of a significant incident.

Procedures such as the below can be customized to your particular circumstances.

In case of accident:
1. Get everyone into a safe location. Contact emergency medical services if anyone is injured.
2. Stay at the scene and notify the police. Make sure an accident report gets filled out.
3. Make no comment regarding the accident to anyone except the police, the organization's administration, or the motor vehicle insurance carrier. Do not plead guilty or assess or admit fault. Do not argue.
4. Contact the appropriate program administrator. You may be directed by them to contact the company's motor vehicle insurance provider. If you cannot reach an administrator, call the insurance company on your own to report the accident.
5. Fill out the "Vehicle Accident" form if your accident involved other vehicles. An Incident Report should also be filled out by the driver or responsible party.
6. If the vehicle is safely drivable and everyone is uninjured, inform the office and proceed to your travel destination.
7. If an employee, volunteer or participant is injured, a staff person should accompany them to the nearest medical facility and immediately notify program administration staff per the notification sequence in the emergency call guide.
8. If the vehicle is off to the side of the road, do not endanger participants or passengers by attempting to push the vehicle back on the road.

9. If the vehicle is not safely drivable, immediately notify program administration so alternate transportation arrangements can be made.

Some organizations may have a policy stating that if an accident review determines driver negligence, a charge may be assessed to cover a portion of the organization's property damage.

Figure 11.11 provides an example of a sample Accident Form. Your motor vehicle insurance company may have additional resources and recommended procedures to follow in case of accident.

Vehicle Accident Report Form

Check off the following as they are completed:

☐ Collect information from each driver involved and fill it in below.
☐ Fill in the on-scene accident information and if possible take pictures.
☐ On a separate piece of paper write a summary of how the accident occurred.
☐ Check organization's Vehicle Manual for more information.

ON-SCENE ACCIDENT INFORMATION

Date and time of Accident:
Location of Accident:
(Street or Highway, City, State)
Accident Investigated by:
Accident Report #:

DRIVER INFORMATION

Driver of Organization's Vehicle_____
License
Address
Phone
Policy #
Company
Address
Phone
Vehicle Make
Model
Color

Driver #2_____
License
Address
Phone
Policy #
Company
Address
Phone
Vehicle Make
Model
Color

Driver #3_____
License
Address
Phone
Policy #
Company
Address
Phone
Vehicle Make
Model
Color

Figure 11.11. Sample accident form. A document such as this can be used to exchange information with other drivers and record police information.

11.2.2. Passengers

Seatbelts. All passengers, including the vehicle operator, should wear their seatbelts while the vehicle is in motion. With certain populations of participants, such as youth, it can be a good idea to confirm that seatbelts are applied before driving. Rarely, seat belts will not be available, for example in certain contexts in low-income countries. If participants will be asked to travel in a vehicle without seatbelts, they (and their parents or guardians, if the participant is a minor) should give informed consent, in writing, well before this situation occurs. This means that in low-resource situations transportation options, including during contingencies and emergencies, should be assessed in advance.

Figure 11.12. Operators should ensure all passengers are wearing seat belts when the vehicle is in motion.

Ride in Vehicle. Passengers should be instructed to ride with their body entirely in the vehicle. Vehicle operators should observe passengers to make sure heads, arms, or other body parts stay inside the vehicle.

Driver Distractions. Occupants should not engage in rowdy, boisterous play (roughhousing) or noisemaking that might distract the vehicle operator, while the vehicle is in motion.

11.2.3. Fleet Managers

A vehicle "fleet" can be as small as one occasionally rented car, or multiple yards of many vehicle types. A fleet can include cars, trucks, and busses, but also other vehicles such as watercraft, snowmobiles, or aircraft.

The term "fleet manager" applies to outdoor programs large and small. It encompasses both a team of specialized professionals who exclusively handle transportation, and a part-time program coordinator who juggles transportation, staffing, marketing, and more.

Insurance. Fleet managers should be aware of insurance requirements, and ensure they are complied with. Documentation of compliance should be kept; it may be important to produce in case of an accident. Fleet managers should also ensure insurance is obtained on rental vehicles during the period of rental.

Record-keeping. Fleet managers are responsible to maintain records of vehicle purchase, inspection, maintenance, repair, and disposal. This can help demonstrate proper care in case of accident. Records may include:

- Purchase of vehicle, including proof of ownership (vehicle title)
- Inspections: pre-drive inspections by operators, periodic safety checks by maintenance staff
- Use logs: a recording of beginning mileage, ending mileage, and name of driver, for each trip
- Maintenance requests or complaints from operators or occupants
- Routine maintenance provided, including what was done, on what date and by whom (example shown in Figure 11.13)
- Repairs made, including what was done, on what date and by whom

Maintenance / Repair Log

The intention of the Maintenance/repair Log is to document routine maintenance or any maintenance or repairs that are done before scheduled routine maintenance or scheduled seasonal inspection.

Procedures

1. A professional maintenance and safety check shall be made of each vehicle before each season and repairs or adjustments/maintenance be made accordingly.
2. Maintenance receipts and records shall be held in the company office.
3. Fill out the Maintenance/repair Log any time any maintenance is performed.
4. Record in the Logbook any items purchased for a vehicle.
5. Record dates tire(s) are rotated, balanced or replaced.

Date_____ Mileage_____

Maintenance Performed (include quantities and type)_____

Name of Technician_____ Phone #_____

Shop name_____ Address_____

Comments_____

Date_____ Mileage_____

Maintenance Performed (include quantities and type)_____

Name of Technician_____ Phone #_____

Shop name_____ Address_____

Comments_____

Figure 11.13. Sample maintenance log form.

Maintenance and Repairs. Routine vehicle maintenance should be done according to the recommendations of the original equipment manufacturer (OEM). If deviations from OEM recommendations occur, they should be justifiable by fleet management. (For instance, if the OEM recommends frequent vehicle washing and waxing for aesthetic reasons, this can be disregarded without compromising safety.)

Figure 11.14. Vehicle maintenance should generally follow original equipment manufacturer recommendations.

11.2.4. Administration

Record-keeping. Program administration should keep the following items on file at the organization's office location:

- Roster of currently approved drivers
- Copy of current driver's license for each approved driver
- Proof of satisfactory driving record
- Records of motor vehicle violations from motor vehicle department ENS, if available
- Completed Driver Assessment forms

Insurance. Business administrators should ensure that they or fleet managers have obtained the appropriate insurance policy with suitable coverage for owned, leased, and rented vehicles. Relevant requirements from the insurer should be transmitted to fleet managers and vehicle operators.

Culture. Executive administration should set a culture of vehicle safety. Administrators should comply with safer driving practices themselves, to set a good example. They should ensure that policies and procedures are followed and follow up promptly, transparently, and firmly when they are not. Communications—such as in messages to employees or periodic safety reports—can establish a safety culture as well, for instance by reminding drivers it is preferable to be late than to drive over the speed limit, and by publicly recognizing operators for employing good driving practices.

Regular Review. Administrators should review fleet management policies regularly, for example each year, to insure compliance with applicable laws and insurance regulations.

Transportation Planning. Organizational leaders should shape the business and its programs to minimize the need for transportation in the first place. For instance, conducting program activities at one location near a population center or transportation hub is preferable to driving from one activity area to another, or traveling long distances to reach an activity area in the first place. Expedition routes that begin or end at a program headquarters can elegantly eliminate the need for road travel.

Structural planning to minimize travel distances and avoid travel in diminished conditions should also be conducted. A few examples:

- A program activity area could be shut down seasonally when weather makes driving less safe.
- When two equally suitable climbing site or other activity areas are available, the closer one should generally be selected.
- Activity leaders might drive back to program headquarters the following morning, rather than at night after a long and tiring day of activities, even if it means slightly greater time or expense.

11.2.5. Vehicles

Trailers. The use of trailers to haul boats, packs and outdoor equipment is common in outdoor program transportation. Most people have limited or no experience with trailer driving, and the special techniques and hazards that come with hauling trailers.

Procedures should be developed to address trailer use, and staff adequately trained in them. This may include:

1. Recognizing some trailers may flip over in high winds, so extra precautions on windy roads should be taken.
2. Trailers add weight, so braking should start earlier than when driving without a trailer.
3. Backing trailers successfully is a challenge for all but the most skilled drivers. Learning how to back trailers and sufficient practice in an open area is important. A second person acting as guide should assist the driver when backing.
4. Items in trailers need to be secured well to prevent them from blowing off the trailer.
5. Care should be taken to properly use the trailer hitch. The hitch, brake lights and turn signals should be inspected before travel.
6. The correct ratio of trailer tongue weight to gross trailer weight must be observed when loading trailers.

Figure 11.15. Safe loading, unloading, backing, hitching, and driving with trailers require training and practice.

Personal Use of Company Vehicles. It's recommended that vehicles owned, leased, or rented by the program should not be used for personal business.

Business Use of Personal Vehicles. Since personal vehicles may not be maintained or insured at adequate levels, it's generally advisable to avoid business use of personal vehicles.

If personally owned vehicles are used for program purposes, the following criteria may be considered:

1. Personally owned vehicles are only to be used if a suitable vehicle is not available from the business.
2. The owner of the vehicle has a current insurance policy meeting the requirements of the organization for coverage and limits, or the organization has insurance that covers personal vehicles used for business use.
3. The owner and operator of the vehicle agree that if damage or other loss occurs to the vehicle caused by the negligence of the operator, the organization has no liability.
4. The vehicle is suitable for the task requiring transportation, and maintenance and emergency equipment are verifiably adequate.

Documents in Vehicle. Vehicle operators should carry in the vehicle documents required by the jurisdiction being traveled through. This may include driver's license, vehicle registration, and proof of insurance sufficient to meet local requirements. A copy of the program's vehicle manual including emergency instructions and vehicle log book should also be carried, if applicable.

Emergency Evacuation Vehicles. Emergency evacuation vehicles are sometimes temporarily placed at trailheads, watercraft takeouts, or other strategic locations close to backcountry travel routes. They can be accessed relatively quickly in case of urgent need to transport a patient to the hospital or other time-bound need, in cases when bringing in a vehicle from the outdoor program's headquarters may take a long time.

Tips for emergency vehicle use include:

- When participants are part of an intact group, such as a school or corporate team, work with the group to determine if they or you will be leaving emergency vehicles.
- Secure the key to the emergency vehicle in a pre-arranged location where it can be found by trip leaders, but is unlikely to be located by passers-by.

- To reduce the risk of theft, avoid leaving items of valuable visible in the vehicle.
- Use caution in storing food in an emergency vehicle where bears or other wildlife might damage the vehicle in an attempt to access the food.
- Avoid leaving emergency vehicles areas known to be prone to vandalism or theft.
- It is preferable to have company vehicles—which have verified maintenance, inspection and insurance status—rather than staffs' personal vehicles, if they do not have such verification, serve as emergency vehicles.

11.2.6. Emerging Issues

New Hazards. In a changing climate, attention should be paid to increased risk of wildfires, floods, and other factors that can affect transportation, and the implications should be considered in transportation planning.

Similarly, just as smart phones have increased the risk of accident from distracted driving, transportation managers should stay alert to technology and related factors that bring increased risk.

Emerging Technologies. Advances in electronic stability control, advanced braking systems, collision avoidance systems, and other technology have reduced driving risk. Transportation managers should consider new safety technology when making choices regarding vehicle acquisition and transportation planning.

Although they are not covered here, autonomous (self-driving) vehicles, flying cars, and similar new technologies should have a risk assessment and development of appropriate policies, procedures and guidelines before use.

Van Rollover Risk

Since 2002, the US National Highway Traffic Safety Administration (NHTSA) has issued a cautionary warning to users of 15-passenger vans because of an increased rollover risk under certain conditions. The NHTSA does not state that 15-passenger vans are unsafe. These vehicles meet federal standards for passenger transportation. Their overall rollover "ratio" is acceptable.

Driving more slowly and allowing space between vehicles are the most important ways the driver can positively impact driving safety.

SPECIFICS

Recent analysis by the NHTSA revealed the 15-passenger vans have a rollover risk that is similar to other light trucks and vans when carrying a few passengers. That risk increases dramatically as the number of occupants increases from as few as five occupants to over ten passengers. The analysis indicated that, with 10 or more occupants, the vans had a rollover rate in single vehicle crashes that is nearly three times the rate of those that were lightly loaded.

The physics involved in the problem are called under-steer and over-steer, neither of which is so dangerous in and of themself. They combine with design features, load distribution, road characteristics, and speed to cause trouble, however. The physical characteristic responsible is a top-heavy design for the vans. Under-steer is exacerbated by increased van weight or by loading a 15-passenger van to its gross vehicle weight rating. Both under-steer and over-steer are exacerbated by lateral acceleration, the side force exerted on the van as it rounds a turn or swerves to avoid an unexpected obstacle.

UNDER-STEER

Under-steer is when the vehicle's front wheels are describing a larger curve than the rear wheels. Most passenger cars are designed to understeer for safety reasons; it gives the driver greater control. When cornering too fast in a van or making an avoidance maneuver, it feels like the vehicle is plowing straight ahead in the turn despite the driver's steering input. Slower speeds minimize understeer problems. Since the van is rear-wheel drive, this has the effect of settling the van down over the front wheels and giving the driver more control.

OVER-STEER

Over-steer is when the rear wheels are describing a larger curve than the front wheels. This happens during a sharp turn at high speed or an avoidance maneuver when the van's relatively high center of mass leans the vehicle toward the outside of the curve. It feels as if the van's rear end will "kick out." This can result in spinning out, which increases the chance of rolling over. Entering a turn at slow speed decreases the negative effects of oversteer.

Fifteen passenger vans have a higher rollover rate partly because they drive well and predictably at low speeds,

and then suddenly become difficult to handle at higher speeds. When making a corner at slow speed, a heavily loaded van's under-steer characteristics are similar to its lightly loaded condition. They are dramatically and dangerously different when making an avoidance maneuver at high speeds.

While cornering at high speed or instinctively overcorrecting after an avoidance swerve, the loaded vehicle will exhibit over-steer, possibly resulting in a rollover.

Key risk management practices include: drive slowly and under control, and take care when loading.

Chapter Summary

1. Transportation risk can be transferred by having subcontractors, participants, or their parents or guardians provide transportation.

2. Prospective motor vehicle operators should be assessed for eligibility through written and practical testing, driving record checks, and compliance with government regulations.

3. Operators should be regularly and verifiably trained in transportation risk management.

4. A culture of safety throughout the organization is an important element of transportation risk management.

5. Operators should follow safety practices, including not driving when impaired, using headlights, obeying speed limits, loading and unloading properly, complying with hours of service rules, and avoiding electronic distractions.

6. Organizations should obtain appropriate vehicle insurance coverage and have required documents available.

7. Operators should use a pre-drive checklist and vehicle log, respond appropriately to adverse driving conditions, and know how to perform emergency braking, shoulder driving and backing.

8. Routes should be selected to reduce transportation risk.

9. Breakdowns and vehicle accidents should be handled with passenger and bystander safety in mind, and in accordance with insurance company and police requirements.

10. Passengers should wear seatbelts, stay completely in the vehicle, and not cause driver distractions.

11. Fleet managers should comply with insurance requirements, keep detailed and comprehensive records, and ensure repairs and maintenance are done to manufacturer or other established recommendations.

12. Administrators should ensure complete records are kept, see that appropriate insurance policies are in force, maintain a culture of safety, regularly review policies, and design transportation needs to minimize risk.

13. Vehicle policies should address trailer use, personal use of company vehicles, business use of personal vehicles, and emergency evacuation vehicle use.

CHAPTER 12

BUSINESS ADMINISTRATION

LEARNING OBJECTIVES

1. Geographical variation in business risks
2. Compliance with laws and regulations as general risk management approach
3. Workplace health and safety risks
4. Physical plant risks
5. Protection, privacy and secure storage of data and information
6. Compliance with corporate registration and similar requirements and restrictions
7. Financial management and controls
8. Seeking legal advice
9. Discouraging fraud, theft and compromise of physical items and intellectual property
10. Human resources considerations
11. Risks in marketing communications
12. Strategic, long-term risks
13. Addressing structural risk in the outdoor industry
14. Administrative risk treatments
15. Sources of additional information

12.1. INTRODUCTION

The domains of risk covered in preceding chapters have focused on risks generally closely and directly associated with outdoor programming. Here we turn to risks that similarly affect the wellbeing of outdoor programs and their participants, but are also shared by most businesses in any industry.

We will cover both immediate risks associated with business administration and also more distant or long-term strategic risks.

Management of business administration risks is not the focus of this book. Therefore, these issues are treated in summary format only. Sources of additional information are provided at the end of the chapter.

12.2. IMMEDIATE BUSINESS ADMINISTRATION RISKS

What counts as a risk in the business administration context, and how it should be managed, varies widely by jurisdiction. Nations and their subdivisions may all have different expectations. The enumeration below is a list of potential example risk areas to consider, and is neither definitive nor exhaustive.

Risks considered to be administrative in nature are also found in other chapters. Insurance is covered in Chapter 13, Risk Transfer, for example; safety culture, a risk domain whose management is overseen by executive managers, is addressed in Chapter 5, Culture.

Many administrative risks are treated in the same manner as are outdoor risks. The core process remains the same: identifying and implementing policies, procedures and systems to manage risks to acceptable levels.

One good place to begin with addressing risks of an administrative nature is to identify and comply with all applicable laws and regulations. Established best practices exist for some areas that may not be covered by regulation, such as intellectual property protection.

12.2.1. Workplace Health and Safety

Risk areas and recommended treatments in workplace health and safety are often covered extensively by occupational safety and health agencies. Topics to address may include, but are not limited to:

1. Engineering controls
2. Hazardous tools, equipment, and substances
3. Personal protective equipment
4. Lighting
5. Cleanliness
6. Storage
7. Food service
8. Signage
9. Hygiene facilities and supplies
10. Ergonomics (design of work spaces, processes and equipment to best fit users)
11. Accident management and investigation procedures
12. Electrical safety
13. Fire prevention and response
14. Emergency exits

Figure 12.1. A number of outdoor program basecamps and offices have burned down. Fire extinguishers can help.

12.2.2. Physical Facilities

This applies to offices, employee housing, equipment warehouses, structures housing animals used in programming, classroom and related structures, and any other relevant built structures. Issues to consider include, but are not limited to:

1. Code compliance: fire, building, and electrical codes
2. Structural integrity and safety
3. Fire inspections
4. Occupancy permits/certificates, commercial use permits, and other facilities-related permits
5. Zoning

12.2.3. Information Security

Considerations here include, but are not limited to:

1. Security, protection and privacy of protected data and information such as:
   a. Financial data, for example credit card information
   b. Personally identifiable information, for example government identification information and passport numbers
   c. Confidential personal information, for example criminal history records and medical history
2. Protection of trademarks, service marks, copyrights and similar intellectual property
3. Documentation, secure storage, and records retention, for example for personnel file information and legal documents

12.2.4. Corporate Compliance

This refers to requirements related to the corporate structure as a whole. Subject areas include, but are not limited to:

1. Legal corporation formation, certificates of formation, operating licenses, corporate registrations and permits, and reporting requirements for corporations

2. Non-profit and charitable organization restrictions on activities such as lobbying and certain fundraising (for instance, raffles, prohibited in some areas as gambling)

The importance of following corporation management regulations

One outdoor organization neglected to pay a very small fee to the regional government as part of its annual corporate registration process. Because of this simple oversight, the organization ceased to officially exist and—in the middle of a busy season with participant groups in the outdoors—technically was unable to do business. (The fee was eventually paid and registration was restored.)

12.2.5. Finance

Financial management concerns include, but are not limited to, embezzlement, maintenance of proper financial controls, appropriate management to budget, sound investment policies, and payment of taxes and fees.

12.2.6. Legal

Areas where qualified legal advice can mitigate business risk include, but are not limited to, contracts, leases, charters, licensing agreements, and other legal documents.

Areas of illegal activity that pose business risks include, but are not limited to:

1. Fraud (wrongful deception to secure unfair or unlawful gain)
2. Theft and related security concerns, for example:
   a. Theft of physical items
   b. Theft or compromise of intellectual property, such as counterfeiting and information technology hazards including viruses and ransomware

12.2.7. Human Resources

A variety of human resources topics should be considered, including, but not limited to:

1. Liability considerations for giving and receiving professional references
2. Illegal discrimination
3. Non-compete agreements (for employees, and also for partners, franchisees, approved providers and others)
4. Minimum wage requirements
5. Criminal background checks
6. Protections for working with minors and vulnerable adults
7. Conflict of interest on the part of staff, including volunteers such as Board members
8. Applicable legal duties, such as the duty of care on

the part of staff, and any other legal duties such as duty of loyalty or duty of obedience
9. Accountability, including established single points of accountability for risk management, and clear roles and responsibilities for risk management in org charts, job descriptions, work plans, and other documents
10. Employee handbook topics such as discrimination, harassment, assault, alcohol and drugs, weapons, bloodborne pathogens, grievance procedures, evaluation, and termination.

12.2.8. Marketing

Marketing and sales staff may want to advertise an outdoor adventure as safe, and promise that participants will have fun. Neither is advisable. "Safety" can imply a complete absence of risk or harm; no outdoor program is completely safe. Likewise, participants may or may not have fun (or enjoy the program or love the experience or any similar wording), and dissatisfied customers claiming fraud or demanding refunds can be avoided by being careful with marketing language.

The importance of accuracy in marketing

One outdoor enthusiast successfully sued a ski area after skiing into a tree and injuring himself. The marketing brochure showed a photo of a snow slope without trees, and the plaintiff claimed that he therefore did not consent to assuming the risk of hitting a tree.

12.3. STRATEGIC RISKS

Management of strategic risks is a function of administrative leadership and governance bodies. Examples of these complex, systemic risks include:

1. **Climate Change.** How does a changing climate affect an organization's long-term sustainability? An outdoor program in a dry area experienced a wildfire which burned its activity areas and damaged its facilities, making programs impossible. More fires are expected. Far from a theoretical reality, climate change leads the organization to assess whether it is advisable to attempt to re-open, or to stay closed forever.
2. **Demographic, Market and Social Shifts.** In some areas individuals may be less interested in the outdoors due to urbanization, electronic entertainment, attention span shifts, or other factors,

leading to a decline into unprofitability for outdoor programs.

3. **Geopolitical Conflict and Instability.** The emergence of international conflicts, nationalism, and authoritarian governments with limited rule of law and civil rights may impact local and international outdoor programs.

These risks are not suited to management through procedures and controls, as one might manage the risk of overheating on a warm-weather hike. Risk management in this context instead may begin by using tools such as strategic planning, stress testing and scenario planning to identify potential risks on the horizon. Approaches to reducing or transferring risks may include diversifying product lines or making fundamental changes to business models.

Smaller organizations may have limited capacity to engage in addressing these strategic risks.

12.4.   ADVANCING THE INDUSTRY

Systems thinkers identify risks facing outdoor programs and the outdoor industry at levels higher than activity leaders, activities, or the organizations themselves. These risks include the relatively low social priority of outdoor programs in some parts of the world, compared to some other professional fields. This results in relatively low resource allocations to support sustainable careers, training, and development of the industry, which has a negative impact on safety.

Executives, Board members, and other leaders in the outdoor industry have an opportunity to advocate for prioritizing outdoor education and related pursuits in domains of government investment, compensation regimes and other areas.

12.5.   PROTECTION FROM ADMINISTRATIVE RISKS

Approaches for understanding and managing the risks in the administrative domain of outdoor programming include:

1. Research regulatory and other expectations, including through consultation with reliable, credible specialists

2. Act in the best interests of customers, employees, the organization, and the larger community
3. Act as a reasonable and prudent person would in a similar situation
4. Stay up to date on standards, regulations and best administrative practices
5. Take effective action on identified risk management issues
6. Document administrative procedures and activities, to facilitate demonstration of compliance with regulations and standards

12.6.   FURTHER RESOURCES

Additional information, training, individual support and other resources are widely available. Sources include:

1. Health and Safety governmental authorities. Free trainings, consultation, and extensive written and other resources are often available.
2. Other relevant governmental authorities. For instance, officials responsible for ensuring criminal history background check records are securely stored may provide guidance and in-person consultation.
3. Legislation and regulations on relevant topics, which may be available online, in libraries, or from government sources
4. Individual qualified specialists, such as lawyers, accountants, bankers, and insurance agents
5. Associations specific to particular activities, such as human resources management associations or societies
6. Business associations, which promote commercial activity and often offer professional resources

Chapter Summary

1. All businesses, regardless of type, face certain business administration risks.

2. The nature of administrative risks varies widely by jurisdiction.

3. Compliance with laws and regulations can address many administrative risks.

4. Administrative risk areas include:
   a. Workplace health and safety, such as hazardous items and signage
   b. Physical facilities issues, such as code compliance and zoning
   c. Protection of data and information, including personal information and intellectual property
   d. Storage and retention of documents
   e. Corporate registration and related requirements
   f. Financial management and controls
   g. Legal documents
   h. Illegal activity such as fraud, theft and counterfeiting
   i. Human resources concerns such as discrimination and conflict of interest
   j. Making inappropriate promises in marketing materials

5. Managing strategic, long-term risks such as climate change and social change requires thoughtful planning.

6. Structural risks in the outdoor industry include low rates of pay and other investments.

7. Administrative risk management approaches can include research, acting in the best interests of stakeholders, staying up to date on requirements, and good documentation.

8. Further resources are widely available.

Part Three

RISK MANAGEMENT SYSTEMS

RISK TRANSFER

13.1. INTRODUCTION

Risk transfer is one of the four ways to manage risk we discussed in Chapter 1: eliminate, reduce, transfer, or accept risk. Risk transfer is the strategy of passing off risk of loss to another party. There are three principal entities to which an outdoor program might pass of risk:

1. Insurance company
2. Participant
3. Subcontractor

We'll discuss each one below.

How risk can be transferred to others varies very significantly by jurisdiction. The concepts here are based off of legal frameworks in the USA. They may be partially or completely inapplicable to your context. In addition, legal requirements and their interpretations regularly change, so what was accurate at one time may not be accurate later. You should consult with trusted and qualified insurance and legal specialists and other resources as needed to obtain guidance that may be applicable to your particular situation.

13.2. TRANSFER OF RISK TO INSURANCE COMPANY

Multiple types of insurance exist: for example, liability insurance, auto insurance, and property insurance. Within a single type of insurance, there are variations in what's offered: coverage, exclusions, deductibles, and so on. It is important to carefully consider what types of insurance coverage your organization requires, and what your desired policy limits and other terms are. Insurance markets are complex. In addition, not everything than an agent might be interested to sell you may be necessary for your specific circumstances. The use of a trusted, capable insurance broker and independent research can be helpful.

Some insurance coverage is required by law in some local, state/provincial, or national jurisdictions or situations, such as operating vehicles or hiring employees. Legal requirements should be understood and followed.

Insurance coverage for a loss ideally is rarely needed. However, in the case of major losses, the right insurance policy can be an essential element in helping your organization survive.

13.2.1. Types of Insurance

Several types of insurance coverage that an organization may obtain are briefly described below.

Liability Insurance. Liability insurance is designed to protect organizations from losses stemming from legal liability, such as with committing acts of negligence. In many jurisdictions this is an essential insurance.

Automobile Insurance. Automobile insurance can provide coverage to damage caused to motor vehicles or by vehicle operations. In some locations certain coverage is required by law, and proof of coverage must be in vehicles. If needed, operators should be listed as such on the organization's vehicle insurance policy prior to operating a vehicle.

Property Insurance. This insurance can cover loss to property such as buildings and their contents including office equipment and outdoor gear.

Other Insurance. Numerous other options are available and may be considered for your situation. Not all may be available in your area. These options include, but are not limited to, participant accident insurance, volunteer insurance, medical insurance (such as for certain employees), directors and officers insurance, unemployment insurance, disability insurance, and worker's compensation insurance.

13.2.2. International Considerations

Some insurance policies do not cover international settings. If this is the case, acquisition of appropriate coverage for your international programs should be obtained prior to travel.

Specific areas of insurance coverage to consider include but are not limited to:

1. Medical and dental
2. Evacuation and transportation, including for those accompanying the evacuee, and including air ambulance/air transport
3. Repatriation
4. Motor vehicle insurance
5. Liability insurance

13.2.3. Where to Procure Insurance

Insurance policies can be obtained from government sources or private insurance companies, depending on the situation. Outdoor programs part of a larger institution such as a university should consult the relevant department in the institution. A qualified insurance agent, qualified attorney, or other specialist can assist you with further information about how these insurance options may apply to you and how coverage can be obtained.

13.3. TRANSFER OF RISK TO CUSTOMER

A variety of instruments may be available to transfer risk from the outdoor program to the customer, client, participant, or minor participant's parents/guardians. An attorney familiar with outdoor-related law and the jurisdictions that pertain to you may be able to help you determine which if any of the following may or may not be applicable to your situation.

13.3.1. Types of Risk Transfer to Customer

Indemnification. This is an agreement to protect someone or something against loss, or not hold that entity responsible for loss.

For example, a customer agrees to indemnify the outdoor company. If the customer is hurt and their family sues the company, the company may not be responsible to pay damages.

In a common example using an individual's personal situation, the insurance company issuing an auto or homeowner's insurance policy typically indemnifies the policyholder against certain loss to their auto or home.

Hold Harmless and other terms. Hold harmless is related to indemnification. Other terms that may be used in connection with this type of risk transfer include exculpatory agreements, save harmless, and agreement to defend.

Release of Liability. This pertains to an agreement that may release an entity (such as your outdoor program) from being held liable in the case of loss by another (such as a participant).

For example, a participant signs a release of liability provided by an outdoor organization. If the customer is hurt during the program, the customer may be restricted by the release of liability from suing the organization.

Assumption of Risk. Depending on the particular language in the Assumption of Risk, this generally refers to the signer agreeing that participation in the activity contains risk, that the signer understands those risks, and that the signer agrees to participate despite those risks.

Risks described here should generally be listed and explained for each activity (climbing, boating, etc.) that is part of the outdoor program. Risks listed typically should include illness, injury and death.

This is also known as "informed consent."

13.3.2. Ample Time for Consideration

Participants (for minors, also including the participants' parents/guardians) should have the opportunity to review the agreements they are being asked to make, consider the risks, and easily get answers to their questions and obtain further information if needed. They should have the opportunity to decline to participate without difficulty or inconvenience. (This means the agreements should not be presented right at the boat launch or trailhead after driving hours out to the activity site, but ideally days to weeks in advance, before travel to the area.)

13.3.3. Limitations and Variations

Some written agreements that transfer risk to participants may be written to apply to simple negligence only, but not situations of gross negligence. (An example of simple negligence may be an honest mistake. An example of gross negligence may be intentionally causing harm.) In some settings, agreements that release liability in the case of gross negligence are unenforceable, meaning they are not legally valid.

Release of liability agreements are limited or prohibited in certain situations, such as in some U.S. states and federal public land settings.

Specific language required by law in your area to make the agreement legally binding should be included.

Documents generally should be signed by the participant (unless the participant is a young child), and the participant's parent or guardian, if the participant is a legal minor.

In order for risk transfer agreements to be effective, the risks must be accurately described. This does not mean that every single possible hazard and risk must be listed. However, marketing, sales, enrollment and registration materials must realistically describe the risks of program participation. It may take several paragraphs for the risk transfer agreement to do this, and the total document may several pages long. Describing a program as "safe," which could be interpreted as free from possibility of loss, is generally inadvisable. I

In addition, the risk transfer documents should be written in plain language and with formatting that is easily understandable by the reader. Waivers or other forms crafted with dense legal terminology may be ruled to be invalid. The print size should be large enough to be easily legible. Important clauses should be emphasized, for instance by using capital letters, boldface, or underlining, or by placing them at the beginning or end of the document.

There are numerous other considerations when drafting these agreements. A qualified legal advisor should be consulted during creation of these agreements, and the documents should be reviewed periodically by a qualified legal advisor as well.

13.4. TRANSFER OF RISK TO SUBCONTRACTORS

Subcontractors are used by outdoor programs for a number of reasons, including:

1. To conduct specialized outdoor activities the program is unable or unwilling to do itself, for example due to lack of suitable permits, equipment or trained staff
2. To provide transportation to participants or others
3. To provide access to specialized facilities such as accommodations or a high ropes course that an outdoor program is unable to provide itself

The risks associated with the services or goods provided by the subcontractor should be borne by the subcontractor. A bus company, for instance, should be responsible if there are damages due to their errors while transporting participants to an activity site. The provider of lodging accommodations or a high ropes challenge course should bear the liability if there are certain injuries or other losses at their facility.

In order for the risk to be appropriately transferred to the subcontractor, a written agreement with appropriate language should be signed by both parties. The agreement might indemnify your program and release your program from liability against claims related to the subcontractor's negligence.

In addition, the subcontractor could be required to provide proof of liability or other insurance coverage, to limits acceptable to you, and should list your program as additionally insured, as applicable.

As with documents transferring risk to customer, written agreements between the outdoor program and subcontractor should be reviewed by qualified legal counsel if there are any questions.

Further information on subcontractors is in Chapter 10, Subcontractors.

Chapter Summary

1. Risk transfer is a way to manage risk, along with approaches to eliminate, reduce or accept risk.

2. Risk transfer varies widely by jurisdiction and an organization's unique circumstances.

3. Some of the concepts presented here may not apply to your situation.

4. Suitable insurance and legal specialists should be consulted before, during and after developing risk transfer plans.

5. Risk can be transferred to insurance companies, in exchange for payment of premiums.

6. Legal requirements regarding insurance should be followed.

7. Liability insurance, automobile insurance, property insurance, and other types of insurance are available.

8. Ensure insurance coverage applies to your international settings, including for medical, dental, transportation, evacuation, repatriation, motor vehicle and liability insurance as needed.

9. Insurance can be procured from government sources or private companies.

10. Risk can be transferred to customers through instruments including indemnification, release of liability, and assumption of risk.

11. Customers should have sufficient time to evaluate agreements before signing, and be able to decline to agree without inconvenience or difficulty.

12. Risk can be transferred to subcontractors through written agreements with indemnification, liability release, or other terms, and through subcontractor insurance.

13. Qualified legal specialists should be consulted in drafting and reviewing risk transfer agreements so they are effective for your particular circumstances.

CHAPTER 14

INCIDENT MANAGEMENT

LEARNING OBJECTIVES

1. Purpose of Emergency Response Plan (ERP)
2. Organization of ERP
3. ERP review and approval
4. ERP relationship with other plans and documents
5. Initial field response to emergency
6. Fatality management
7. Communications methods
8. Search and Rescue
9. Role of subcontractors
10. Administrative roles
11. Initial administrative response to emergency
12. Logistical support
13. Supporting survivors
14. Working with next of kin
15. Incident reviews
16. Legal and cultural considerations
17. Training on and testing the ERP
18. Disaster Drills

14.1. INTRODUCTION

The best incident is the one that never occurred. Despite efforts at prevention, however, emergencies will sometimes happen. When a major incident occurs, it's important to be able to effectively respond in the minutes, hours, and months that follow.

A written Emergency Response Plan (ERP), and staff who are trained on and competent to execute it, can fulfill this need. The plan should:

- Identify criteria for emergencies that require activation of the plan
- Clarify roles and responsibilities for both staff in the field and administrators
- Provide protocols and information to guide the actions of those in the field, the office, and elsewhere
- Address emergency care, scene management, and evacuation; communication between relevant entities, and documentation
- Cover both the immediate emergency response and long-term follow-up

Incidents can be frightening, confusing and stressful. But when staff are suitably trained in a well-developed emergency plan, then victims, responders, and the organization are set up to experience the best outcomes possible.

14.2. EMERGENCY RESPONSE PLAN CHARACTERISTICS

By their nature, emergencies are characterized by incomplete information, extreme time pressure, and insufficient resources such as people, transportation, rescue equipment, and medical resources. Emergencies may change rapidly and in unpredictable ways. An Emergency Response Plan—also known as an Emergency Action Plan, Situation Response Plan, Emergency Response System, Crisis Response Plan, or by other names—brings structure to a chaotic situation. Yet a good plan also provides sufficient flexibility to allow for adaptation and the good judgment of responders.

Emergency Response Plans outline a series of steps that should be taken in emergencies, in roughly chronological order. Plans typically are divided into two sections: one guiding the response by staff in the field, at the site of the incident, and a second part, guiding the actions of administrators and governance personnel. In some cases, two separate Emergency Response Plans exist, one for each group.

ERPs should be customized for each outdoor program's unique circumstances. These include the organization's particular program environments, outdoor activities, legal and cultural contexts, participant characteristics, and staff capacities, as well as the emergency services that are available.

Any plan, however, should outline systems for responding to serious medical issues as well as behavioral and motivational concerns such as assault, running away, self-harm, or drug use that might reasonably be anticipated to occur.

The plan should be readily available to all persons who might need it. Activity leaders in the field should carry a copy with them at all times. (The ERP might be embedded as a special section in the activity leader's field handbook.) Copies should be easily accessible throughout the administrative offices, and accessible to persons even when not in the office. Board members and others only peripherally involved in day-to-day operations should also have copies if they will ever be called to participate in incident response, for example in working with the media.

The plan should be formally reviewed and approved annually by the organization's executive leadership. Regular reviews may also be done by the organization's Risk Management Committee, legal counsel, risk management officer, and insurance representative, as appropriate. As outlined below, all persons throughout the organization should be familiar with the plan, understand the role they play in emergency response, and be capable of fulfilling their responsibilities.

The Emergency Response Plan, as one element of an outdoor program's risk management infrastructure, may be referenced by or even included in the organization's Risk Management Plan, depending on how the organization's documentation is structured. The ERP is designed to be used with accompanying documents, such as incident reports, SOAP notes, medical facility visit forms, evacuation reports, medical protocols, and information on telecommunications and other emergency equipment use.

14.3. DEFINITIONS

The plan should outline the organization's definition of an emergency deserving activation of the plan. This might include not only fatalities, but also serious injuries, illnesses, property damage, criminal activity, and lost person situations, or any incident likely to attract media attention or potentially cause reputational harm.

14.4. FIELD RESPONSE

14.4.1. Initial Field Response

The plan should provide guidance for immediate response to an emergency by activity leaders or others at the site of the emergency. This may include:

Assess the situation. Is the scene safe? What happened? How many persons are involved? Address scene safety issues for victims, rescuers and bystanders.

Provide emergency care. Provide first aid for urgent medical problems. Provide shelter from the elements as needed. Ensure the supervision and safety management of others at the scene. Once emergent medical issues are stabilized, provide information, reassurance and care to meet the psychological needs of bystanders and survivors.

Initiate emergency services response. Contact emergency medical services, search and rescue, law enforcement, and emergency evacuation/transportation services as necessary. Specifics will vary widely depending on the context so this should be customized for the organization and its activity areas and circumstances. For instance, initial contact may be made by VHF or other radios (Figure 14.1), satellite phone, mobile phone, runner, emergency beacon or messenger, or otherwise. Contact might be with maritime authorities, land management agency emergency dispatch center, regional law enforcement entity, national emergency number regional dispatch center, or other. In some situations a medical advisor or contracted private international medical/rescue service may be contacted. The plan should provide an Emergency Call Guide with detailed information on how to initiate contact, whom to contact, and what to expect in response. Information on how to operate telecommunications technology such as radios (as described in the telecommunications section of Chapter 8, Equipment) should be available.

Figure 14.1. Radio use requires training on assembly, storage, adjustment, features, and communication protocol.

Contact outdoor program administration. Advise the organization's management of the emergency. Inform administrators about the nature of the incident and the response so far. Concisely ask for support as needed. This could include organizing or coordinating search, evacuation or other responses. The plan should remind field staff to be organized and efficient in these communications, as emergency telecommunications technologies may not be completely reliable, and battery life, limited reception (in caves, canyons, and elsewhere), and other factors may limit the time available for communication. It may be useful to suggest that incident information and support requests be written down before calling, to improve communications efficiency and accuracy.

The Emergency Call Guide should provide an extensive and detailed list of whom at the organization to contact, and how. It should include multiple backup contact persons in case the primary contact is unavailable. If the organization has a rotating 24-hour on-call person, relevant contact information should be provided.

Control the scene. Continue to supervise and provide for the logistical, safety, and psychological needs of uninjured group members. Manage bystanders or others who might enter the area, for safety. If media representatives arrive, ensure they do not disrupt emergency operations or pose a safety hazard, and keep in mind the organization's media relations protocols (see Chapter 20, Media Relations).

Secure physical evidence (such as damaged rope or

malfunctioning camp stove) for investigators, in case of serious incident or law enforcement issue.

Plan evacuation. Assess the need for evacuating victims. The ERP should list conditions requiring evacuation, such as certain medical conditions at particular levels of severity, and other issues such as harassment, bloodborne pathogens exposure, or suicidal ideation.

Determine if a self-evacuation can be made, or evacuation should wait for the arrival of additional resources. Determine the urgency of evacuation based on patient condition (Figure 14.2).

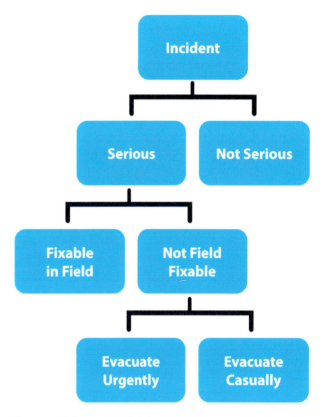

Figure 14.2. Evacuation decision tree.

In general, simpler evacuations are preferred. Aircraft evacuations can be hazardous, and should be requested only when necessary. Work with program administrators or directly with external rescue services on evacuation coordination as appropriate.

In order to guide staff in the field conducting self-evacuations, the ERP should list local medical facilities and provide driving directions, contact information, and a description of relevant services such as 24-hour emergency department or availability of antivenin (Figure 14.3).

Figure 14.3. Medical facility capacities should be assessed in advance.

If evacuation by aircraft is expected, a suitable landing zone should be arranged. Information on preparation and assessment of landing zones for helicopters or fixed-wing aircraft used in the area should be documented. Working around aircraft landing zones can be dangerous so safety measures should be clearly described. Radio or other telecommunications with pilots can increase safety and efficiency.

Transmit specific location coordinates to incoming rescuers. If necessary, prepare to attract the rescue party by making the victim location evident.

Document. Once first aid and other urgent concerns are addressed, write an incident report. Have witnesses separately write, sign and date statements, ideally before they have time to speak with each other. Complete SOAP notes (medical report forms). Particularly for major incidents, write a chronological incident log describing what occurred and at what time, as appropriate, while memories are fresh.

14.4.2.　Fatalities

In the event of a fatality, the body should be protected from predators or other hazards. The body should not be moved, if possible, to preserve evidence for investigators. If it is necessary to move the body, take photographs from multiple angles, mark the incident site, collect and preserve evidence, and consider measuring and sketching the incident site.

Psychological care of survivors is vital. Providing comfort, an opportunity and emotionally safe space to talk and express emotions, early access to a counselor, prompt evacuation from the field and connection with family members, and long-term opportunities to share, process and make meaning of the incident should all be considered.

14.4.3.　Runners

In many cases, telecommunications technology provides the most efficient and least hazardous means of contacting emergency resources. In increasingly rare situations, such as in cave rescues or in which telecom gear is missing or nonfunctional, sending a small team of persons for help is necessary.

These "runners" should be capable to travel safely in their small group. Typically the most senior leader stays with the main group, and a second leader leads the runner team, often of two to three people. Runners should bring necessary safety supplies, such as first aid materials, emergency camping (bivouac) supplies, sufficient food and water, outdoor essentials such as lighting and maps, and appropriate clothing.

The group should also carry a copy of the incident report, along with information about the situation, including but not limited to victim location, equipment and people at the scene, evacuation plans, local weather and terrain conditions, landing zone options, and telecommunications capacities at the site.

14.4.4.　Lost Person

The ERP should describe procedures in case an individual or travel group is lost or late. It should reference operating procedures designed to prevent lost persons, such as appropriate screening, supervision, and participant training.

That training should include instructions for persons who find themselves lost to stay calm, stay together, and not move (Figure 14.4). The group should be in a visible area if possible. Lost persons should take appropriate safety steps to avoid environmental hazards like hypothermia and dehydration.

Figure 14.4. Individuals should be instructed on what to do if they become lost.

The ERP should describe when activity leaders should call for additional help, for example after a hasty search is completed. Depending on the situation, additional support should generally be called two to 12 hours after determining a person is lost.

Procedures should also cover management and supervision of group members who are not lost, including while initial searches are under way.

Search Procedure. Procedures for conducting initial searches in the field should be documented in the ERP, and may include:

1. Gather information. Interview bystanders. Establish and document point last seen, direction of travel, equipment carried, behavior, and state of mind. A Missing Person Report (example provided in Figure 14.5) can be used to record this information.
2. Begin a hasty search of areas such as trails where subject is most likely to be found.
3. Attempt containment of search area, for example by posting individuals along the search area perimeter.
4. Call for additional help if the initial hasty search is unsuccessful, and no later than the required timeframe (as mentioned above).
5. Begin grid search, often with the assistance of external searchers.

More detailed information on search and rescue procedures is widely available and should be included in the Emergency Action Plan as required.

Missing Person Report

Fill out a separate form for each missing person. Attach a complete copy of the missing person's Medical History Form to this report. Use additional sheets for documentation if necessary.

Activity Leader Name: _____ Field Supervisor Name:_____

Client Organization (if a group customer): _____

Program Dates: _____ Program Location: _____

Missing Person's Name: _____ Nicknames: _____ Sex:☐ M☐ F☐Other Age: ____

Exact Point Last Seen: _____ Date and Time Last Seen: _____

Direction of Travel: _____ Specific stated reason for leaving: _____

Possible motives for leaving: _____ Unusual comments prior to leaving: _____

Physical Description of Missing Person

Race: _____ Complexion: _____ Eye Color: _____ Facial Hair: _____ Height: _____Weight: _____

Hair Color: _____ Hair Length: _____ Build: _____ Facial features, shape: _____

General appearance: _____ Distinguishing marks, scars, features, tattoos: _____

Health/Character Traits

Mental Condition: _____

Physical handicaps:☐ Y ☐ N Description: _____

Known medical, psychological problems:☐ Y ☐ N Description: _____

Requires medication: ☐ Y☐ N Description: _____ Amount and duration of medication probably

in possession: _____ History of running away:☐ Yes ☐ No Known current family/significant other

problems:☐ Yes ☐ No _____

Experience

Familiar with area:☐ Yes ☐ No   Person informed of what to do if separated from group: ☐ Yes ☐ No

Experience level with this mode of travel: ☐ Beginner ☐ Intermediate ☐ Advanced

General camping skills:☐ Beginner ☐ Intermediate ☐ Advanced Other relevant areas of experience: _____

Person has driver's license:☐ Yes ☐ No Person has keys to nearby vehicle:☐ Yes ☐ No Location:_____

Training in ☐ First Aid ☐ Outdoor Survival ☐ Other: _____

Clothing: style, color, description

Hat:_____ Jacket: _____ Shirt: _____

Pants: _____ Gloves, mittens: _____ Other: _____

Footwear, incl. sole type: _____ Sample available:☐ Yes ☐ No Location: _____

Eyewear:☐ Glasses ☐ Contacts ☐ Prescription Description: _____Scent articles available:☐ Yes ☐ No

Equipment/Food: style, color, description

Pack: _____ Sleeping bag: _____ Tent: _____ Lighting: _____

Emergency equipment: _____ Water: quantity, container description: _____

Food type & quantity: _____ Other: _____

Witnesses

Name: _____ Name: _____

Contact info: _____ Contact info: _____

Relationship to missing person: _____ Relationship to missing person: _____

Details of Search Plan (include routes marked on map, anticipated timetable, and return of search teams) _____

_____

Figure 14.5. Sample Missing Person Report.

14.4.5. Subcontractors

The role of subcontractors in emergency management should be made clear when the subcontractor agreement is established. The Emergency Action Plans of both organizations can be compared and discussed at that time.

When an incident occurs in which subcontractors are involved, it may be helpful to quickly review with the subcontractor who is responsible for what. This includes which party is in charge of communications with emergency services, the family, media, and law enforcement, in both the short and long term.

14.5. ADMINISTRATIVE RESPONSE

14.5.1. Administrative Roles

On receiving the initial call from the field, program managers should initiate the administrative components of the Emergency Response Plan.

The ERP should outline which persons are responsible for the administrative coordination duties of the incident. Every person should be clear on

1. What their job is,
2. Who their supervisor is, and
3. Whom they are supervising.

A management model based on the Incident Command System with a clear hierarchy of responsibilities and authorities is often the most effective approach.

The ERP should describe who is responsible for working with the following groups:

1. Activity leaders in the field at the incident site
2. Emergency medical and rescue services
3. Organizational medical advisors and contracted rescue services
4. Law enforcement
5. Family members of victims and survivors
6. If the participant group is an intact group, the client organization
7. News media
8. Other individuals making general incoming inquiries
9. Other groups in the field
10. Individuals in the organization. This includes employees and volunteers in the outdoor program and employees in any parent organization or headquarters offices.

11. Insurance, legal, safety management, and communications/public relations specialists, either in-house employees or external entities
12. Health and safety agency representatives, in the case of a notifiable incident
13. Other entities such as embassy or consular officials for international situations

14.5.2. Initial Administrative Response

When administrators receive initial notification of the incident, immediate action steps generally include the following.

Document the call. Begin an incident log (ranging from a special form to any piece of paper or electronic record) documenting the time of the call, who called, the message contents, and any other relevant information.

Figure 14.6. Document every phone call (electronically or on paper) and its details.

Alert others in the organization. A notification sequence should begin right away, with staff, Board members and other relevant stakeholders in the organization being alerted to the incident.

Support the field team. Determine the needs of staff in the field. Share information about emergency services activation. Send resources into the field, such as rescue equipment, searchers, counselors, and backup staff. As the hours go by, staff in the field may be overwhelmed, stressed, and exhausted, and need rest, emotional support, and logistical support. It is difficult to provide too many resources.

Activate emergency services. Unless this has already been done from the field, coordinate with emergency medical, search and rescue services (Figure 14.7). It is sometimes easier for managers with dependable communications access and other resources to coordinate this response, rather than leave it to individuals in the field.

Figure 14.7. A rescue team prepares for a mission.

Contact client representative. Reach out to the client group, if the participant was a member of an intact larger group that is the outdoor program's customer, such as a student on a school group program or an employee on a corporate team-building adventure. Provide information as soon as it is available. Maintain regular and close contact for as long as needed. (In some cases, this can involve months of collaboration on investigation, legal proceedings, and closure.)

Contact family members. When the participant is a minor, contact the parents or guardians even if the incident is relatively mild, such as a broken arm requiring a trip to the clinic. For more significant incidents, see below.

Contact legal, insurance and communications resources. Larger institutions such as universities with an outdoor program may have specialists in these areas in-house. Other organizations should contact their business lawyer and insurance representative. If overwhelming media attention is anticipated, engaging a crisis communications firm should be considered.

Contact regulatory authorities. In some jurisdictions, an occupational health and safety agency, worker's compensation insurance program authority, or other governmental entity should be notified. Applicable agencies can provide guidance as to what incidents require notification.

Attend to the victim. If a patient is transported to the hospital, a representative of the organization should be there as well, to provide support to the patient and work directly with family members if they are present. Organizational staff should be prepared to stay at the hospital for hours or days, if needed. In addition to serving

as a communications link between the organization and the victim and their family, an attentive, caring presence at the hospital sends an important message of support and compassion.

14.5.3. Lost and Late

Administrators can provide support and coordination roles in organizing in-house search efforts, and liaising with external search and rescue entities. Administrators should have access to and refer to participant and field staff medical forms and emergency contact information, the group's expected and potential alternate itineraries, and information on equipment and supplies with the group.

14.5.4. Logistical Support

Administrators are well-positioned to support staff in the field with logistical assistance. Managers can help coordinate re-insertion and reunification of a previously evacuated participant who is ready to return to their group in the field. Administrators can help provide resupplies of medical items, outdoor gear, food, or other materials to the field team.

14.5.5. Supporting Surviving Field Staff and Participants

Individuals in the outdoor group who did not directly suffer injury, illness, or loss of life need and benefit from support. Their physical safety and psychological well-being should be looked after by program managers, which may mean evacuating the entire group from the field and providing ongoing structured support.

One resource for reducing the sometimes powerful trauma of experiencing extreme or prolonged stress is Critical Incident Stress Debriefing (CISD). This technique often begins with a structured group debriefing of the incident. Led by a trained facilitator, participants are encouraged to discuss their feelings and work through the emotional aftermath of the incident. CISD helps reduce post-incident stress, which can be life-altering and debilitating if not skillfully addressed.

The organization should identify trained counselors or CISD specialists in advance. The organization should have plans to promptly connect counselors or CISD practitioners with the survivors of major incidents, in a location and format that is convenient to the survivors. The organization is also well-served to continually foster an organizational culture of emotional competency, where expression of emotion is encouraged. This can be particularly important in settings where certain staff may face cultural conditioning to appear tough and invulnerable.

CISD is appropriate with fatalities, serious incidents involving friends or family members, serious injuries to children, incidents of brutality, mass casualty incidents, and any other incidents likely to elicit emotional distress.

CISD is often made available promptly after an incident. In addition to CISD support, the organization may choose to help survivors engage in long-term counseling, perhaps at the organization's expense.

Employees may also be offered paid or unpaid time off, in order to process the event. The organization should arrange work schedules to make this possible.

In addition, the organization may facilitate visits by staff or participants in the affected group to victims recovering in the hospital or to a memorial service in the case of fatality. Managers may enquire of survivors about what ways the organization can be of support and help them through the experience.

The incident doesn't end when the victim reaches the hospital; in some ways, it is only beginning. When the leadership of the organization sincerely and diligently seeks ways to help the uninjured to grieve, process, and find meaning, and invests institutional resources in making this possible, the benefits are valuable for all.

14.5.6. Working With Family Members and Next of Kin

This is an area that calls for skill, tact, and sensitivity. Successfully working with family members of those seriously hurt or killed can provide to those family members solace, meaning, and support in working through a grieving process. It can also benefit the outdoor program by reducing animus and potential legal exposure.

Contact information for family members or emergency contacts may be on the participant's medical form or other documentation. If a fatality or serious injury or illness occurs, the family should be notified as promptly as possible. The organization should not wait until all the information about the incident has been received. It is preferable to provide initial information early and

call back later with additional details, rather than have a family member learn about the incident from social or broadcast media.

The person who notifies family members should be a very senior member of the organization, for example the CEO. The caller should be direct but tactful when providing the information. It may be helpful to think through, or better yet, write an outline of what is to be said prior to delivering the news. Communicating with utmost respect and attention to the family members' feelings is important.

The message should communicate:

1. The facts of the situation, accurately
2. The sincere and deep condolences from the caller and the organization

The caller should give as much information as is available. When further information arrives, it should be communicated to the family. The caller should assiduously, and always, tell the truth.

After delivering the news, the caller should provide their contact information so they can be reached by family members. The caller should typically advise that updated information will be provided as soon as it is available, and establish a plan with the family to provide that information and continue communications.

It is good practice to ask family members what support they need, and be prepared to help provide it. This might include support with logistics, transportation, and contacting others. The caller may encourage family members to get support from friends.

The organization should have a plan for what to do if family members are not immediately available. It is also good to consider the timing of the call and the implications of reaching family members at night, at work, or inconvenient situations.

An appropriate approach in the event of fatality is to invite the next of kin to travel to the incident location at the program's expense, if they desire. The organization should offer to handle travel logistics, such as airline tickets and air transportation into the wilderness.

If the organization holds a memorial for the deceased participant, it is gracious to invite the family to attend, at the organization's expense. The organization may also offer to help pay for the funeral, and send flowers and messages of condolence. For family members, meaningful and respectful expressions of compassion are valued and deeply appreciated.

The organization should also consider an in-person visit to the family at their home. This is another opportunity to express condolences, provide information, offer emotional support, and build a positive and respectful relationship.

In general, maintaining a positive relationship with the family is enhanced by providing the family with the results of internal and external incident reviews. Although some legal specialists may express concern this exposes the organization to legal liability, many agree that good communication—including about errors made by the organization—is helpful for the family in finding meaning and closure, and of long-term benefit to the organization.

The organization should be prepared to maintain contact with family members for months or years. This ideally is made by the initial caller or another senior member of the organization, who stays consistently in this role for as long as required.

One of the responsibilities of the organization is to support the family members in finding meaning in their loss. Outdoor programs have been successful in supporting this aim by taking steps such as establishing a scholarship fund in the name of the deceased participant, or organizing a conference to disseminate outdoor safety information to others with the aim of preventing future fatalities.

Key points to remember when building and establishing relationships with family members:

- Be open, truthful, and transparent
- Provide as much information as possible
- Express sincere compassion and concern

When compassionate, respectful relationships with family members are established, it can be a healing process for everyone involved. Family members of individuals who lost their lives on an outdoor program have even become generous and long-term donors to the organization, for example endowing a scholarship in the name of the participant. Rather than seeking relief through legal channels, families have partnered with outdoor programs to honor and learn from tragedy.

14.5.7. Incident Review

Internal and external reviews should be initiated, as described in Chapter 16, Incident Reviews. Often, when review results are widely shared with staff, family members and stakeholders in the broader community, then opportunities for growth, finding meaning and closure are enhanced.

14.6. LEGAL AND CULTURAL CONSIDERATIONS

Legal and cultural environments vary dramatically around the world. Researching and understanding the context your program operates in, particularly in international environments, can help inform incident management.

In some settings, for instance, it is inadvisable to stop and help a bystander in trouble, as described in Chapter 4, Legal Considerations. (In other instances, however, it's legally required.) Would-be helpers who have stopped to provide assistance have been attacked by crowds, as they are assumed to be the perpetrator, for example in parts of East Asia.

For managing incidents in international settings, organizations may wish to work with their embassy, legal advisors, or private medical/rescue contractors.

14.7. TRAINING AND TESTING

A well-written Emergency Response Plan is only the beginning of appropriate incident management. It is essential that staff be thoroughly and repeatedly trained in the plan, and the plan be rigorously tested, examined, and continually improved.

This is particularly the case because of the experience of well-meaning outdoor programs that have what they believe to be a high-quality Emergency Response Plan. They are grievously shocked with a disaster occurs, and in mounting a response, the Emergency Response Plan is found to be deeply inadequate.

In part this stems from the unpredictable nature of incidents, and the limited capacity of persons to anticipate and respond to extraordinary challenges. In part it is due to the fact that the plan is rarely, if ever, put to use. Often, however, contributing factors are complacency, under-investment, and over-confidence on the part of the organization, leading to a flawed or incomplete plan, and failure of the organization to suitably invest in training its staff in effective emergency response.

14.7.1. Competent Staff

Staff should have the capacities to effectively implement the organization's Emergency Response Plan. This means they must understand the plan, and have opportunities to practice implementing the ERP.

All staff—employees, volunteers, and anyone else with a potential safety responsibility—should be provided with an opportunity to thoughtfully read the plan, and then do so. They should receive answers to any questions about the plan. And they should document that they have read and understood the plan, for instance by signing a written agreement to that effect. This should be done in the earliest days of a staff person's engagement with the organization.

In addition, staff should review the plan each year, and again sign an agreement stating they have re-familiarized themselves with the ERP.

Staff must then have an opportunity to practice the plan, at least annually. This can be done in the format of a Disaster Drill, described below.

Even highly trained and experienced professional emergency responders can struggle in the face of major disasters. They rely on continual training to help them be their best. For outdoor leaders called only rarely to manage a crisis, repeated and high-quality training can make a great difference.

14.7.2. A Well-Tested Plan

The Emergency Response Plan should be regularly tested to identify strengths and opportunities for improvement. The plan should be strengthened accordingly.

Testing should involve a rigorous examination for weak links. Does the plan take into account recent changes to the program? Are new staff capable of implementing it? If one link—for example, the chief risk management officer—is removed, is the plan sufficiently resilient to continue to work?

DISASTER DRILL

Introduction

Conducting a disaster drill provides the opportunity to test an organization's Emergency Response Plan, build emergency response skills in staff across the organization, and identify opportunities for improvement in the organization's crises response systems.

The drill is an immersive, experiential and whole-organization exercise that simulates, as realistically as possible, an actual emergency. It tests the organization's response in the field, administrative, and governance levels. Drills often take several hours to a half-day or more.

A full-scale disaster drill (Figure 14.8) can be held at least annually. Smaller exercises may be held seasonally or as needed. A standard to consider is that each staff member should participate in a disaster drill once a year. While the drills can be exciting, and even fun, they provide an essential and serious purpose of improving the real capacity of the organization to effectively respond to a serious incident.

Following the drill, a debrief with all players is held, identifying strengths and growth areas for the organization's crisis response capacity. An action plan is then made and implemented to build on the strengths and improve in areas needing development.

Figure 14.8. Disaster simulation with outdoor adventure guides in Iceland.

General Format and Progression

The drill can contain many variations, and may be scaled up or down depending on the needs of the organization.

It should be custom-designed to the activities, program areas, and organizational structure of the outdoor program. In general, the more comprehensive and realistic it is, the better the learning opportunity is.

In some circumstances it is convenient to conduct the drill during the timeframe of an activity leader staff training session, so that all field staff are already assembled and can easily participate in the exercise.

1. **An accident occurs.** This simulated accident could be a fall while rock climbing, near-drowning, lightning strike, motor vehicle accident, or anything else appropriate to the organization's context. A group of activity leaders in the outdoor environment responds. The field team begins extrication, medical care, patient packaging, and evacuation of the individual(s) acting as the patient(s), depending on the situation. (This can be similar to simulations in wilderness medicine training courses.)
2. **Notification sequence begins.** The field team contacts the administrative headquarters to advise managers of the incident, according to the procedures in the organization's Emergency Response Plan.
3. **Administrative response.** Office staff begin the administrative response in accordance with Emergency Response Plan procedures. This may include:
   a. Activating the notification sequence so others in the organization, from employees to key Board members, are made aware of the incident.
   b. Supporting the field team with evacuation logistics, land manager liaison, emergency medical services coordination, and other coordination and assistance as required.
   c. Contact with the client organization (if the incident simulates an accident with a member of an intact group such as a school class or corporate team).
   d. Preparation of media messaging.
4. **Emergency responder contact.** If part of the drill, the field team interacts with real-life emergency medical services, land managers, or search and rescue entities. For example, an ambulance could meet the evacuating group at a trailhead, or a helicopter could land at a suitable landing zone. This involves pre-planning with EMS and coordination with land managers as necessary.
5. **Media contact begins.** Volunteers acting as media representatives (such as reporters, Figure 14.9) contact administrators and volunteers such as Board or Risk Management Committee members,

requesting information. If it can be arranged, individuals acting as media representatives appear at the incident site, and attempt to interview rescuers or the victim. This tests the ability of staff to manage potentially intrusive reporters, and keep good discipline in maintaining conformity with the organization's media relations procedures. (Note that media interaction of this nature is generally not applicable in settings with state-controlled media.)

Figure 14.9. Practice working with the media is useful.

6. **Customer contact begins.** Customers (clients) can include representatives of current or potential client groups or parents of current or future minor participants. Volunteers acting as customers contact various staff or volunteers such as Board members, demanding information. Actors can range from concerned to belligerent. Unpredictably over the course of hours, these volunteers call or physically appear at the locations of administrators or others. They may make demands or request information that is or is not available.
7. **Conclusion.** The field team completes the evacuation of the patient (or other emergency response activity, depending on the situation), perhaps within two hours of beginning. The simulation ends.
8. **Debrief.** Either directly after the simulation ends, or later that day, the field team, administrators, and others involved (such as Board members) debrief the experience, by conference call and/or in person. Volunteers who acted as media representatives and customers participate as possible. A record of what went well and opportunities for improvement is generated.
9. **Improvement plan.** An action plan to build on Emergency Response Plan strengths and improve in areas needing development is created and implemented, in the days and months that follow.

Figure 14.10. Interface with rescue services increases realism.

VARIATIONS

- Field liaison with real emergency services units (Figure 14.10) is optional but can help the organization understand what to expect and how to work effectively with these groups.
- Consider stress-testing the Emergency Response Plan by removing key elements and checking for redundancy and resilience. For example, make the organization's designated media representative unavailable. Rescuers can experience (simulated) injuries. Communications technology can break down.
- Determine if there are elements of the organization's emergency response capacity that deserve closer examination, and strategically design the simulation to test and explore those areas. The simulation might test technical rescue capability by staging the accident on top of the high ropes challenge course. Complex long-distance negotiation can be examined in a drill involving a (simulated) legal entanglement on an international program. Ability to manage rescues with a particular outdoor activity or program area can be tested by simulating, for example, a flash flood in a popular canyon route.

ROLES

Disaster Drill Coordinator.
- Develop and write the scenario, and run the simulation.
- Decide how many media representatives and concerned customers or family members will be involved in the drill, write short profiles for each person (aggressive reporter, tearful parent, threatening customer, etc.), and recruit and train volunteers to fill those positions.

- Determine whether to involve real emergency medical services, search and rescue, or land management entities, and work with them to participate in the drill. (This can be time-consuming to arrange, but ultimately rewarding.)
- Days or weeks in advance, alert office staff and other persons such as Risk Management Committee or Board members that an unspecified simulated disaster will happen on a certain day and they may be contacted.
- Advise land managers and others who may encounter the drill in the field that a disaster simulation will be occurring, and not to mistake it for a real emergency.
- Review the organization's Emergency Response Plan before the drill.

Activity Leaders.
- Handle the emergency from the field.
- Coordinate with emergency services, the office, and others as necessary.
- Supervise the scene during the drill so that any passers-by do not mistake the exercise for a real emergency and contact emergency services.
- Ensure safety management during the rescue simulation.

Administrators.
- Coordinate emergency response with staff in the field, emergency services, land management, and others as necessary, following the Emergency Action Plan.
- Communicate with media, volunteers such as Board and committee members, customers, minor participant parents, and others.

Board members, other volunteers, or other staff.
Who this is varies widely depending on the organization. A small non-profit outdoor program might include Board members or Risk Management Committee members in the exercise. An outdoor program part of a university or school district might include corporate communications department employees or other institutional administrators.
- Receive communications from media, customers, and concerned parents, and respond appropriately in accordance with the organization's Emergency Response Plan and media relations protocols.

SAFETY AND LOGISTICS

- A code phrase may be employed so that if a real incident occurs during the drill, it is not considered part of the exercise. A phrase such as "this is for real" may suffice.
- To avoid confusion, radio and telephone communications should start with language such as "this is a drill."

NOTES

Real-life disasters are generally managed less successfully than simulated emergencies, where individuals are less stressed and conditions may be less challenging. Responding to real disasters is often scary, confusing, frustrating, and emotionally taxing. The psychological after-effects of responding to tragedy can be profoundly life-altering for both rescuers and survivors, particularly if things did not go well.

Uncovering unknown weaknesses in an organization's risk management plans and emergency response can be very difficult, but well-developed disaster drills can help. In order to maximize learning, and help real life incidents and their aftermath go as positively as possible, it is useful to have the drills be as complex, realistic, and challenging as possible.

Chapter Summary

1. Preventing incidents is better than responding to them.

2. An Emergency Response Plan is a written document describing who does what when in an emergency.

3. ERPs provide structure yet flexibility.

4. The ERP has separate field and administrative sections.

5. ERPs should be regularly reviewed and approved.

6. The initial field response includes: assess the situation, provide first aid, contact emergency services and the office, manage the scene, plan for evacuation, and document.

7. Bodies of the deceased should be protected and not moved.

8. Small groups of "runners" can go for help if needed.

9. Search and rescue procedures for lost persons should be described.

10. Roles with subcontractors should be clear.

11. Roles for administrators should be established in advance.

12. Initial administrative response includes: document, contact others, support field staff, alert emergency services, and attend to the victim.

13. Managers should provide for psychological support for survivors.

14. Be clear, direct, compassionate, and truthful with family members of those affected.

15. Promptly provide as much information as possible to those family members.

16. Support family members to understand and make meaning from the incident.

17. Conduct incident reviews for serious incidents.

18. In some situations, it is best to not give help to others encountered who are in need.

19. All relevant persons should be thoroughly, experientially, and repeatedly trained in the ERP.

20. The ERP should be continually reviewed and improved.

CHAPTER 15

INCIDENT REPORTING

LEARNING OBJECTIVES
1. The purpose and value of incident reporting
2. Components of an incident report form
3. When to write and not write an incident report
4. How and where completed reports are distributed
5. Analysis of aggregated incidents for trends, patterns and action items
6. Creation and dissemination of incident statistics and reports
7. Documents accompanying incident reports
8. The value of an organizational culture supportive of incident reporting
9. Industry-wide incident reporting efforts
10. Legal considerations

15.1. INTRODUCTION

A focus of outdoor program risk management is the prevention of the occurrence of incidents in the first place. This is a wise approach; however, despite best efforts, at times an incident may transpire. In these situations a loss has already occurred, but a well-developed process for incident reporting can help reduce the frequency and magnitude of future losses.

A robust incident reporting system principally provides a tool by which the organization can learn from the incident and thereby improve risk management systems and future outcomes. In addition, it provides information to defend individuals and the organization against legal claims arising from the incident.

An organization's incident reporting system should be comprehensively documented in a written risk management plan.

15.2. THE INCIDENT REPORT FORM

An important component of an incident reporting system is the incident report form. The form may be initially filled out on paper, then transcribed into an electronic incident database. The content of the incident report can vary, but should generally include:

1. **What happened.** A description of the incident.
2. **When it happened.** A specific chronology of activity.
3. **Who was involved.** Victims or subjects, responders, and others.
4. **Immediate causes.** This assists in addressing factors that might lead to future incidents.
5. **How could the incident have been prevented.** This important element provides an initial analysis of opportunities to make organizational changes.
6. **Name and signature of person completing form; comments and sign-offs from administrators.** Commentary from the immediate supervisor of activity leaders can add a useful perspective; administrator sign-off encourages and records evidence of incident review by executive staff.

There are many varieties of incident forms, and yours should be customized for your situation. Figure 15.1 provides an example of a two-page incident report form.

Incident Report

Attach a complete sheet of the subject's Medical History Form to this report. Attach SOAP Note as applicable.
Use additional sheets for documentation if necessary. Fill this form out completely and neatly in blue or black ink.

Subject Name: _____ ☐ Staff ☐ Student Sex: ☐ Male ☐ Female Age: ____ Program Type: _____
Primary Caregiver's Name: _____ Course Director's Name: _____
Client Organization: _____ Day of Course Incident Occurred: _____
Incident Date: _____ Time: _____ a.m. / p.m. Geographical Location of Incident: _____
Course Location: _____ Course Dates: _____ # Staff ____ # Participants ____ # Program Days ____

Type of Incident: ☐ Injury ☐ Illness ☐ Motivational/Behavioral ☐ Property Damage
(check all that apply) ☐ Near Miss ☐ Evacuation ☐ Missing Person ☐ Fatality

Course Format: ☐ Residential ☐ Basecamp ☐ Backpacking ☐ Canoeing ☐ Kayaking ☐ Challenge Course
☐ Other: _____

Type of Injury or Property Damage: (check all applicable)
☐ Muscle sprain ☐ Ligament sprain ☐ Dislocation ☐ Fracture ☐ Tendonitis ☐ Laceration ☐ Puncture
☐ Blister ☐ Avulsion ☐ Sunburn ☐ Burn ☐ Frostbite ☐ Skin ☐ Eye injury
☐ Dental ☐ Bruise, contusion or similar soft tissue trauma ☐ Head injury (without loss of consciousness)
☐ Head injury (with loss of consciousness) ☐ Near drowning ☐ Other_____
☐ If property damage, describe_____

Anatomical Location of Injury:
☐ Head ☐ Shoulder ☐ Wrist ☐ Upper Back ☐ Thigh ☐ Foot/toe ☐ Face ☐ Knee ☐ Upper Arm
☐ Neck ☐ Hand/finger ☐ Eye ☐ Chest ☐ Pelvis ☐ Lower Leg ☐ Forearm ☐ Abdomen ☐ Hip
☐ Ankle ☐ Lower Back ☐ Elbow ☐ Other: _____

Type of Illness: check all applicable
☐ Abdominal or other gastrointestinal problem (without diarrhea) ☐ Diarrhea
☐ Allergic reaction (to: _____) ☐ Apparent food-related illness
    ☐ Mild or localized ☐ Skin infection
    ☐ Severe, generalized or anaphylaxis ☐ Eye infection
☐ Upper respiratory illness (runny nose, congestion, "cold") ☐ Chest pain or cardiac condition
☐ Lower respiratory illness (asthma, bronchitis) ☐ Altitude illness
☐ Hypothermia (specify core temperature if known ____ °C) ☐ Nonspecific fever illness
☐ Heat illness (specify core temperature if known_____ °C) ☐ Urinary tract infection
☐ Heat cramps
☐ Heat exhaustion
☐ Heat stroke
☐ Other_____

Environmental Conditions at Time of Incident:
Temperature: _____°C Precipitation ☐ None ☐ Rain ☐ Snow Wind Speed: ____kph
Visibility: ☐ Clear ☐ Limited to_____ ☐ feet or ☐ miles
Surface &Conditions: check all that apply
☐ On trail ☐ Off trail ☐ Even ☐ Uneven ☐ Sloped ☐ Wet ☐ Dry
☐ Grass ☐ Sand ☐ Dirt ☐ Rock ☐ Mud ☐ Snow ☐ Ice

Immediate Cause: Prioritize major applicable categories 1, 2, 3 etc.
____ Altitude ____ Avalanche ____ Carelessness ____ Cold exposure
____ Dark/poor visibility ____ Dehydration ____ Exceeded ability ____ Exhaustion
____ Fall/slip on trail ____ Fall on rock ____ Fall on snow ____ Falling rock
____ Failure to follow instructions ____ Falling tree/branch ____ Hazardous animal/insect (specify _____)
____ Hostile bystander ____ Immersion/submersion ____ Improper screening ____ Misbehavior
____ Inadequate equipment ____ Inadequate instruction ____ Inadequate supervision ____ Poor hygiene
____ Inexperience/poor judgment ____ Missing/Lost ____ Lightning ____ Sunburn
____ Intoxication (alcohol/drugs) ____ Overuse injury ____ Plant poisoning/toxicity ____ Weather
____ Preexist. medical condition ____ Poor Techn ____ Psychological ____ Unfit
____ Tech. system failure ____ Unknown ____Other (explain)_____

Continued on next page.

Incident Report Continued

Program Activity at Time of Incident:

☐ Backpacking   ☐ Canoeing   ☐ Cooking   ☐ Day Hike   ☐ In Camp   ☐ Initiative/Game   ☐ High Ropes
☐ Low Ropes   ☐ Rappelling   ☐ River Crossing   ☐ Rock Climbing   ☐ Sea Kayak   ☐ Solo
☐ Swimming   ☐ Unaccompanied Travel   ☐ Unstructured Time   ☐ Vehicle/Van   ☐ Other: _____

Briefly describe incident: What happened and how? Who was involved? Where? When? Why?

_____
_____
_____

Analysis: Include any observations, recommendations or suggestions regarding prevention.

_____
_____
_____

Outcomes of Incident:

Did the participant leave the field? ☐ No ☐ Yes Date: _____
If yes, type of evacuation: ☐ Walk ☐ Vehicle ☐ Boat ☐ Backboard Carry ☐ Aircraft ☐ Other _____
If yes, evacuation or runner team leader_____
Was outside assistance used? ☐ No ☐ Yes If yes, name of organization(s): _____
Name of primary contact person: _____ Contact Phone Number: _____
Did participant go to medical facility? ☐ No ☐ Yes Date: _____ If yes, Facility Name: _____
Arrival date: _____ Arrival Time: _____ Address: _____
Phone Number: _____ Fax Number: _____ Attending Physician's Name: _____
Diagnosis: _____
Was physician permission granted for patient to return to course? ☐ Yes ☐ No If yes, obtain in writing and attach to incident report.
Were there any physical activity restrictions for patient returning to course? ☐ Yes ☐ No
If yes, explain _____
Was it necessary for patient to leave the course? ☐ Yes ☐ No If yes, Pickup Date: _____ Pickup Time: _____
Location where evacuee was picked up: _____
Full name of person who picked-up evacuee: (print) _____
Signature of person who picked up evacuee: _____

Notification Log

Initial call to base: Date: _____ Time: _____ Contacted Person: _____
Response: _____
Parent/Guardian: Date: _____ Time: _____ Contacted Person: _____
Response: _____
Other Calls: Date: _____ Time: _____ Contacted Person: _____
Response: _____
Other Calls: Date: _____ Time: _____ Contacted Person: _____
Response: _____

Details of Primary Evacuation Plan

Include routes on marked map, anticipated timetable and return of evacuation or runner team.

_____
_____

Details of Backup or Contingency Plan

_____
_____

Number of days on course (until evacuation date): _____ Number of days missed: _____

Date this report was completed: _____ Full name of person completing this report: (print)_____
Title: (print)_____ Signature of person completing this report: _____

Field Risk Mgt. Officer comments; initial & date: _____
_____
_____

Executive Director signature: _____ Date: _____

Figure 15.1. Sample Incident Report, front and back (two pages).

15.2.1. When to Report

Incident reports should be filled out for events such as a nontrivial injury, accident, illness, fatality, property damage, or near miss. A near miss or "close call" is an incident without injury or property damage, where the potential for serious loss was present but did not occur.

Incident reports may be filled out for:
1. Any nontrivial first aid given
2. Any loss of program time by participant due to accident/incident
3. Any accident/incident or near miss that may be relatively minor but would be useful to document for analysis of trends (for example, uncomplicated bee stings, slips/falls, mild contact dermatitis)
4. Any accident/incident or near miss that might result in a recommended program or policy change

Recording near misses is useful as these can give early warning and an opportunity to prevent more serious future incidents.

When in doubt as to whether or not completing an incident report is warranted, it is often useful to fill out an incident report.

15.2.2. When a Report May Not Be Necessary

For trivial occurrences, an incident report may not be necessary. An example might be a tiny paper cut on a finger in a circumstance unlikely to lead to infection or other issue, such as on a one-day hiking trip in good weather. (If the individual had a bleeding disorder, was immunocompromised, or was in an environment conducive to infection, for instance, an incident report might then be important.)

Organizations may provide a medical log or trip log book where a brief note might be recorded in lieu of a full incident report. In the example provided here, the note might indicate the person's name, the date, the location of the cut, and document that a 3 mm long superficial cut was washed off, a disinfectant and bandage were applied, and the subject instructed to observe for signs of infection.

15.3. THE INCIDENT REPORT PROCESS

15.3.1. Documentation and Dissemination

When an incident occurs, documentation is not the first priority. Instead, the scene should be made safe, first aid should be administered, and bystanders should be managed, as per the organization's incident response plans.

Once the scene has been stabilized and urgent needs have been addressed, an incident report can then be generated. Other documents, such as a SOAP note (medical incident report form), evacuation report, medical facility visit report, or chronological narrative, may be created as well. (See Section 15.4, Other Documents, for details.)

The incident report should be written and delivered to program management within 24 hours, if possible. This allows for an administrative response in addition to the in-the-field activity. (This helps prevent a situation in which an administrator first hears about an incident from an irate family member of an injured party demanding answers regarding an incident about which the administrator knows nothing.)

If prompt delivery of a written report is not feasible, then a verbal report should be given by phone or other communication system.

Once delivered to the supervisor of activity leaders, the incident report then is distributed to all relevant outdoor program staff in the organization's chain of command, up to the top program officer. The report should also be forwarded to staff responsible for admissions, participant screening, facilities/equipment, or other relevant departments, depending on the nature of the incident.

The incident report should also be provided to members of the organization's Risk Management Committee. And if the incident is very serious—for example, a fatality, permanently disabling injury or extensive property damage—the report should go to the highest levels of the organization, such as the CEO and members of the Board of Directors.

In addition to the internal dissemination described above, incidents sometimes must be reported to health and safety entities, coast guard or other maritime authorities, the police, child protective service agencies, or other entities, depending on the nature of the incident and the jurisdiction.

15.3.2. Immediate Action

Immediate action should be taken if the nature of the incident indicates this is appropriate. This might include notifying others, modifying safety policies, altering activity plans of other groups to avoid similar hazards, inspecting potentially faulty equipment or facilities before further use, or other responses.

15.3.3. Analysis, Synthesis, and Longer-term Response

Each facet of the organization that has a role in responding to the incident and preventing future occurrences should thoughtfully consider its response to the incident. This includes program activity leaders, coordinators, managers, and directors; logistics/facilities staff; safety officers and insurance managers; and sales, marketing, and executive staff, among others. The Risk Management Committee is also involved. Organizational leadership should decide how responsibilities are divided between the Risk Management Committee and staff teams.

In addition to a review of each incident, incidents should be looked at in the aggregate, and assessed for trends or patterns. For instance, a significant number of skin rashes from plant-related contact dermatitis might be occurring in a new activity location. Synthesis of multiple dermatitis-related incident reports might uncover a trend that should be addressed.

A useful tool in facilitating the analysis and synthesis of incident data is the aggregation of incident data in chart format, allowing examination by location, subject age, activity, proximate cause, and other factors. Figure 15.2 provides a simple example of such a chart; well-developed incident databases can generate sophisticated dashboard reports with colorful graphs and pie charts.

Type of Incident	Sum	Avg
Injury	7	0.006
Illness	0	0
Motivation/Behavior	0	0
Evacuation	0	0
Property Damage	4	0.004
Near Miss	6	0.005
Number of Participant Days	1115	
Number of Days Lost (Total)	0	
Number of Incidents	16	
Type of Injury		
Bruise	0	0.001
Ligament sprain	0	0.001
Muscle Sprain		
Frostbite		
Fracture		
Dislocation		
Head Injury w/o Loss of Consciousness		
Head Injury w/ Loss of Consciousness		
Near Drowning or Other Submersion Problem		
Other	2	0.002
Immersion Foot		
Tendinitis		
Eye injury		
Dental or Tooth Related		
Burn		
Blister		
Laceration		
Abrasion		
Sunburn		
Anatomical Location		
Head		
Face		
Eye injury		
Neck		
Shoulder		
Upper Arm		
Elbow		
Forearm		
Wrist		
Hand/fingers	2	0.002
Chest		
Abdomen		
Lower Back		

Anatomical Location Con't.	Sum	Avg
Pelvis		
Hip		
Thigh		
Knee	2	0.002
Lower Leg		
Foot		
Ankle	2	0.002
Toe		
Type of Illness		
Allergic Reaction: Local or Mild		
Allergic Reaction: Anaphylaxis		
Altitude illness		
Acute Mountain Sickness		
Pulmonary Edema		
Cerebral Edema		
Hypothermia		
Heat Illness		
Heat Exhaustion		
Heat Cramps		
Heat Stroke		
Chest Pain or Cardiac Condition		
Upper Respiratory Illness		
Lower Respiratory Illness		
Abdominal or GI problem w/o diarrhea		
Diarrhea		
Apparent food related illness		
Non-specific fever illness		
Urinary tract infection		
Skin infection		
Eye infection		
Other		
Program Activity		
Backpacking	3	0.003
Camp		
Canoe		
Caving		
Cooking		
Hike Without Backpack		
Initiative Game		
Portage		
Rafting		
River Crossing		
Residential Camp	2	0.002
Challenge Course		

Program Activity Con't.	Sum	Avg
Rock climbing		
Run		
Service		
Sea Kayak		
Solo		
Other		
Motor Vehicle	4	0.004
Immediate Cause		
Cold exposure		
Carelessness		
Dark/Poor Visibility		
Dehydration		
Inadequate Equipment		
Exceeded Ability	1	0.001
Exhaustion		
Fall/Slip on Trail	2	0.002
Fall/slip on Rock		
Falling Rock		
Failure to Follow Directions		
Falling Tree/Branch		
Immersion/Submersion		
nexperience/Poor Judgment		
Intoxicated		
Inadequate Equipment		
Inadequate Instruction		
Improper Screening		
Inadequate Supervision		
Lightning		
Animal/Insect		
Misbehavior		
Overuse Injury	1	0.001
Poor Hygiene		
Preexisting Condition		
Plant Poisoning		
Poor Technique		
Psychological		
Sunburn		
Technical System Failed		
Unfit		
Unknown		
Weather		
Missing/Lost		
Other	2	0.002

Figure 15.2. Example incident data spreadsheet.

As trends and patterns emerge, appropriate systemic responses can be developed. In the previous example, the surge in contact dermatitis might trigger the addition of a suitable skin cleanser to the first aid kit and enhanced training to help program participants avoid contact with the offending plant.

If a pattern of behavioral incidents on urban youth programs is noticed, systemic changes to participant screening, qualifications of activity leaders, staff training, and sales activities might be made.

Incident report data can be compiled into written reports that provide a narrative synthesis and make recommendations for action. The content, timing, and dissemination of these reports vary depending on each organization's needs. An outdoor program might choose to distribute quarterly safety reports to all staff, for example. The report might include incident statistics, brief descriptions of key incidents, an analysis of causes, and recommendations or directives for activity leaders or others.

An annual safety report might also be published for a slightly different audience and with a higher-level discussion and analysis. And episodic "safety memos" or brief messages might be distributed on an as-needed basis to activity leaders and managers with incident notes, tips, and messages encouraging a culture of safety.

In this way, information generated in the outdoor activity locations moves up the organizational chain of command. The data undergoes analysis and is synthesized to produce recommendations or directives for action. Those responses then filter throughout the organization, including back to the field level where the incident occurred and the initial incident report began (Figure 15.3). When this is done well, the program acts as a "learning organization" where information is generated, spreads through the organization, and is analyzed, and where learning from synthesis of the data is disseminated and implemented throughout the organization.

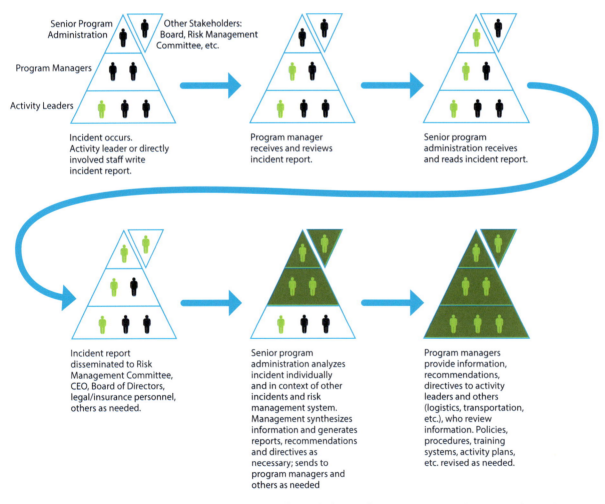

Figure 15.3. Flow of information in incident reporting. Black figures lack any information on an incident. Green figures have raw incident data only. Green figures/background have synthesized data processed into improved practices.

Section 3: Risk Management Systems

15.4. OTHER DOCUMENTS

In addition to the incident report, incident-related information may be recorded on other documents. Organizations should develop the information-gathering formats that best work for them. Figure 15.4 provides an example of one such form, used when visiting a medical facility.

Medical Facility Visit Form

Use this form as an outline for your role in a participant's visit to a medical facility. Return this form to your supervisor. Attach a complete copy of the Incident Report, Evacuation Report, and SOAP note (as applicable) to this report. Use additional sheets for documentation if necessary.

Participant's name:_____   Client group:_____

Date of visit:_____   Time of visit:_____

Course area/program type:_____

Course Director:_____

Before visiting medical facility:

☐ Have a copy of participant's "Medical Information & Release for Treatment" form on hand

☐ Get Incident Report, SOAP note, and other pertinent information from field staff to provide to treating medical staff

☐ Consider getting payment resources or information from participant/participant family/client for payment for prescriptions

At the medical facility:

Fill out this section of the form, or ask physician/nurse/physician assistant to do so.

Treating physician: _____

Diagnosis:_____

Instructions for care:_____

_____

_____

_____

Participant cleared for return to program? ☐ Yes   ☐ No Reasons: _____

_____

_____

If a participant must leave the program on a physician's advisement, have the physician affirm this in writing on letterhead identifying the medical facility. (This may be important for airline acceptance, if necessary.)

Before leaving medical facility/town:

☐ Ensure form is completely filled out.

☐ Obtain any necessary prescriptions (participant/participant's guardian to pay)

Date this report was completed: _____

Full name of person completing this report: (print) _____

Title of person completing this report: (print) _____

Signature of person completing this report: _____

Field Risk Mgt. Officer comments; initial & date: _____ _____

_____

_____

_____

Executive Director signature: _____   Date: _____

Figure 15.4. Example of a Medical Visit Report Form.

Examples of additional documents include:

1. **SOAP note (medical incident report form).** These documents, widely used in medicine, record information about medical patients.
2. **Evacuation report.** An evacuation report can be used in the process of removing a participant from the field to a program headquarters, medical facility, or elsewhere. Data fields may include evacuee name and location, reason for evacuation, detailed evacuation plan, information on entities assisting, a notification/call log, information on the receiving medical facility, and details on participant departure from program (such as date, time, and who picked up evacuee).
3. **Chronological narrative.** This is simply a log of who did what when during an incident or emergency. It can be written on a simple blank piece of paper or an established form. For complex incidents, one or more persons maintaining these activity logs help bring clarity during and after the incident.

15.5. CULTURE

It is important to maintain an organizational culture that supports, rather than suppresses, reporting incidents when they occur. Incident reporting is best when it is understood to be an important and valued part of a process of continual learning and improvement for individual staff and the organization as a whole. It is therefore important that individuals not be punished for making mistakes and documenting those errors in an incident report. Ideally, staff are proud to write incident reports, and to thereby take a leadership role in improving safety and helping the outdoor organization best meet its mission.

Some organizations have an established safety objective to reduce the number of incidents that occur. This can be an appropriate aim; however, care must be taken to ensure that a culture that suppresses incident reporting does not result.

15.6. INDUSTRY-WIDE INCIDENT REPORTING

Efforts are made to gather incident reports from a wide variety of outdoor programs and compile them into a master database of incidents, from which all organizations can learn. These efforts generally are voluntary and industry-led (rather than being government-mandated). Reporting systems are made in different parts of the outdoor industry and in various geographies. These databases have the potential to provide significant value.

Organizations may choose to assess the current state of multi-organization incident compilation applicable to their area and determine for themselves if it is beneficial to participate.

Some government-managed incident report databases and investigation report depositories may provide useful information for your situation. These can be in the form of coroner's report depositories, marine incidents report repositories, and the incident report databases of workplace health and safety agencies. An example is the repository of reports compiled by the Marine Casualty Investigation Board in Ireland.

15.7. LEGAL CONSIDERATIONS

Incident reports are generally considered private and confidential documents. However, in certain circumstances, such as some legal proceedings, they may become open to inspection by others. Despite this potential, it is widely considered appropriate to be honest, thorough, and candid in these reports. An organization's legal counsel can provide opinions on the organization's particular situation.

Chapter Summary

1. Incident reporting can help organizations understand incident causes and improve safety.

2. Incident reports can be used to defend against legal claims.

3. Incident reports should include the who, what, where, when, how, and why of an incident.

4. Incident reports should be generated following any nontrivial injury, accident, illness, fatality, property damage, or near miss.

5. A brief log entry in place of a complete incident report is sufficient for very minor incidents.

6. Incident reports should be delivered to program managers within 24 hours if possible.

7. Incident reports should be distributed to all relevant organizational staff and the Risk Management Committee.

8. Appropriate immediate action should be taken after each incident.

9. Incident data should be aggregated and analyzed, and action steps developed.

10. Learning from the incidents, including recommendations and directives, should be distributed to all stakeholders.

11. Statistical analysis charts and reports summarizing incident information are tools to understand and learn from incidents.

12. Medical facility visit forms, SOAP notes, evacuation reports, and chronological narratives may be used in incident documentation.

13. It is important to maintain an organizational culture that supports full and candid incident reporting.

14. Organizations may choose to join industry-wide initiatives to collect and share incident data.

15. Incident reports may not be private documents in some legal proceedings, but complete, thorough incident reporting is generally advisable; legal counsel can provide guidance.

INCIDENT REVIEWS

LEARNING OBJECTIVES
1. Why and when internal and external incident reviews are carried out
2. Who carries out incident reviews and their qualifications
3. Assembling potential external reviewers in advance
4. Incident reviews by insurance companies and government officials
5. Steps in the review process: gather and analyze information, develop conclusions, make recommendations
6. Organizational response to incident review reports

16.1. INTRODUCTION

It was late in the afternoon on a beautiful spring day at the high ropes challenge course. The final camper to head down the zipline was unclipped from the tether holding her to the launch platform. Group members gave encouraging cheers. She accelerated down the cable, gaining speed as she got closer to the lowest point of the element. Once she came to a stop there, some three meters above the ground, a massive wooden ladder would be wheeled into place for her to descend.

As the 11 year old girl sped down towards the bottom, encouraging cheers turned to horrified screams. "The LADDER!!" The girl slammed into the heavy ladder structure, which somehow had not been moved out of the way. She hung limp and unmoving, folded almost in half, her tiny hands dangling below her feet. The ladder, smashed and lying on its side, lay below her.

The camper was eventually rescued from the zipline and transported by ambulance to the hospital, where she was diagnosed with bruises and released. She returned to her group that evening. Questions turned to: how could this have happened? How can we prevent it from occurring again?

Formal incident reviews are conducted following occurrences resulting in significant loss. Examples of significant loss include fatality, permanently disabling injury, serious illness, and major property damage. The purpose of the incident review is twofold: 1) understand what led to the event, and 2) provide recommendations that can help prevent similar incidents from occurring in the future.

Incident reviews are different from risk management reviews. Incident reviews are carried out in response to a major incident and focus on issues related to that incident. Risk management reviews are carried out proactively and on a periodic basis, with an aim to prevent incidents—especially major ones—from occurring in the first place.

Specific procedures for when and how an incident review should be performed, and by whom, can be developed by each outdoor program. One approach is as follows:

1. *Minor incidents*. An incident report is generated. The incident reporting process (see Chapter 15) is carried out. No separate incident review is made. Possible examples: many near misses; small, superficial, uncomplicated lacerations; superficial frostbite; property damage of US $50.
2. *Medium-impact incidents.* In addition to incident reporting, an internal incident review is held. Possible example: four-meter fall while rock climbing leading to brief loss of consciousness and emergency transport to hospital, where patient is assessed with mild traumatic brain injury and released.

3. *Major incidents.* In addition to incident reporting, an internal incident review is conducted, and an external review is completed as well. Example: fatality.

Other considerations in deciding whether or not to initiate an incident review might include the potential consequences to persons, property, the organization, or other entities if a similar accident were to re-occur, and the assessed probability of re-occurrence.

Any incident review system should be recorded in an organization's risk management plan documentation.

16.2. INTERNAL REVIEWS

Internal reviews are generally conducted by senior program staff within the organization. Members of the organization's Risk Management Committee might also be part of the review team, providing a useful perspective. A team of up to three or four persons often suffices.

Each review team member should be suitably qualified. Review team members as a group should have an understanding of the standards for proper conduct of the outdoor activity in question. They should understand how to conduct incident investigations thoroughly, effectively, and impartially. They should have an understanding of legal and other implications of incidents. And they should have the ability to obtain, process and synthesize complex data streams in a relatively short period of time.

Internal reviews often take place over a period of days or weeks, depending on the nature of the incident, availability of review team members, and the requirements of the review.

At the conclusion of the review, a written report is provided to senior leadership and/or the organization's Risk Management Committee, as determined by the organization's incident review process.

16.3. EXTERNAL REVIEWS

External incident reviews are led by a team of independent outside experts, generally with extensive specialist knowledge in the outdoor activity that is the subject of investigation, and with experience conducting incident reviews. In addition to providing expert knowledge of the activity, external reviewers can provide fresh perspectives uncolored by potential conflicts of interest or cognitive biases and logic traps such as confirmation bias.

External reviews are often conducted along with internal reviews, to provide multiple perspectives following very serious incidents. They can take several months from start to finish, and may require a significant budget.

The external review team, as with the internal review group, should have an understanding of relevant standards, a knowledge of how to conduct reviews, and the capacities needed to identify, access, and interpret the information needed to create a comprehensive set of findings and insightful recommendations. In some circumstances, nationally or globally recognized leaders in the relevant outdoor activity (such as whitewater canoeing or mountaineering) may be retained to be part of the team for part or the entirety of the review process. Team members optimally are senior, mature individuals with decades of industry experience and a background in incident response and review.

It is useful for organizations to consider beforehand who they might call upon to assist with an external review. Having a roster of individuals who have agreed to serve on a review team if they are called upon and available can be helpful in a crisis. Larger outdoor organizations and industry groups may be useful in assisting you in assembling prospective team members in advance.

External reviews may follow a similar process to that employed in internal reviews. In some cases, external reviews may be more probing and extensive than their internal counterparts.

It can be useful to consult with the organization's insurance providers and legal counsel before, during and after the review.

At the conclusion of the external review, a report with findings and recommendations is made to the organization's executive leadership, Board of Directors, or others as appropriate.

16.4. OTHER REVIEWS

In addition to internal and external reviews commissioned by and controlled by the outdoor organization, other reviews may occur, particularly with serious incidents such as fatalities. Insurance companies, coroners or medical examiners, law enforcement agencies or other authorities may conduct reviews.

The contents of these reviews may be useful to the organization as it conducts its own reviews and determines a course of action following completion of all reviews.

16.5. THE REVIEW PROCESS

16.5.1. Gather and Analyze Information

Determining the facts of the situation is the first part of the review process. All relevant aspects of the organization and the incident should be looked into.

Subjects of investigation may include:

1. *Activity Location.* Assess hazards, risks, environmental conditions, available rescue resources. How well does the nature of the incident site match the location-related risk assessment and related procedures in the organization's risk management documents and systems? Review weather reports. Reviewers may travel to the site, by fixed-wing aircraft or helicopter for some remote sites.
2. *Activities.* Were activities conducted to standards? Were they appropriately matched to the participants, staff, location, and environmental conditions?
3. *Documents and Systems.* Review informed consent documentation, participant gear lists, written or other pre-event communications to participants, program gear inventories, emergency plans, policies and procedures, risk assessments, training syllabi, evidence of training of staff, safety briefings, permits and other authorizations, SOAP notes, incident reports and narratives, police reports, medical examiner or coroner's reports, previous incident reports, previous incident reviews or safety reviews, maps, photographs, and written approvals for activities and use of activity areas.
4. *Staff.* Evidence of appropriate training, certification, knowledge, skills, attitudes, experience, and judgment.
5. *Participants.* Pre-event information and preparation. Informed consent. On-program training and briefings.
6. *Equipment.* Availability of needed equipment. Condition, quantities, location of equipment. Was equipment used, and used appropriately? Were persons suitably trained in equipment use and management?
7. *Contractors.* Qualifications, vetting, and performance during activities.

8. *Culture.* Culture among field staff, participants, contractors, program administrators. Attitudes towards taking risks. Pressure to meet financial aims over safety objectives.
9. *Other Parties.* Information from bystanders, witnesses, survivors. Accounts from responders and emergency dispatchers. Information from program administrators, risk managers, land managers, involved officials.
10. *External Resources.* Information from reliable, qualified specialist consultants. (For instance, an organization might assess if the National Lightning Safety Institute, based in the US, would provide suitable expertise for an electrical storm incident.) Gear manufacturers. Consensus standards set by established standards-setting bodies.

In the case of the zip line accident, written incident narratives and medical reports from staff on site, communication with the patient's family, and information from the hospital were assessed. The challenge course operations manual and staff training plans were reviewed. The organization's insurance agent and legal counsel provided guidance.

16.5.2. Synthesize Information and Develop Conclusions

In this step information previously assembled is reviewed to identify immediate (proximate) and underlying, or root, causes. A systems approach to information analysis, and an investigation of cultural elements underlying behavior, can both be helpful to uncover root causes.

One root cause analysis approach begins by asking why an incident occurred. It is then asked why that proximate cause occurred. The next question is why that underlying cause leading to the proximate caused occurred. This continues for five or so iterations. This method of inquiry can help clarify underlying causes and therefore more effective responses.

Let's consider an incident where an activity leader did not use proper technique or provide adequate supervision, leading to an injury or other incident. Why did this occur?

An initial analysis uncovers that the activity leader's training was minimal, and that the leader had very little experience, both of which led to providing inadequate supervision. In addition, the organizational culture seemed supportive of not closely following industry standards, equipment manufacturer recommendations (which were not even known by the activity leader), or the organization's own guidelines. Why was this?

There was significant turnover in the organization's administrative positions, and the current program mangers had little background in risk management. Financial pressures led to low pay for activity leaders, and resulted in high turnover in employee positions throughout the organization. The Risk Management Committee had few members and rarely met; it was generally ineffective in assessing corporate culture or advocating for strong risk management systems. Administrative leadership was focused on marketing, sales, and keeping things fun and free of burdensome paperwork and procedures for field staff in order to keep up morale and field staff retention.

When we put the pieces together, a deeper understanding appears. It now becomes clearer that simply reprimanding the activity leader for not following the rules in insufficient. Grappling with financial, cultural, and systems issues is necessary to fully address the underlying causes of the incident.

Figure 16.1. Reviewer and program staff discuss issues and review findings.

Conclusions from analysis of the zip line incident included that staff were inadequately trained, volunteer chaperones where inappropriately tasked with moving the ladder, and the ladder structure was excessively heavy and bulky.

16.5.3.   Make Recommendations for Action

In the next step, recommendations are made to address the conclusions about the range of causes of the incident. Actions that effectively address the underlying causes are most helpful in preventing a reoccurrence of the incident over the long term.

Recommendations are generally provided in a written report, which summarizes the entirety of the review:

1. Description of the incident
2. Relevant facts uncovered in the investigation
3. Positive elements of the organization's risk management systems and incident response
4. Immediate and root causes of the incident
5. Recommendations

Recommendations are addressed to the organization that experienced the incident. Since the organization exists in a larger context, however, recommendations for the outdoor industry as a whole or relevant industry associations and regulatory bodies may be offered if relevant to the situation.

Recommendations for improving zip line and challenge course safety included making certain improvements to staff training, reducing staff turnover, better documenting roles and responsibilities of adult leaders on site, lowering the zipline to enable a smaller and lighter ladder to be used, and adding a formalized "all clear" communications system for the zip line.

16.5.4.   Organization Response

The outdoor program then responds to the review findings. This is often in a written format and within a reasonably prompt timeframe following receipt of the report.

The organization's response may address each recommendation separately. The response can indicate if the organization agrees with the recommendation, agrees only in part, or disagrees. Broad approaches to implementing recommendations can be outlined.

For internal reviews of less serious or complex incidents, a written response to each of the report's findings may not be made.

The organization then should develop and implement strategies and tactics to act on the recommendations. This may include changes to policies and procedures; improvements to staff training; revision of qualification requirements of activity leaders; adjustments to gear, activities, or approved activity sites; shifts of organizational culture, or any number of other changes.

As a final step, the organization reviews the effectiveness of its actions in addressing the report recommendations, and makes adjustments as necessary. This occurs on an ongoing basis for as long a time as needed.

Sharing What's Learned with Others. Openly sharing the results of the report with activity leaders and others throughout the organization has numerous benefits. It can help those psychologically or otherwise affected by the incident to process their experience. It can build buy-in for the changes that follow. And it can enhance the integration of new systems, procedures and perspectives needed to put in place the recommended changes.

Sharing report findings with family members of those affected and past, current and potential future customers can also have benefits. When done well, this can show the organization's commitment to quality risk management of activities it offers. It can build goodwill and has the potential to reduce the probability of damaging legal action against the organization.

Providing information about the incident and from the report to others in the outdoor industry can help them learn from your experience. Redacted report summaries and case study presentations, when sensitively and thoughtfully presented, can elevate the outdoor field as whole without offending those affected by the incident.

When sharing report findings with others, care should be taken to respect the confidentiality of those involved, for example by not including names of individuals who were part of the incident. In addition, consideration should be given to liability implications of disclosing errors or negligence committed by the organization. Qualified legal counsel can provide guidance relevant to your situation and jurisdiction.

Case Study: Kayaking Tragedy

The Incident

It was a beautiful morning to be out on the water. At around 10 am, eight students and their teacher launched from the sandy harbor, accompanied by two professional outdoor guides, for a two-hour kayak trip. They would paddle a few kilometers down the shore, then return. They'd be back by lunch.

Not long after launching, one of the participants capsized. As one instructor worked with him, the second instructor rafted the other kayakers together in a group. Winds pushed the flotilla of kayaks so far from the first participant they could not longer see each other.

The wind-blown waves were now one meter high. One of the kayaks was swamped, then another. Eventually, all nine kayakers were in the eight degree Centigrade water. They were swept out to sea and became separated from each other, spreading over an eight-kilometer area.

Noon came and went. Although the group was supposed to have returned by now, nobody at the outdoor program initiated a search and rescue process or alerted the authorities.

An upturned boat was discovered by a fisherman, who called the coast guard. A lifeboat and helicopter went to rescue the boaters. The rescue began close to four hours after the group was supposed to have returned to shore.

Four of the students drowned.

Analysis

An investigation reported that the kayak instructors were not highly experienced, with one only having paddled a total of 400 meters previously. The instructors were not carrying flares or a VHF radio. The victims blew their emergency whistles but this was not effective.

Conclusions

The tragedy was found to be preventable. The outdoor program failed to properly organize the kayaking program. It failed to employ appropriately trained guides. And it failed to put in place and properly use emergency procedures.

Recommendations and Action

The owner of the outdoor program was convicted of "gross negligence manslaughter," and was jailed for between one to two years.

Also as a result, a governmental regulatory body was created to control commercial adventure activities. Government regulations then replaced voluntary codes that could be used by outdoor activity organizations.

Chapter Summary

1. Incident reviews are conducted following serious incidents with significant losses.

2. Incident reviews should uncover incident causes and make recommendations to prevent future incidents.

3. Internal incident reviews may be held for medium-impact and major incidents.

4. External incident reviews may be held for major incidents.

5. Internal incident reviews are led by staff and volunteers from within the organization.

6. External incident reviews are led by outside experts not a part of the organization.

7. Reviewers should understand the applicable outdoor activities, know how to conduct incident reviews, and have the capacity to synthesize complex data into recommendations.

8. It can be helpful to make arrangements for potential external reviewers prior to an incident occurring.

9. Consult with insurance representatives and legal counsel before, during, and after reviews.

10. Insurance companies and government entities may also conduct reviews.

11. The first step in an incident review is to gather and analyze relevant information.

12. The next step is to synthesize the information into conclusions about incident causes.

13. Next, reviewers make written recommendations about how to prevent future similar incidents.

14. Finally, the organization responds to the reviewers' report.

15. The response can include an action plan on how to implement recommendations.

16. The response should include a continual assessment of the organization's capacity to prevent incident recurrences.

17. Information from the review may be shared with others, when confidentiality and liability considerations are made.

CHAPTER 17

RISK MANAGEMENT COMMITTEE

LEARNING OBJECTIVES
1. Risk Management Committee purpose
2. Typical composition of Committee membership
3. Standard Committee activities
4. Structure of the Committee
5. Legal requirements for safety committees
6. Professional development opportunities for Committee members

17.1. INTRODUCTION

A Risk Management Committee is an important tool for any outdoor program. It offers a team of individuals who work alongside key employees to provide a valuable and powerful resource to help the organization anticipate, understand, and manage risks.

Risk Management Committee structures can vary depending on the needs of each outdoor organization. The committee may go by other names, such as Safety Committee. Whatever the form and title, however, to be effective, top management must provide full and unwavering support for an active, high-functioning Risk Management Committee.

17.2. ROLES OF A RISK MANAGEMENT COMMITTEE

A Risk Management Committee serves several roles:

1. **A resource for staff** seeking guidance about risk management topics
2. **A check on staff**, providing oversight regarding key risk management decisions
3. **A force pushing for excellence** in risk management, by encouraging best practices
4. **An external perspective.** Members from outside the ranks of the organization's employees provide fresh views and ideas.

5. **A high-level view.** While employees sometimes get stuck in the day-to-day details, the Committee, acting in a governance role, can ask, are we successfully managing risk? What trends should we be paying attention to? What is our long-term strategy?
6. **Provides support where needed.** The Committee can jump in to assist with an incident investigation or accreditation self-study, and bring resources wherever needed to help the organization meet the goals and objectives of its risk management program.

17.3. COMMITTEE MEMBERSHIP

The Risk Management Committee typically has members internal to the organization (employees), and external members from the broader community.

Internal members may include:

1. Outdoor program coordinators, managers or directors with a risk management responsibility
2. The organization's risk management officer
3. Risk management department staff, such as medical screening staff
4. For facilities-intensive programs, a facilities manager
5. The organization's insurance administrator, if the organization is sufficiently large to have this position
6. An activity leader, who can bring a valuable in-the-field perspective

7. Board representatives, if the Risk Management Committee is a committee of the Board

External members are generally experienced, senior professionals who can sit in an advisory and governance position and provide reasoned, deliberate guidance. Examples may include:

1. An attorney, to provide legal advice and perspective
2. A physician. The medical doctor can serve as the organization's Physician Medical Advisor (as mentioned in Chapter 18, Medical Screening). The Physician Medical Advisor, however, does not need to sit on the Risk Management Committee. The organization, depending on need, may have one or multiple Physician Medical Advisors for different situations: a neurologist, psychiatrist, orthopedist, infectious disease specialist, or other. Specific medical roles can include:
   a. Guidance with difficult medical screening situations
   b. Real-time guidance during medical emergencies regarding medical treatment decisions, evacuation, and related issues
   c. A source for prescriptions for first aid kit medications
   d. Review and approval of first aid kit contents
   e. Review and approval of medical (health history) forms, screening manual, medical follow-up questionnaires, and other medical screening infrastructure
   f. Review of medical aspects of significant incidents
   g. Approval of medical protocols for use by activity leaders
3. Outdoor specialists such as those with expert technical outdoor skills, for instance sailing or climbing experts (if the organization has a sailing or climbing program)
4. Others. This can include insurance specialists, transportation experts, land management officials, or others.

Figure 17.1. Committee meeting.

17.4. RISK MANAGEMENT COMMITTEE ACTIVITIES

The Risk Management Committee should have clearly defined responsibilities, documented in writing. This can help ensure effectiveness and provide focus, motivation, and purpose.

Activities can vary depending on the particular needs of each organization, and may include:

1. Review incident reports, on an individual basis, and analyze aggregated incident statistics
2. Review New Element Readiness Assessments for approval
3. Review risk management policies, procedures, and guidelines
4. Review the organization's Risk Management Plan document
5. Act as a resource and source of guidance on questions posed by employees
6. Research and render an opinion on complex risk management topics, as requested by staff
7. Review risk management training systems
8. Take on selected initiatives, for example assessing and improving the organization's culture of safety
9. Participate in internal risk management reviews, often in a leadership capacity
10. Participate in external risk management reviews, for example as interviewee
11. Participate in accreditation reviews, through meeting with reviewers
12. Review inspection reports such as challenge course inspections
13. Participate in internal incident reviews, often in a leadership capacity
14. Participate in external incident reviews, for example as interviewee
15. Make requests of staff or provide recommendations to staff based on the information the Committee receives
16. Track overall success in meeting the organization's risk management mission and specific objectives

17.5. RISK MANAGEMENT COMMITTEE STRUCTURE

The Risk Management Committee should have a chartering document describing its purpose, structure, and functioning. This may include the Committee's overall purpose, specific objectives, frequency of meetings, composition of members, membership terms, roles and duties of officers, activities and outputs (such as regular reports), and responsibilities.

The Risk Management Committee should meet regularly, with sufficient frequency to be able to have appropriate awareness and exercise appropriate oversight of risk management topics. This may be monthly, quarterly, or otherwise.

The Committee should develop agendas before each meeting, and generate and retain minutes of meetings.

Officers of the Committee may include Chairperson (who provides overall leadership and facilitation), Vice Chair (to support the Chair and step in as necessary), Recording Secretary (to take and store meeting minutes), or other roles as necessary.

The Committee may provide periodic and as-needed reports to the Board, CEO, or other entities, as the Committee or organizational leadership determines to be appropriate.

Larger organizations may have multiple Risk Management Committees. There may be a main Committee that includes Board member representation; different sub-divisions of the organization may have their own Committees as well.

If the Risk Management Committee is officially a committee of the Board of Directors, the Committee may be described in the organization's bylaws (as applicable).

The Risk Management Committee is generally advisory in nature, without formal authority. In a well-developed organizational system, however, the guidance and recommendations of the Committee are taken very seriously by the organization's Board, senior executives, and other staff.

17.6. REQUIREMENTS

In some jurisdictions, a Risk Management Committee (or Safety Committee) is required by health and safety regulations. Requirements may vary depending on the size of the organization or its accident rate. In some cases, particularly with smaller organizations, safety meetings between front-line employees and management may be required in place of a full committee.

The purpose of these workplace safety committees is generally to provide for good two-way communication between management and on-the-ground employees regarding safety issues. Some regulations have requirements about the minimum number of employees required on the committee, the terms of members, how often the committee meets and for how long each time, required topics, recordkeeping, and other parameters.

These safety committee structures are often in place to ensure the safety of employees, particularly in heavy industry settings and with contentious relations between management and workers/labor unions. Regulations regarding these committees should be followed. However, the thrust and tone of the Risk Management Committee typical of an outdoor program are often somewhat different from these industrial safety-focused groups.

17.7. PROFESSIONAL DEVELOPMENT

Members of the Risk Management Committee are most effective when they have access to continuing education around various risk management topics. Support to attend outdoor safety-related conferences, access to media on outdoor program risk management, and similar resources for professional development are beneficial, should the organization be able to provide these to Risk Management Committee members.

Chapter Summary

1. A Risk Management Committee provides support and resources to an organization's staff for the management of risk.

2. Risk Management Committee structures and title can be customized for the organization's needs.

3. The Committee should have the support of the organization's top leadership.

4. The Committee can serve as a resource and as an oversight body, and provide an external and high-level perspective.

5. Committee members internal to the organization are often program managers, risk management and insurance specialists, and Board members, among others.

6. Committee members external to the organization may include legal, medical, outdoor, insurance or other experts.

7. Physician Medical Advisors, who may or may not sit on the Committee, can support medical screening, medical emergency management, selection and acquisition of medical supplies, and review of medical incidents and protocols.

8. The Committee may review safety-related reports, documents, and systems; conduct research; provide recommendations; approve New Element Readiness Assessments; participate in reviews, or perform other tasks.

9. The Committee, which is often advisory in nature, should meet as often as required and keep records of its meetings.

10. Regulations require safety committees in some jurisdictions.

11. Professional development opportunities for Committee members are desirable.

MEDICAL SCREENING

18.1. INTRODUCTION

A person with a history of seizures wishes to enroll in your whitewater paddling expedition. A young adult who has thoughts about committing suicide applies to go on the long, strenuous wilderness expedition you offer. An older person with a history of heart problems enrolls in your high ropes challenge course experience. Will you permit them to participate?

Medical screening can help you answer these kinds of questions.

Medical screening is a useful tool to help ensure that the participants in your outdoor program are medically and psychologically suitable for participation. The purpose of medical screening is not to screen out people, but to screen in as many as possible. The screening process helps ensure that participants are well matched with the characteristics of your program, and are most likely to have a positive and successful experience.

In addition to participants, activity leaders and any others involved directly in the activities should go through a medical screening process at a level appropriate for their involvement. In this chapter, staff and others are included when applicants or participants are discussed.

18.2. THE MEDICAL SCREENING PROCESS

The medical process often begins with applicants filling out and submitting a medical form. Medical screening staff review the information on the form against screening criteria. Additional information from medical tests or specialists may be sought as needed. The screener makes a decision to permit full participation, permit limited participation, or reject the applicant.

The organization's physician medical advisor(s) and the applicant's physician can both assist in making screening decisions.

18.2.1. Medical Form

The medical form provides relevant information about the applicant's medical condition, including allergies, medications, and health history. These forms should be developed and approved by a qualified physician who understands the nature of your outdoor programs and the general characteristics of your participants. The specific content of forms can vary widely, depending on the nature of the outdoor activities, distance from medical care, characteristics of participants (such as age or special needs), and other factors. An organization may have one form for all program offerings or have different forms for different programs or participant populations.

Figure 18.1 provides an example of a two-page medical form. Forms your program uses may vary substantially from this example.

Consent for reasonable and customary medical treatment should also be secured from the participant or their parent or guardian. Section V of the medical form example in figure 18.1 requests such permission.

Medical Information and Release for Treatment

Follow-Up	Approval

I - General Information

Information requested in this form is vital to an effective response if a medical emergency occurs while you are participating in the program. **All parts of this document must be filled out completely.**

Course Location and Date(s):

Name (print clearly) _____ Address _____

City _____ State _____ Zip _____ Email _____

Phone (_____)_____ Fax (_____)_____ Birth date_____/_____/_____ Age_____ Sex ____

Person to be notified in case of emergency _____

Address _____ City _____ State _____Zip_____

Relationship _____

Home Phone (_____)_____ Work Phone (_____)_____Other Phone (_____)_____

Fax (_____)_____Physician _____Office Phone (_____)_____

Restrictions for medical treatment? _____

Medical Insurance Company _____

Medical Insurance Company Tel. No. (_____)_____ Policy Number _____

Name of Policy Holder _____

II – Medical Information

A. Allergies (including medicines, foods, bites and stings):

☐ No allergies **OR** list below:

Allergy	Reactions	Medications Required

B. Medications

☐ No medications **OR** list all, including prescription and over-the-counter:

Medication	Condition	Dosage (size and freq.)	Current side effects

C. Current Exercise Activity:

Activity	Frequency	Time / Distance	Pace (easy / moderate / strenuous)

III - Health Profile

Height _____ Weight _____ Blood Pressure _____ / _____ Pulse Rate _____ Date Taken_____(within past 6 months)

Have you been in counseling with a psychiatrist, psychologist or other therapist within the past two years?

Yes _____ No_____ Detailed description, including symptoms and restrictions: (use add'l pages if required)

If Yes, Therapist's Name _____

Therapist's Phone (_____) _____ Fax (_____) _____

Address _____

City _____ State _____ Zip _____

Do you have a history of:

		Yes	No			Yes	No
1.	Seizure within past year	☐	☐	9.	Special dietary needs, (e.g. vegetarian, vegan, kosher, lactose intolerance)	☐	☐
2.	Hospitalization w/in past 2 years	☐	☐				
3.	Emergency Room visit within past year	☐	☐	10.	Claustrophobia, acrophobia, agoraphobia, depression or hysteria	☐	☐
4.	Family history of heart attack	☐	☐				
5.	Head / neck / back / shoulder / arm / hand / leg / knee / foot pain, injury, stiffness or swelling	☐	☐	11.	Smoking	☐	☐
				12.	Pregnant within past year	☐	☐
				13.	History of alcohol or drug abuse	☐	☐
6.	Asthma or shortness of breath	☐	☐	14.	Other medical illnesses / symptoms / requirements	☐	☐
7.	Date of last tetanus shot	_____					
8.	Medical equipment requirements	☐	☐				

Issue #	Detailed description, including symptoms and restrictions (use additional pages if necessary)

IV – Health Problems   Do you have any of the following conditions?

	Yes	No	
A	☐	☐	Resting pulse rate over 100
B	☐	☐	Systolic blood pressure over 150 and/or diastolic blood pressure over 90
C	☐	☐	Experiencing chest pain and/or pressure
D	☐	☐	Heart disease past or present (including high blood pressure)
E	☐	☐	Abnormal heart murmur (if you have a normal or functional murmur, written confirmation by your physician is required. Only abnormal murmurs require a physician's exam.
F	☐	☐	Diabetes
G	☐	☐	Seizure disorder (If "yes" your physician must confirm that you are seizure free for one year.)
H	☐	☐	Fainting / Dizziness
I	☐	☐	Chronic illness or physical infirmity

Issue #	Detailed description, including symptoms and restrictions (use additional pages if necessary)

If you have checked "yes" on any of the above conditions, you must contact our office at least two weeks prior to your start date.

V – Consent for Treatment

I give my consent and permission for any emergency anesthesia, operation, hospitalization or other treatment that might become necessary. I certify that the information on this form is correct to the best of my knowledge and that there is no other medical or psychological information I am withholding that will in any way affect my performance while participating in the program.

Participant Signature _____ Date _____

Parent or Guardian Signature _____ Date _____
(parent or legal guardian only must sign if participant is a minor

Figure 18.1 Sample Medical Form (two pages).

Organizations often find it useful to obtain completed medical forms at least two weeks prior to the start of the event, in order to provide sufficient time for screening and follow-up. Applicants may not all submit forms prior to the deadline, so systems should be established to respond appropriately should this occur.

Applicants may submit inaccurate and incomplete information. This may be in an effort to be admitted to an experience despite the presence of a medical condition that would preclude participation. Note that in an effort to address this issue, the example form in figure 18.1 requires applicants or their guardian to certify that the information is correct and complete.

Medical forms hold confidential information, access to which may be restricted by law. Forms should be secured from unauthorized access during pre-program screening, the duration of the program, and in storage after conclusion of the outdoor experience.

18.2.2.   Screening

The details of certain medical conditions should be reviewed to ascertain if an applicant is eligible for participation. Figure 18.2 gives an example list of such conditions. The medical conditions your organization chooses to consider may be different from this list.

MEDICAL CONDITIONS

Amputation
Anorexia nervosa
Ankle
Asthma
Bladder infection
Bleeding disorder
Blood disorder
Broken bones
Bulimia
Cancer
Chest pain/pressure
Circulatory problems
Heart disease
Current pregnancy
Diabetes mellitus
Difficulty urinating
Dizziness/fainting
Endocrine problems
Frostbite
Headaches (incl. migraines)
Hearing impairment
Heart murmur

Heatstroke
Hepatitis
Hernia
High blood pressure
Hips
Hypoglycemia
Intestinal problems
Irregular heartbeat
Jaundice
Kidney problems
Knee
Medication
Motion sickness
Neck and back
Seizure disorder
Shoulder
Skin condition
Sleepwalking
Special diet
Stomach ulcer
Thyroid problems
Tuberculosis
Vision impairment

Figure 18.2. Example medical conditions to consider in screening.

An individual without special training can conduct initial review of medical forms. If the forms are completely clear of any medical concerns, the subject may be considered medically qualified for participation. If there are concerns then a trained medical screener should review the form.

The medical screener should have sufficient medical training to understand the meaning and significance of medical terms and other information provided in screening materials. Screeners should have a thorough understanding of the screening tools at their disposal, such as a screening manuals and follow-up questionnaires, and know when and how to access extra support from physicians or others as required.

Screening Manual. A screening manual can provide essential guidance to a medical screener responsible for making complex medical judgments. It can reduce the need to employ the services of highly trained (and expensive) medical professionals such as physicians. Development and maintenance of the screening manual should be led by a competent physician closely familiar with the nature of your outdoor activities and participant population types. Organizations may create their own or seek a license to use an existing screening manual.

Figure 18.3 provides an example of an algorithm in a screening manual for outdoor adventure programming. In this case, heart disease is the condition under consideration. Several caveats apply. This is provided as an example only and this particular decision matrix may not necessarily apply to your or any other current situation. Different fully qualified medical professionals may employ different but equally valid screening approaches. Different outdoor programs may have more exacting or lenient screening criteria depending on their unique situation. Medicine is constantly evolving, so medical screening should as well.

HEART DISEASE			
Related information to look for on Participant Medical Record pertaining to this condition			
Participant Medical Record – 6 Page; 4 Page; 2 Page Youth and Adult			Physician's Section Only
IDENTIFICATION History/current status: heart attack, angina. Related symptom(s): chest pain, abnormal cardiac rhythm	**HISTORY** Surgery/procedures: angioplasty, stent placement, CABG Current medication(s) Hx, hospitalization/ER Tx	*LIFESTYLE* Smoker Height/Weight Activity Level	**PHYSICIAN FEEDBACK** Assessment— Referral— Restriction(s)—

ACCEPTANCE CRITERIA:

MANDATORY ACTION:

RED FLAGS:
- History of or continued chest pain/pressure, shortness of breath, heart palpitations, sweat or exertional dizziness or faint spells
- History of procedure (CABG, angioplasty, stent)
- History of a myocardial infarction (MI)
- Recent medication change
- History of risk factors
- Use of anti-coagulants (e.g. warfarin)

CONTRAINDICATIONS:

STATUS	BACKCOUNTRY	FRONTCOUNTRY
1. **Myocardial Infarction (MI, Heart Attack)** a. Within the past 3 months (with or without procedures) b. Between 3-6 months ago c. History of an MI with no symptoms and good activity level d. History of an MI with no symptoms and sedentary lifestyle	1. **Myocardial Infarction** a. **Medical Rejection** b. Accept if applicant has good exercise and approval of the applicant's physician. Medical Rejection if any of the above is not met c. **Accept** with approval of the applicant's physician d. **Accept** with approval of the applicant's physician	1. **Myocardial Infarction** a. **Medical Rejection** or **Limited Participation Status** b. **Accept** if applicant has good exercise and approval of the applicant's physician. **Limited Participation Status** if any of the above is not met c. **Accept** d. **Accept** with approval of the applicant's physician
2. **History of chest pain/ pressure, shortness of breath, heart palpitations, sweats or exertional dizziness or faint spells** a. Cardiac condition b. Non-cardiac condition	2. **History of chest pain/ pressure, shortness of breath, heart palpitations, sweats or exertional dizziness or faint spells** a. **Medical Rejection** if symptoms are not remedied. b. **Accept** with approval of applicant's physician	2. **History of chest pain/ pressure, shortness of breath, heart palpitations, sweats or exertional dizziness or faint spells** a. **Limited Participation Status** if symptoms are not remedied. b. **Accept**
3. **History of angioplasty, stent.** a. Within 1 month. b. More than 1 month, with no MI within 6 months. c. Coronary bypass surgery within 6 months. d. Coronary bypass surgery greater than 6 months.	3. **History of angioplasty, stent.** a. **Medical Rejection** b. **Accept** with approval of applicant's physician c. **Medical Rejection** d. **Accept** with approval of applicant's physician	3. **History of angioplasty, stent.** a. **Medical Rejection** b., c., d. **Accept** with approval of applicant's physician. Applicant may choose **Limited Participation Status** if they physician will not approve active participation.

ADDITIONAL INFORMATION: There are a variety of different ways to assess for coronary artery disease including exercise/stress testing. For one of these tests, the heart rate can be increased by exercising on a treadmill or bicycle or by stimulating the heart with a drug. Cardiac function can be assessed by reading an EKG or echo cardiogram or a cardiac image generated after the injection of a radioisotope.

Staff—Same as above

Figure 18.3. Medical screening example.

Creation and maintenance of a screening manual and related screening infrastructure can represent a substantial investment for a small outdoor program to undertake, particularly if it travels to remote areas, engages in high-risk activities, or works with certain special populations.

Supplemental Questionnaires. The presence of certain conditions on a screening form may raise the need for additional information. For instance, with applicants who have a history of certain current behavioral or psychological issues, a supplemental questionnaire may be requested from the applicant's psychologist, psychiatrist, or other psychological care provider. This confidential questionnaire might describe your program and its activities and potential stressors. It might request information regarding the applicant's psychological diagnoses, treatment, progression, and anticipated response to and suitability for full or limited participation in an outdoor program such as yours.

Similarly, an orthopedic questionnaire might be required for an applicant to a backcountry program with an ankle fracture, history of patellar dislocation with recent surgery, or certain other orthopedic issues.

Separate topic-specific screening manuals applicable only to the subjects addressed in these supplemental questionnaires may accompany the questionnaires.

Physician Referral. The medical screener may at times find it useful to obtain the expert judgment of a physician who understands the nature of your outdoor program and the applicant's medical conditions. The physician is commonly either a consulting medical advisor for the outdoor program, or the personal physician of the applicant.

Especially with situations in which an applicant's suitability for participation is not immediately obvious, a recommendation from a qualified physician can be particularly helpful. One standardized format in which to request this recommendation is a physician referral form. An example is provided in Figure 18.4. Such a form should be customized for the circumstances of each individual organization using this tool.

Examples where physician referral may be useful include an applicant with a history of mitral valve prolapse with arrhythmias, an implantable pacemaker/defibrillator, or a recently repaired hernia, among others.

Physician Referral

To: Dr._____

We seek your assistance in the medical screening of: _____

This individual has applied to participate in [organization's] outdoor program. During this program, the individual may be subjected to a variety of stresses, physical and psychological, due to strenuous activities in the out-of-doors. In addition, the individual may be in a situation of delayed and/or prolonged transport to a medical facility.

The program this individual is applying to participate in includes the following elements
(Organization medical screener to check applicable boxes):

- ☐ **Low ropes Challenge Course**—traversing obstacles relatively close to the ground
- ☐ **High ropes Challenge Course**—traversing obstacles up to 15+ meters in trees or poles
- ☐ **Backpacking**—including carrying a backpack of 20+ kg over rugged, uneven terrain, in a mountain or desert environment
- ☐ **Dayhiking**—including carrying a daypack of 7+ kg over rugged, uneven terrain
- ☐ **Sea kayaking**—paddling in a kayak within two km of shore, facing strong winds, waves or other obstacles
- ☐ **Canoeing**—expeditionary flatwater canoeing in remote environments
- ☐ **Rock climbing**—scaling cliffs 15+ m high using ropes and technical safety equipment
- ☐ **Remote travel**—backpacking, canoeing or other travel in a wilderness environment where medical assistance may be several hours or rarely days away
- ☐ Other _____
- ☐ Other _____

(If applicable) We are seeking your guidance in regards to the following medical condition(s):

_____

_____

_____

Please indicate if there are any restrictions to activity below by checking the appropriate box and initialing and dating the appropriate area:

- ☐ No restrictions to activity _____(initial) _____(date)
- ☐ The following restrictions apply: _____
  _____ _____(initial) _____(date)
- ☐ Participation is not advised or not permitted. Details/explanation: _____
  _____ _____(initial) _____(date)

Name of Physician:_____ Telephone: _____

Please fax this form back to [organization] at [fax]. Call [phone] with any questions.

Thank you for your assistance in this matter.

Fig 18.4. Example Physician Referral Form.

Additional Testing. In some situations, the applicant may be required to provide results of additional medical tests before being admitted onto the program. For instance, an applicant with a history of ventricular tachycardia, who is taking medication but currently asymptomatic, may require a stress test before acceptance.

Essential Functions. Another tool that can be considered for screening use is a list of essential functions required of all participants. These may include fundamental capabilities such as:

- Ability to eat, dress, and use a toilet or latrine independently
- Ability to follow adult supervision
- Ability to express needs
- Ability to walk three to five miles per day without assistance

These requirements should be made evident to applicants (and their parents or guardians, in the case of minors) well in advance. For instance, they could be available in promotional materials such as on the program's website, and in application forms.

If the prospective participant may not be able to meet the essential functions, then the applicant (or guardian) and the organization may explore potential solutions. These might include the involvement of a Personal Care Attendant, sign language interpreter, or appropriately skilled and credentialed medical caregiver. The organization and participant or guardian should determine which party would be responsible for obtaining and paying for the services of these individuals.

Whether or not the organization is required to make or accept such accommodation depends on the jurisdiction and particular circumstances.

18.2.3. Screening Decisions

The screening process can result in one of several decisions:

1. *Medical acceptance.* The applicant is cleared to participate in the outdoor program.
2. *Acceptance with conditions.* The applicant may participate in the program subject to certain restrictions regarding activities, locations, intensity of involvement, environmental conditions, or other factors.

3. *Medical rejection.* The applicant may not participate in the experience.

In the case of medical rejection, it is generally prudent to have a clear, thoughtful and empathetic two-way conversation with the applicant or guardians regarding the reasons for medical rejection. Communicating required essential functions and potential screening issues as early as possible can also be useful.

Referring rejected applicants to other potentially more suitable experiences can be helpful as well. Perhaps your organization offers an outdoor experience that is closer to medical care, shorter, or in a less extreme environment. Or you might suggest deferring participation so that more planning for accommodation (such as hiring an assistant) can be made, or so an applicant can better learn how to manage their newly diagnosed condition. A referral to another organization may be helpful; special programs for individuals with diabetes, persons who are deaf, and others may be a better fit for the applicant than the program at your organization to which they initially applied.

These steps can reduce the resistance to accepting medical rejection that might come up. It can also reduce the probability of protest, including public protest to news media, attacking the organization's decision to reject.

18.3. FIELD APPLICATIONS

Activity leaders should review participant medical history forms before meeting participants. They should speak with participants on or shortly after arrival to gather any further information as needed. This might include information on how the participant manages their chronic illness such as diabetes, best approaches if a patient's disease symptoms suddenly increase, and the extent to which other group members should be aware of their medical circumstances.

Activity leaders should have ready access to medical forms for each participant and other activity leaders at all times, and should ensure their security and confidentiality.

18.4. VARIATIONS IN SCREENING

The nature of medical screening can vary widely. The intensity level of screening depends on a number of factors, including:

1. Nature and type of outdoor activities
2. Location, including environmental conditions and access to medical care
3. Nature of population
4. Skill and training of activity leaders
5. Presence or absence of adaptive facilities and equipment for working with populations of all abilities
6. Logistical, financial and other capacity to provide accommodation for certain medical conditions
7. Local standards, i.e. social norms in different countries and regions

The screening regime described in this chapter is moderately intensive, and is designed to be suitable for remote wilderness expeditions. Programs may elect to employ different levels of screening depending on their particular circumstances, as below.

- In a minimal screening system, there may be no pre-participation screening whatsoever. Alternately, a few basic questions about medications, allergies, and activity restrictions may be asked, possibly right before commencement of activity.
- With a basic screening system, participant contact information, insurance information, allergies, medications, relevant health history, and basic psychological information are gathered and assessed.
- With a comprehensive screening system, information in the basic screening regime is gathered and evaluated. In addition, responses may be required to questions regarding activity restrictions, immunizations, hospitalizations/urgent care history, detailed psychological profile, drug/addiction/lifestyle background, exercise level, swimming ability, and blood pressure. Written results of a physical exam conducted by a physician may be necessary. Data on cardiovascular fitness and cardiac risk factors, and other information, may also need to be submitted.

18.5. ACCEPTING SCREENING RISKS

Particularly in litigious societies such as the United States of America, there are liability risks to judging certain persons, for example those with diabetes or asthma, as qualified to participate in an outdoor experience, especially one that is strenuous or remote. If a medical emergency occurs, the organization may be blamed for failing to understand and mitigate the risks of the person's participation in the outdoor activity.

Some tools exist to transfer this risk away from the organization. For example, requesting the applicant's physician to judge whether or not a person be recommended to participate may transfer some risk to that physician.

The organization is assumed to know the nature of its activities, program areas, and hazards better than others. On the other hand, the applicant and their physician presumably know much more about the applicant's medical condition that the organization does. Which side is best situated to make the decision about whether the program and the applicant are a good match for each other?

There are cases where the decision for medical acceptance or rejection is not clearly evident. In these situations a useful approach may be to have thoughtful conversations involving the applicant, the outdoor organization, the applicant's physician, and the organization's medical advisor or advisors. Through informed conversations with the appropriate and qualified individuals, an understanding can be reached as to whether and how an applicant may be suited for participation in a particular outdoor experience.

The foregoing is not legal advice. A qualified legal specialist should be consulted for an organization's questions about screening-related legal liability.

Chapter Summary

1. Medical screening can enhance safety and availability of outdoor programs by efficiently gathering and assessing accurate and relevant medical information.

2. Medical screening uses medical information to determine who is and is not suited to participate in an outdoor program.

3. A medical form filled out by applicants provides important information to medical screeners.

4. Consent for appropriate medical treatment should be sought, and can be documented on the medical form.

5. Screeners match medical form information with criteria in a medical screening manual to determine if an applicant is eligible to participate.

6. Supplemental questionnaires provide screeners with additional information with which to make decisions.

7. An organization may request that the patient's physician or the organization's medical advisor provide a recommendation as to whether or not the participant is medically eligible to participate.

8. Additional medical tests may be required to determine eligibility.

9. A list of essential functions required of participants can provide useful screening guidance.

10. Screening decisions include full acceptance, acceptance with restrictions, or medical rejection.

11. Medical information on participants and activity leaders should be available to, kept secure by, and used appropriately by activity leaders during program activities.

12. The depth and intensity of medical screening systems can vary greatly between organizations, depending on needs.

13. Liability risk in medical screening exists, but can be managed through risk transfer and making thoughtful, quality decisions.

RISK MANAGEMENT REVIEWS

19.1. INTRODUCTION

Risk management reviews provide an opportunity to stop and take a close look at an outdoor organization's risk management systems and actual performance. They help an organization enhance its understanding of what is working well and not so well safety-wise. They provide the basis for an action plan to maintain strengths and invest in improving in areas that need work. Well done, they are a powerful tool for helping organizations committed to quality in safety management to meet their safety-related goals.

In the term "risk management review," the phrase "risk management" is sometimes replaced with "safety," and "review" is sometimes replaced with "audit," "inspection" or "assessment." These terms should be construed generally and outside a strict legal context where one might exist. In any case, regardless of terminology, the purpose and process remain the same.

These risk management reviews generally apply to an entire outdoor program. If a review covers only a selection of an organization's activities, the remaining activities should be similarly assessed within a reasonable timeframe.

In many parts of the world risk management reviews of outdoor programs are considered a best practice but are not mandatory. In other locations, such as New Zealand and the UK, they are legally required for certain outdoor activity providers. The frequency of reviews, who serves as reviewer, and other aspects of reviews may also vary around the world.

19.2. CONTRAST WITH OTHER INSTRUMENTS

Risk management reviews are proactive. That means their focus is generalized and forward-looking, with an aim to prevent future losses from occurring and to reduce the severity of losses that might occur anywhere in the outdoor program. This is different from incident reviews, which are triggered by a significant incident. Incident reviews focus retrospectively on understanding the causes of an incident and making adjustments to reduce the probability and severity of any future similar incidents. Chapter 16 discusses incident reviews.

Risk management reviews are also different from periodic inspections of complex installations such as high ropes challenge courses. These inspections may be required or recommended by a manufacturer, installer, government regulator, industry group, or published consensus standard relative to that particular activity (such as portable climbing wall or canopy tour). They are typically conducted by specialized experts in that particular field, who may not be qualified to assess other aspects of an outdoor program. These inspections should be conducted in addition to the comprehensive risk management reviews discussed here.

Accreditation reviews of experiential adventure programs are also generally not considered to serve as risk management reviews, although they can provide useful safety-related information.

19.3. REVIEW CHARACTERISTICS

Risk management reviews look at all safety-related aspects of an organization. This includes activities, staff, participants, equipment (Figure 19.1), transportation, organizational culture, procedures, emergency plans, and more. The reviews are an integral part of safety management and the continuous improvement process for each of these program elements.

Figure 19.1. Safety-critical equipment gets close inspection during a risk management review.

Reviews typically compare each aspect of an organization to industry standards. An evaluation is made as to whether the organization meets the standard for that particular organizational element. If a standard is not met, an indication may be given regarding how urgent or important it might be to address the deficiency.

The frequency of risk management reviews depends on a variety of factors. Completing a comprehensive review every 18 to 24 months may work well for many organizations which have a generally stable program but wish to keep a close eye on safety. However, it may be useful to conduct a review before that time period elapses if there is a significant institutional change such as a corporate reorganization or major leadership turnover. Conversely, well-established and extremely

stable organizations with an extensive and continuous history of excellent risk management infrastructure and performance might choose to normally hold a review every four or five years.

Reviews are often of two types: internal and external. Internal reviews are typically conducted by an organization's own staff and members of its Risk Management Committee. External reviews are performed by qualified individuals who are not a part of the organization. These reviews can be especially valuable as capable external reviewers may notice issues that those within the organization might not. Budgeting for the expenses of the external review is necessary. In both review types, the organization is assessed to pre-established standards, a written report of findings is provided, and prioritized recommendations for action are made. Organizations often choose to alternate between holding internal and external reviews.

Risk management reviews typically look at all safety-related elements of an outdoor program. Some organizations choose to combine a risk management review with assessments of how well the organization meets non-safety objectives such as education, recreation, or other human development programmatic outcomes.

High-quality external review services may be available from companies or agencies that specialize in providing risk management reviews for outdoor programs. These enterprises should typically have staff with extensive outdoor experience and training in conducting risk management reviews. They may also have well-developed systems and infrastructure for performing such reviews. Candidates for external reviews should be assessed for reviewer qualifications, scope of work, review format, assessment criteria, and history of past performance prior to hiring. It can also be useful to switch external review contractors from time to time in order to obtain varying perspectives.

In some situations, external program reviews are conducted on a peer review basis, with program managers from other organizations that provide similar programming conducting the reviews. These peer reviews are likely to reach the quality of reviews led by experienced specialists only if they are rigorously conducted by qualified reviewers using a well-developed assessment system and without a conflict of interest.

19.4. REVIEW STRUCTURE

Reviews, whether internal or external, benefit from a well-defined structure and approach. External reviewers normally provide an established framework for how the review will occur. Internal reviews can be based off of any suitable template available from resources internal or external to the organization. New Zealand's adventure tourism and commercial outdoor recreation industry resource SupportAdventure, for example, provides review resources intended to be compliant with New Zealand regulatory requirements.

There are many possible review structures that achieve appropriate results. A typical framework might be as follows:

1. The organization conducts a self-evaluation of its performance relative to a comprehensive array of risk management standards (Figure 19.2). An assessment of if and how each standard is met is provided, and evidentiary materials are made available.

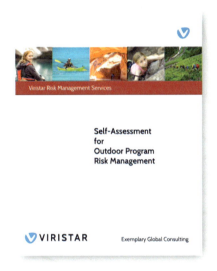

Figure 19.2. Risk Management Reviews often begin with a comprehensive self-assessment to pre-defined standards.

2. Reviewers read the self-evaluation, review supporting evidence, and make initial conclusions for each standard as to the extent to which there is suitable evidence to demonstrate compliance with the standard. Examples of evidence include, but are not limited to, job descriptions, emergency plans, safety policies and procedures, incident reports, Risk Management Committee meeting minutes, personnel file contents, safety reports, installation inspections, incident reviews, participant screening documents, staff training information, equipment management documentation, insurance certificates, and vehicle use and maintenance logs. It is standard for hundreds of pages of material to be reviewed.

3. Reviewers gather further information by interviewing select key individuals. These persons may include program managers, executives, activity leaders, Risk Management Committee members, a medical advisor, or others. Interviews may be done in person or telephonically.

4. Reviewers perform on-site evaluations, including:
   a. Inspection of program equipment and facilities, including vehicles, applicable buildings, and outdoor gear and supplies
   b. Inspection of activity sites
   c. Observation of outdoor programs in action (Figure 19.3)
   d. Interviews of staff, participants, or other stakeholders, not previously conducted

5. Reviewers use information from the site visit to complete their assessment. At the conclusion of the site visit, a verbal report is typically given to the organization's senior management. The report describes the review process and notes which standards have and have not been met. In some cases, a prioritization may be provided regarding unmet standards or unsafe conditions. The organization has an opportunity for immediate response to the verbal findings to ask questions, make comments, or provide additional information if needed.

6. A written report, documenting the findings first outlined in the verbal report, is generated by reviewers in the days following, and provided to the organization.

Figure 19.3. A site visit often involves observation of risk management with groups in the field.

19.5. FOLLOW-UP

After the organization's leadership receives the written report of findings from the review team, follow-up is required. Unless the report finds everything is perfectly in order, an action plan for addressing areas of deficiency should be developed and implemented (shown in figure 19.4). The plan should specify who is accountable for implementation, and set priorities and timelines.

It can also be useful to share the report findings and the implementation plan widely throughout the organization—including Board, Risk Management Committee, and all levels of staff. The information serves as an educational tool and builds the case for investing in improvements to the organization's risk management infrastructure.

In the service of continuous improvement, between review periods, the organization should continue to look for changing standards, new technologies, emerging best practices, and other opportunities to improve its management of risk.

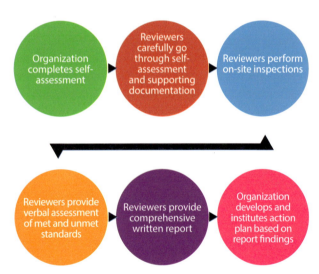

Figure 19.4. The Risk Management Review process.

19.6. LIMITATIONS

Although risk management reviews can be of great benefit, several limitations inherent to reviews should be kept in mind:

1. Reviews do not completely assess every component of an organization. Only a sample of equipment is inspected; only a small number of programs in action may be visited; only select incident reports, personnel files and other documents on file are inspected. Reviews aim to provide a reasonable sense of the organization's practices rather than provide total surveillance.
2. The integrity of reviews depends on the willingness of program staff to share openly. It may not be possible for reviews to overcome intentional deception or other fraud if it should be present.
3. In the sometimes small community of outdoor professionals, there can be a conflict of interest in which reviewers may not wish to criticize or displease their colleagues in the outdoor industry. Reviewers must strive to be candid, accurate, and professional, and neither excessively harsh nor overly forgiving.
4. Although standards are well-developed in some situations (for example, with some outdoor adventure settings in Australia and New Zealand), in other cases the standards against which an organization will be judged are unclear. In most situations, standards have an element of subjectivity and can be interpreted in different ways.
5. Reviews are non-continuous and therefore provide an assessment only at one point in time. If risk management systems decay following the review, the review may no longer accurately represent the organization's risk management performance.

Despite these limitations, however, risk management reviews can be of great benefit. When done well, risk management reviews have an extraordinary power to help an organization understand its strengths, prioritize areas for improvement, and maintain excellence in risk management.

Chapter Summary

1. Risk management reviews provide a close look at the strengths and growth areas of an organization's risk management system.

2. They are also known as safety audits, inspections, or assessments, or by other terms.

3. Requirements for risk management reviews vary geographically.

4. Norms around review frequency, who conducts reviews, and other aspects also vary.

5. Risk management reviews differ from incident reviews, installation inspections, and accreditation reviews.

6. Reviews assess all safety-related aspects of an organization, and compare them to standards.

7. Reviews may occur every 18 months to five years, depending on circumstances.

8. Reviews can be led internally by organizational staff and volunteers, or externally by outside specialists.

9. Organizations may alternate between doing internal and external reviews.

10. Peer reviews can be effective if criteria are met.

11. A typical review process involves: organization completes self-assessment; reviewers go over self-assessment and supporting documentation; reviewers conduct a site view and interviews; reviewers provide verbal and written reports, and organization follows up on report findings.

12. Limitations to reviews include: spot checks cannot catch all issues; fraud may be undetectable, and management of risk may change after the review.

MEDIA RELATIONS

CHAPTER 20

LEARNING OBJECTIVES

1. The differing priorities of news media and your organization
2. Consequences of not working effectively with news media
3. Information news media seek when a newsworthy incident occurs
4. How to help news media do their job
5. Selecting and training authorized spokespeople for your organization
6. Framing your story with messaging points
7. Projecting a caring image and telling the truth
8. Avoiding common media pitfalls
9. Writing press releases
10. Conducting interviews
11. Preparing for the media in advance
12. Bringing in external resources
13. Working with others who are providing news media content
14. The role of an emergency action plan and increased staffing in media response
15. State-controlled media

20.1. INTRODUCTION

When a major incident occurs, expect news media to pay attention. How the media portray the story, and how their story affects your organization, depends in part on how well you work with media outlets.

An aim of news businesses typically is to tell a compelling story about a newsworthy topic that draws in consumers (and ultimately advertisers). Their role is not to tell your side of the story, share the truth as you see it, or act exclusively in your best interests. The media may focus on the most sensational aspects of the story. They may omit information about your excellent safety record and risk management procedures, the inherent nature of some risks, or other items that you think are an important part of the story and that might help maintain a positive perception of your organization by the public.

Your organization's reputation and business interests can be unnecessarily damaged if media relations are not managed well.

If the story that emerges about your incident has negative elements and is not informed by the truthful and well-crafted information you have to share, expect that current and potential future customers may avoid your business. Permits or licenses necessary for business operations may be more difficult or impossible to get. Other problems may arise. The consequences of poor media exposure can range from a minor inconvenience to the termination of your outdoor program.

Of course, if an organization is accurately exposed by the press as grossly negligent, then the shutting down of the program and pursuit of legal penalties may be well-justified.

In this chapter, we'll cover ideas on how to work effectively with the media. (The focus is on environments with a free press; for situations involving state-controlled media, see the noted on state-controlled media at the end of this chapter.)

20.2. WHAT MEDIA REPRESENTATIVES WANT

The public has a right to know about important topics that might affect them. News media are an important conduit for sharing relevant information with the public. When a newsworthy event occurs, the media will want to know:

1. **What** happened
2. **Where** it happened
3. **When** it happened
4. **Who** was involved (that is, names and personal data, not only of those injured, but rescuers and caregivers as well)

Expect the media to want background information on your organization, your programs, and your safety record.

Reporters can be working on very tight deadlines, sometimes of just a few hours. A prompt response to media inquiries helps reporters get a well-rounded picture and share the story in a timely way.

Figure 20.1. When a major incident occurs, news media will want information.

20.3. GUIDELINES FOR WORKING WITH THE MEDIA

20.3.1. Assist the Media with Responsible Reporting

Responsible news outlets play a valuable role in society. You can help them do their job while looking after the legitimate interests of your organization by following these guidelines:

1. Provide the media the what, where, when and who of the incident.
2. Be accurate. Do not guess.

3. If you don't know the answer to a media inquiry, say so. Try to get back to the reporter promptly, ideally in the next few minutes, either with the requested information, or a referral to an alternate source who might be able to provide the information.
4. Ensure that all media outlets and reporters have equal access to information.
5. Correct factual mistakes promptly.
6. Cooperate with the media. If information cannot be released, explain why. For example, perhaps names of the injured cannot be released because relatives have not yet been notified. Or the physician's orders may prohibit an interview of a survivor.
7. Be respectful, courteous, and attentive to reporters' deadlines.

20.3.2. Select Your Messengers

Tightly restrict who is authorized to communicate with the media. Normally only a small number of top people in the organization, such as CEO and chief communications executive, would be authorized. Articulate and charismatic individuals who are well-informed and have the appearance of trustworthiness are ideal.

All staff should be clearly aware of this strict requirement. Measures helpful to ensuring staff are clear on restrictions might include documenting the policy in an employee handbook or similar document, and having staff sign an agreement that they have read the handbook and agree to abide by its contents. Periodically reviewing the requirement, for example annually, may be useful, as can be reiterating the policy when a major incident occurs.

20.3.3. Train Your Messengers

Consider providing specialized training on how to work with the media to those in your organization authorized to communicate with news media. A variety of resources, such as conference workshops and online material, are available for this.

This kind of training may not be realistic for organizations with significantly restricted resources. Larger organizations, on the other hand, may have on staff communications specialists who are career professionals with relevant degrees and extensive media experience.

20.3.4. Tell Your Story

When to Communicate with Media Outlets. If the incident is not a major event, for instance a relatively small-scale internal incident only involving your own staff, you might choose to only respond to media inquiries rather than take the initiative to disseminate information.

In the case of a major and clearly newsworthy incident, affecting the community beyond your organization, it can be useful to promptly and proactively reach out to relevant news media.

Frame the Story. If you do not tell your side of the story, someone else will tell theirs. In order to help ensure that reports are accurate and appropriately favorable to your organization, a well-developed and truthful message, thoughtfully crafted and delivered, is important.

Develop Message Points. Carefully craft message points—generally, three—and stick to them. Key points for initial response with a disaster involving ill or injured participants might be:

1. **Our primary concern is for our participants.** This sets a compassionate tone.
2. **Our Situation Response Plan worked as designed, and participants received medical care.** This highlights positive elements of the emergency.
3. **We are working with the authorities to determine the facts and cause.** This shows you have nothing to hide, and helps you avoid having to say 'I don't know.'

The answer, then, to <u>every question you are asked is one of your three key points</u>.

Reporters may pluck out the most interesting or unusual bits of what you say and repeat it out of context. It is therefore crucial that you have good discipline in sticking to your message points. <u>If you don't want it to be part of the story, don't say it.</u>

Project Caring and Concern. This can positively affect the tone of the story that appears. Emphasize any thoughtful, humanitarian acts taken by the organization. For example, you might talk about how the director visited the scene of the accident, how counseling is provided to those affected, or that the Board Chair visited the family.

Tell the Truth. Not only is this the moral imperative, but also a later investigation may uncover your deception with disastrous consequences. Telling the truth does not necessarily mean full disclosure.

Provide Background. Along with providing the what, where, when and who of the incident, provide background information on your organization. This generally includes the organization's mission, history, activities, and risk management practices. This material should be prepared in advance of any incident.

20.3.5. Circumstances to Avoid

Practices for avoiding traps, minimizing unwanted liability exposure, and responding to errors include the following.

1. Avoid speculation, personal views and opinion, and emotional responses. Expect media to ask for them, however. Stick to the facts.
2. Don't let reporters guide your language. If a reporter says, "So, you're saying…" your best response may be, "No; let me be clear:…" Do not repeat inaccurate information, even to dispute it.
3. Do not allow yourself to be provoked.
4. Do not assign responsibility for an incident; criticize conduct, policy or equipment, or provide estimates of property damage, before speaking with legal counsel.
5. Do not provide names of victims until family members are notified.
6. Do not provide information regarding the nature of injury or illness prior to diagnosis by a licensed medical physician.
7. If media has been given erroneous information, provide correct information as soon as possible. If a media report is in error, contact the relevant reporter and courteously provide the correct information.

20.3.6. Media Channels

Press Release. For major incidents likely to elicit the interest of the news media, proactively send out press releases, emphasizing your established talking points. Distribute the press release to your pre-established list of media contacts, typically via email or relevant messaging app.

A press release is an official statement written in a professional voice describing the who, what, why and where of a newsworthy item such as a major incident. It typically includes a bit of background information relevant to the topic (for example, about your organization, accomplishments, and safety record). It often contains one or more quotes. It is concise—usually no more than 500 words—and written in easy-to-understand language in a standard press release format. A good press release provides a factual, ready-for-publication story about the news item.

Consider having text, image and any video information packaged in formats friendly for the news outlet's multiple platforms: website and various social media accounts, each of which has its own optimal format.

Social Media. Provide information via your website and social media accounts. This information might be distributed at the same time that your press material is to be released.

Interviews. A variety of approaches can help you have an effective interview. See Figure 20.2, Interview Tips.

1. **Prepare.** Ensure you have all the available information. Anticipate what questions might be asked. Practice.
2. **Use multiple ways to say the same thing.** For each of your three talking points, develop three concise responses that help communicate that point. This helps you get the same message across multiple times, in slightly different ways. Ensure the responses can be clearly, crisply delivered in fewer than 10 or 20 seconds.
3. **Key points first.** As with a news release, begin with what is most important.
4. **Use plain language.** Speak in terms people unfamiliar with your field can understand. Talking about Class III water and a single-pitch top-belay will just confuse and frustrate the audience.
5. **No "no comment."** This sounds evasive. Explain why you aren't able to comment: "We're currently gathering that information and will provide it as soon as we're able." "Our policy is not to comment on pending litigation."
6. **Don't speak off the record.** The information may be misused and traced back to you.
7. **Stay calm.** Don't argue, even if the reporter is provocative.
8. **Stay on message.** Stick to your messaging points. Even if an unrelated issue is brought up, guide the conversation back to your themes. "That's an interesting question, and I think that what's really important here is…" or "Well, first, let me say…"
9. **Use sound bites.** Develop memorable phrases and short, catchy ways of summarizing your main message. These can be used as quotes or as broadcast sound bites.

10. **Summarize.** Reinforce your three core messages by concisely restating them as the interview draws to an end.

Figure 20.2. Interview tips.

Other Channels. Press conferences, media advisories, and other formats for providing information can be used as appropriate. Press conferences are rare outside of major and widely publicized incidents.

20.3.7.   Prepare in Advance

If possible, build relationships with media representatives and institutions well before a newsworthy incident occurs. Regularly send out press releases and other media communications about good-news stories. Invite reporters to events. This level of media contact may be unrealistic for smaller organizations. When reporters contact you, however, use that as an opportunity to build a collaborative, mutually beneficial, respectful, long-term relationship.

Assemble relevant media contacts in advance of a newsworthy incident. Contacts include reporters, editors, news directors, and producers for local newspapers, broadcast stations, and news agencies (newswires). Your list may also include industry media such as prominent bloggers or staff of industry publications. Keep a record of the names of media outlets and relevant staff along with their contact information. Since staff turn over and the media landscape is dynamic, regularly update the list.

As discussed earlier, prepare generic incident-related messaging points in advance of incidents. When an incident occurs, draft messaging points specific to the incident, and multiple ways of saying each messaging point.

Prepare background information to provide to news media. At a minimum, this would be a couple of paragraphs about your organization, risk management system, and safety record. A more extensive press kit might include a marketing brochure, organizational fact sheet, recent annual report, copies of recent press, and access to photo and video resources.

If members of the media visit the incident scene or your offices or facilities, have a plan to keep them away from sensitive areas and persons such as actively working emergency response personnel. Plan for conducting interviews in locations without visual, auditory, or other distractions or disturbances.

20.3.8. Aim for a Short Story

Provide as much detail as possible, as early as possible. This helps make the incident a short one-day story rather than something that continues for days. A continuing series of headlines and features dragging out over days and weeks keeps your unfortunate incident in the minds of the public longer.

20.3.9. Employ Outside Expertise

In complex situations, enlist legal counsel and public relations advisors to provide guidance on what information should be released, and how.

In a major incident, consider contracting with a crisis management company to provide expert guidance and communications support.

If your outdoor program is part of a larger institution—for instance, a recreation department within a larger government agency, an outdoor activities office of a major university, or a chapter or branch of a national outdoor organization—access communications, legal, and other specialists in that larger institution to support your media communications.

20.4. MANAGING OTHER MEDIA OUTLETS

If the incident occurs in an area (such as a national park or waters regulated by a maritime authority) managed by a government agency or similar authority, communications and public information officers from the agency may communicate with news media and the public regarding the incident. Search and rescue authorities, law enforcement agencies, and other authorities may release information as well. Be aware of what these agencies are communicating, respect their authority, and avoid providing conflicting information.

Personal social media posts from participants and bystanders can broadcast unedited information about an incident with great rapidity. Management of information flowing from a scene via social media and similar channels is important. Consider providing guidance to participants about what is and is not appropriate to share, and managing the scene to reduce unhelpful bystander social media.

Promptly contact parents, guardians, sending institutions (in the case of corporate, school group or similar customer types), and upper administrators in the outdoor program's parent institution (such as a university with an outdoor club), as applicable, with relevant incident information. This helps avoid a situation in which those persons learn about the incident from social media or from family members of participants posting on social media.

20.5. OTHER FACTORS

Emergencies are characterized by the presence of insufficient information. In order to best respond to requests for information from the media and others, it is useful to have a good emergency action plan. The plan should have provisions to provide for the best possible information flow between persons at incident sites and with those affected, and spokespeople.

Be prepared to rapidly increase your organizational capacity to manage communications through social media and other channels, work with parents, sending institutions, and concerned other customers. Adding additional staff resources to your communications efforts for as many hours or days as needed will help reduce stress, diminish confusion, and improve the flow of information.

20.6. CONCLUSION

News media play an important and valuable role in society. This does not extend, however, to a responsibility to help your organization, or present information about you in the most favorable light. But by working cooperatively and skillfully with media outlets, you maximize the probability that media exposure of your incident will be as accurate as possible and the most favorable to your organization.

News media is not best considered your friend or your enemy, but an important element in the business landscape. By managing interactions with media well, you can support their legitimate needs, the legitimate interests of your organization, and the public interest.

State-controlled Media

The rules are different when news media are controlled by the state rather than acting as a free press not subject to direct government control. (Reporters without Borders' World Press Freedom Index and others provide nation-by-nation rankings of press freedom.)

When the news media is state-controlled, the aims of the state may be to promote stability and ensure the state is perceived well—for example, by highlighting the quick and efficient response of rescue teams, or by publicizing a forceful crackdown on those immediately responsible for the incident.

In the case of a major incident, expect the police to conduct an investigation, the results of which may be influenced by state authorities. The state-controlled media may then release information from the police report that meets the state's aims for stability and civic harmony. At no point does your organization initiate contact with the news media.

Chapter Summary

1. The media will be interested in your major incident, but their goals are different from yours.

2. Skillful interaction with news media can benefit your reputation and organization.

3. When an incident occurs, news media will want to know the what, where, when and who of the incident, and background information on your organization.

4. Help news media by providing accurate, timely information to all media agencies.

5. Carefully select and train media spokespeople.

6. In an incident, craft three main message points, and a few ways to communicate each one. Communicate only these message points.

7. Be truthful, and portray a compassionate, caring image.

8. Avoid speculation, opinion, or emotional responses.

9. Do not assign blame, provide names of victims prematurely, or make your own medical diagnoses.

10. Correct factual errors.

11. Distribute concise, factual press releases in standard format to media contacts.

12. Disseminate information via website and social media channels along with press releases.

13. In interviews, prepare in advance; focus on core messages; use easy-to-understand language; avoid "no comment," and don't speak off the record.

14. Prepare for news media in advance by building relationships with media representatives, developing messaging points, and creating background information.

15. Attempt to keep news reports to one day in length by promptly providing comprehensive information.

16. Employ legal, public relations, and other specialists as needed.

17. Coordinate with government authorities who are communicating with the media, and manage unofficial social media posters as possible.

18. Develop plans for good communication between the incident scene and administrative headquarters during emergencies.

DOCUMENTATION

21.1. INTRODUCTION

Documentation provides an important official record of two things: 1) what should be done, and 2) what has been done. The former is the collected wisdom of others regarding best practice. The latter shows us the extent to which that good guidance was faithfully followed.

Examples of documentation include, but are not limited to, written material recorded on paper, electronic, or other media; images, audio & video, and electronically stored information such as databases. Our focus here is primarily here on the written word.

Figure 21.1. Paper documentation is being replaced by electronic files.

21.1.1. Expectations

Legal requirements vary widely by jurisdiction. Some documentation is required by law, such as in some situations in the UK, documented risk assessments.

A certain level of documentation is expected in order to conform to outdoor industry standards. The presence of safety policies and procedures for conducting outdoor activities is an example.

In this chapter we'll discuss principles of documentation that are generally applicable. Details may vary for your particular situation.

21.2. DOCUMENTATION: PROVIDES DURABLE, RELIABLE GUIDANCE ON WHAT TO DO

The first of the two principal purposes of documentation we'll discuss here is the role of documentation in defining what should be done.

Risk management systems should not be individually people-dependent, as staff at some point leave the organization. Rather, knowledge of systems should be based in the organization and in its records, not solely in people's heads.

Similarly, risk management practices should not solely exist as oral history. Relying exclusively on verbal transmission of expectations is insufficient, as memories are imperfect.

And risk management guidance should not be contained in a flurry of scattered memos or random slips of paper with no chain of custody that may be misplaced or forgotten about.

The most appropriate reservoir of risk management guidance is in securely and permanently stored documents in clearly established locations where document integrity can be assured. This can take the form of an original field manual, employee handbook, risk management plan, or other document on a secure and backed-up computer server, with printed or electronic copies available to staff so as to be easily accessible when needed. Figure 21.2 below outlines certain documentation practices for risk management documentation.

As a general principle, if you want outdoor program personnel to verifiably and durably know something about risk management, it should be written down. When coupled with high-quality, verifiable, repeated training and reinforcement, this maximizes the probability that the risk management information will be retained and appropriately used.

Important Outdoor Program Practices

- Not just in people's heads
- Not just communicated verbally
- Not distributed by disjointed memos or updates

+ All critical information comprehensively recorded
+ In written or other documentary format
+ Consolidated in central locations such as handbooks, policy registers or comprehensive plans
+ Easily accessible to those who need it
+ Essential safety-critical information highlighted
+ Version control clarifies which revision is in effect

Figure 21.2. Select principles regarding documentation of important outdoor program practices.

21.3. DOCUMENTATION: PROVIDES A RECORD OF WHAT WAS DONE

The second of the two principal purposes of documentation is to provide a record of what was done—and not done. This can help to show if the organization's duty of care was met.

Examples include, but are not limited to:

1. **Training sign-in sheets** proving people were exposed to the content of the training.
2. **Signed documents** saying that staff have read safety-critical written materials, for example an employee handbook, risk management plan, field manual, readings required to be reviewed by activity leaders prior to each season, or the most recent annual safety report.
3. **Test results:** written evidence of passing written or practical exams such as driver tests.
4. **Check-off sheets** completed by a qualified person attesting they have observed an individual and that individual has been assessed to have the requisite knowledge, skills, and attitudes to conduct a certain outdoor activity or lead groups in a certain activity area.
5. **Certificates** or other evidence of passing a training. (In order for the certificate to be credible, the training should have a written curriculum with goals, lesson plans, and assessments.)
6. **Safety briefing checkoff sheets** where checked boxes record that each topic was mentioned during a safety briefing, and where the sheet is signed and dated.
7. **Rope logs**, showing inspection, usage and climbing rope retirement per organization's retirement schedule.
8. **SOAP notes and incident reports** for medical and other incident recording.

21.4. PUTTING IT TOGETHER: DOCUMENTATION SYSTEM IN ACTION

Let's consider a couple of examples of a comprehensive documentation system in an outdoor program context.

21.4.1. Example 1: Training On Emergency Procedures for New Activity Leaders

A chain of documentation gives guidance for the training of new staff on emergency procedures.

Documentation Describing What to Do. In this case, four documents provide the information:

1. **A written safety policy** stating that the outdoor programs' staff shall be adequately trained for their jobs.
2. **A written training plan** describing training requirements for all staff. The plan indicates that newly hired activity leaders are to be trained in emergency procedures before they work with participants.

3. **A written training syllabus** (outline of topics) for the new staff training noting the subjects covered. Emergency procedures are included in the listing of topics addressed.
4. **The actual emergency procedure.** This may be included in the risk management section of the activity leader field manual.

Documentation Showing What Was Done

1. **A written lesson plan** may provide detailed information on the emergency plan training. Alternately, it may be sufficient to have an unwritten practice of providing a copy of the plan, discussing it, and providing an opportunity for questions.
2. **A sign-in sheet** for the training shows who was physically present for the training.
3. **Finally, a document signed and dated** by the trainee states they were provided with a copy of the risk management system documentation for activity leaders, including emergency procedures, and that they have read it, understood it, and agree to comply with it.

This can provide convincing evidence that staff were successfully trained in the cognitive aspects of emergency procedures. Similarly documented participation in practical training such as an emergency simulation may meet the psychomotor training requirement and complete the training process for the season or the year, until re-training begins.

Documentation as Legal Protection: a Case Study

A participant on a guided whitewater kayaking trip in the US through his own fault was cut on the leg by a sharp rock while carrying his kayak. The guide properly cleaned and bandaged the wound and advised the client to get the injury checked out at a medical facility. This was documented on a signed and dated incident report. About six months later, the outdoor program got a letter from a lawyer. The letter claimed the boater's wound became infected and required significant and expensive treatment. The lawyer blamed the kayaking program, and demanded thousands of dollars. A copy of the incident report showing that the incident was handled properly by the kayak guide was sent to the lawyer by the outdoor program's administrative staff. The claim was dropped and organization never heard from the lawyer again.

21.4.2. Example 2: Driver Training

Documentation Describing What to Do. As with the emergency procedure training described above, a written policy states staff shall be adequately trained for their job. The organization's written training plan indicates that approved drivers must, among other things, successfully complete a driver training. The organization's Vehicle Manual specifically states that as part of the training, drivers must read the Vehicle Manual, discuss its contents with the transportation manager, agree to comply with its contents, and in addition pass written and practical vehicle operation exams.

Documentation Showing What Was Done. A document signed and dated by the vehicle operator states they have read the Vehicle Manual, understood it, and agree to abide by its contents. This document is on file. A copy of the written test and a check-off sheet completed by the transportation manager demonstrating successful completion of the practical on-the-road driving assessment are also on file.

Figure 21.3. Documentation must be securely stored for years in case it is needed to verify compliance.

21.4.3. Conclusion

The documentary links described in these two examples create the necessary chain of verifiable proper action. They demonstrate that the outdoor program has proper safeguards such as appropriate training. And they demonstrate that the person has verifiably and successfully completed the required training.

One step in helping ensure that outdoor program activity leaders understand appropriate risk management practices is to have all relevant information documented or referenced in the activity leader field manual. The same principle can apply to other activity leader information (such as outdoor leadership and programmatic material). It can also apply to information for those in managerial positions.

21.5. APPLICATIONS

21.5.1. Learning and Improvement

The primary application of risk management documentation is to help ensure the organization conducts quality programs that meet safety performance objectives. The ability to continually learn and improve is an important element of this aim. For instance, documenting incidents enables the organization's current and future staff, and potentially others in the outdoor industry, to learn from those incidents.

This including documenting errors made, and ideas about how the incident could have been avoided. In the case of serious incidents, thorough and searching incident reviews with comprehensive written reports can also help the organization and others learn and improve.

21.5.2. Legal Defense

When an accident occurs, good documentation showing that staff acted appropriately can help provide a defense against legal charges of wrongdoing such as a claim of negligence.

Simply stating that a certain thing—such as inspecting a first aid kit for completeness of inventory prior to embarking on a wilderness expedition—was done is less strong than having a written document—such as a signed and dated first aid kit inventory check form—showing that the thing in question was done. Without such documentation, it can be more likely to appear that what should have been done was not actually completed. The saying "if you didn't write it down, it didn't happen" roughly expresses this concept.

In some parts of the world, during a legal proceeding, plaintiff's attorneys will dig deeply into the organization's written and unwritten practices. This is done in an attempt to find weaknesses in an organization's risk management systems that can be used to convince a jury of the organization's wrongdoing. Any weakness discovered by opposing attorneys may be pounced upon, brought up for close examination, and repeatedly and aggressively displayed as evidence of the outdoor program's guilt. Good documentation showing that the organization provided appropriate risk management guidance and that the guidance was followed is a powerful tool against these attacks.

In some legal contexts, the smallest fault or evidence of incomplete documentation may be seized upon, magnified far out of proportion, and ruthlessly and repeatedly used as a bludgeon to discredit the organization and its staff. In these situations it is wise to assume that very experienced, articulate and capable attorneys on the opposing side of a lawsuit will attempt to exploit any absence of documentation in an attempt to show wrongdoing. Their job is not to uncover the truth or promote justice, but, within the boundaries of the law, to win, and to ensure the other side loses. These attorneys often are intelligent and capable and have devoted their entire careers to being able to professionally destroy their opponents. They are often very good at what they do.

21.6. LIMITATIONS

Documentation has clear value. All the policies and procedures in the world, however, are not useful if they are not followed. In accordance with the systemic nature of risk management, documentation is only effective when accompanied by a culture of safety, suitable training, and other factors that help ensure that appropriate policies and procedures are actually followed.

In addition, the presence of abundant documentation cannot be expected to exonerate an organization if it has, in breach of its duty of care, caused harm to those for whom it is responsible.

Finally, documentation can provide guidance for addressing reasonably anticipated risks, but it is not possible to document every aspect of every risk management consideration to the tiniest degree. This would be overwhelming. Documentation is best seen as one tool that relies on good judgment and other factors to help ensure quality risk management.

21.7. CAUTIONS

Excessive documentation can lead to a culture of compliance where staff focus on completing paperwork rather than providing the best possible outdoor experience. A suitable balance between written structure and professional judgment must be found. The presence of hundreds of pages of program documentation can be perfectly appropriate. However, the material must be well organized, and users must be trained on how to access the information. Users should also be clear on what elements of the documentation must be absorbed into memory, such as where to find and how to operate emergency equipment. They should likewise understand which parts of a field manual can be referenced at leisure in the manner of an encyclopedia, for example, procedures for camp stove repair.

Outdoor adventurers do not likely enter outdoor professions due to an abiding love for processing paperwork. Nevertheless, some amount of reading materials and filling out forms is inevitable and must be done.

In the section above on continuous learning and improvement, the value of documenting mistakes was discussed. Although some may be concerned that documenting failures can lead to liability, it is generally agreed that understanding what went wrong, sharing that appropriately, and learning from it is appropriate practice, where the benefits outweigh risks.

Interrogation

If a serious incident occurs, a lawsuit may follow. Judicial procedures vary widely around the world. However, as part of the legal proceedings, outdoor program managers may be questioned by attorneys from the opposing side.

Suppose an accident has occurred during an activity, and there is a question of whether or not the activity leader in charge provided an appropriate safety briefing before the activity. Solely on the narrow question of the safety briefing under consideration, you might anticipate being asked questions somewhat similar to the following:

1. Do you require a safety briefing to be given before each activity?
2. Did you specify what should be in that briefing?
3. Did you provide training about the requirement and the contents of the briefing? When?
4. Was the activity leader in question present at that training?
5. Do you have an established procedure for what to do if an activity leader misses the training?
6. How did you determine that the training was well-designed and effective?
7. At the activity site, was the briefing provided?
8. Did the briefing contain all of the necessary information?
9. Was the briefing conducted appropriately—was it audible; were people were paying attention when it was given? How do you know?

10. Was it made clear to the participants they should take the safety briefing seriously? How?
11. How do you assess if participants heard and understood the safety briefing?
12. Was the incident subject present at the safety briefing?
13. How did you determine what should go into the safety briefing?
14. Did you review the contents of the safety briefing? How often do you do this?
15. Whom did you consult in deciding what to include in the safety briefing?
16. Have staff always given the full safety briefing?
17. Do you have any disciplinary consequences established if an activity leader fails to deliver a complete safety briefing? What are they? Have they ever been administered? When?
18. Do you have any way of knowing if a staff person in the field does not complete the full safety briefing?
19. Have any staff ever given an incomplete safety briefing?
20. Do you feel it's acceptable to not know if your staff are giving incomplete safety briefings?
21. Does the safety briefing cover all the potential risks and hazards of the activity?
22. Why are some risk and hazards not covered?
23. How did you determine which risks and hazards to include in the safety briefing?
24. Did you or anyone else speak with the activity leader about the importance of giving this safety briefing? Who? When?
25. Have all the safety briefings you've given been complete?
26. Have you ever given an incomplete safety briefing?

Some questions may appear unreasonable, but they may still be asked. Questions may be designed to make your outdoor program look bad. This might be done to make the jury less likely to find in your favor, following the idea that "perception is reality." Questioning can go on for days and days in a legal proceeding. Good documentation can help you show your organization is doing the right things.

Chapter Summary

1. Documentation provides an official record of what should be done, and what has been done.

2. Documentation can be in written, audio, video, still image or other forms.

3. Legal requirements for documentation vary per jurisdiction.

4. Outdoor industry standards require certain documentation.

5. Documentation should be securely and durably recorded in established locations.

6. Examples of documents showing what should be done include field manuals, employee handbooks, and risk management plans.

7. Having written documentation on a subject is useful if it is important for individuals to have knowledge of that subject.

8. Examples of documents showing what was done include sign-in sheets, check-off forms, rope logs and incident reports.

9. Documentation of incidents and mistakes helps organizations learn and improve.

10. Documentary evidence that appropriate practices were followed can help in legal defense.

11. Documents alone are not helpful without a culture and system to ensure they are used.

12. Documentation may not absolve one from negligence.

13. Excessive documentation should be avoided.

14. Documenting failures may alter exposure to liability; it has value in promoting continuous improvement.

ACCREDITATION

22.1. UNDERSTANDING ACREDITATION

Accreditation is recognition by an accrediting body that an entity conforms to widely accepted standards. The process of applying for and receiving accreditation is generally voluntary. (In contrast, licensing, permitting, and other legal and regulatory compliance is mandatory.) Accreditation can be provided by a government body or, more often, by a private entity, commonly a not-for-profit institution.

In some parts of the world, accreditation has been formalized for institutions in certain industries such as hospitals and universities (and specialty departments within them). In some of these situations accrediting bodies must be reviewed and approved by governmental authorities. This is generally not the case with organizations that accredit outdoor programs.

22.2. THE VALUE OF ACCREDITATION

Accreditation of outdoor programs helps ensure that the program is of good quality, meeting socially acceptable standards for program design, safety, and ethics. It indicates that the organization is likely to provide well-crafted experiences that meet organizational goals around education, recreation, and other outcomes, and manages risk in a reasonable and prudent manner. Accreditation from a high-quality accrediting institution is of real value. However, accreditation comes with limitations. It is not a guarantee of safety. It does not guarantee that every participant will have a positive experience. It provides assurances of quality at the time of accreditation but a guarantee of future quality.

Accreditation schemes are generally voluntary in nature and employ standards set by industry. Accreditation systems are only as useful, then, as their designers and implementers craft them to be. When self-regulatory accreditation or similar schemes are found to be deficient, they may be replaced by mandatory government oversight. This occurred in the United Kingdom in the 1990s after multiple fatalities on a boating program exposed deficiencies in outdoor program self-regulation.

Accreditation's value ultimately depends on the extent to which the entity being accredited genuinely seeks to use the accreditation process as a means to improve the quality of their program. Accreditors may be unable to overcome intentional deception on the part of entities seeking accreditation. And since accreditation indicates standards conformity at the time of accreditation, a quality ongoing assessment scheme on the part of the accreditor and sufficient efforts by the accredited entity to maintain adherence to standards are both necessary to insure the integrity and value of the accreditation process.

22.3. ACCREDITING ENTITIES FOR OUTDOOR PROGRAMS

Accreditation in outdoor programs is not widespread. Many organizations remain unaccredited, and the accreditation concept in the industry is dynamic and undergoing maturation. As the value of high-quality accreditation increases in visibility to consumers, providers and other stakeholders in the field of organized outdoor experiences, the role of accreditation can be expected to grow.

The Association for Experiential Education (AEE, Figure 22.1) developed accreditation standards for experiential adventure programs in 1994 and provides a rigorous accreditation process for outdoor programs around the world. AEE also provides accreditation for outdoor behavioral healthcare organizations providing wilderness therapy programming. (Disclosure: the author is a volunteer accreditation reviewer with AEE.)

Figure 22.1. Accreditation by AEE for experiential adventure programming and outdoor behavioral healthcare.

In the UK, the Adventure Activities Industry Advisory Committee coordinates the Adventuremark safety accreditation scheme (figure 22.2) for UK entities providing adventure activities not covered by national regulation.

Figure 22.2. Adventuremark logo for UK adventure programs.

Figure 22.3 the bfu, or Swiss Council for Accident Prevention, helps establish safety standards for outdoor adventure programs in Switzerland.

In Switzerland, the Federal Office of Sport (BASPO) is working to identify a certifying body that will provide government-recognized certification for adventure programs, with the support of the bfu (Beratungsstelle für Unfallverhütung, Swiss Council for Accident Prevention) (figure 22.3).

Accreditation services are also provided by a number of associations, often national in scope, for specific outdoor activities such as climbing and outdoor camps.

A variety of bodies also provide accreditation or certification for practitioners—educators, facilitators, guides and other outdoor activity leaders.

22.4. THE ACCREDITATION PROCESS

Organizational accreditation processes often share common features:

1. **Self-study.** The organization compares itself to published standards.
2. **Peer review.** Other professionals in the field assess the organization against standards.
3. **Site visit.** Accreditation reviewers examine the organization and its programming first-hand.

4. **Decision.** The accrediting body decides to confer full, limited, or no accreditation.
5. **Monitoring and oversight.** The accrediting body performs limited ongoing assessment during the accreditation period.

The self-study is a significant element of an effective accreditation process. This self-examination helps program managers look in depth at their organization's strengths and weaknesses. This process can in some cases provide an organization a more detailed picture of the organization's conformity to standards than can be made in a relatively brief visit by on-site accreditation reviewers, who may be exposed to only a partial sampling of the organization's activities and systems.

The process of applying for initial accreditation, conducting the self-study, completing the site visit, and decision-making can take months or more than a year for rigorous accreditation schemes. Re-accreditation is often more straightforward. Accreditation can last for two to 10 years, with regular reporting to the accrediting body during the period of accreditation.

22.5. STRUCTURES SIMILAR TO ACCREDITATION

Chapter 3, Standards, contains broadly accepted professional practices that can be established, updated, and met through accreditation or without going through an accreditation process.

Chapter 4, Legal Considerations, discusses mandatory expectations. These may or may not be incorporated into accreditation schemes. Conformity with legal and regulatory expectations is obligatory.

In some countries reasonably comprehensive national regulation has been in place for years and may fill the place of accreditation partially or in full.

Certification and accreditation, depending on how the terms are used, can have a similar meaning and impact.

22.6. RELATION TO ACCREDITATION IN OTHER INDUSTRIES

In some parts of the world, hospitals and related healthcare organizations are widely or universally accredited by healthcare accrediting bodies. Some care facilities may offer outdoor behavioral healthcare such as wilderness therapy experiences as part of their patient care. However, the healthcare organization accreditation may not provide the specificity and detail offered by accreditation solely focused on outdoor behavioral health.

Similarly, many universities and other institutions of higher education are accredited by education accrediting agencies. Some of these colleges and universities may have outing clubs, outdoor orientation programs, outdoor adventure centers, or academic courses in outdoor or wilderness settings. As with outdoor programs embedded in larger healthcare organizations, these outdoor programs part of a larger academic institution will likely find a more useful and targeted accreditation process in one specifically designed for outdoor programs.

22.7. ASSESSING ACCREDITATION SCHEMES

When an outdoor program is considering pursuing accreditation, it can be useful to assess the prospective accreditation scheme to determine if it is of sufficient rigor and quality to provide reasonable assurance that accredited programs are meaningfully and verifiably held to relevant and appropriately high standards.

In conducting this assessment, factors to consider include the content of standards, the motivation and profit structure or business model of the accrediting entity, safeguards against deception or fraud, qualifications of reviewers, and the structure of the accreditation process. Accreditation reviews are ultimately not useful if they are conducted by reviewers inexperienced in the industry, have a peer review structure susceptible to conflict of interest, and—even for programs in need of improvement—invariably result in awarding of accredited status.

Indications that an accreditor is of profoundly insufficient quality may include:

1. Accreditation status can be purchased without assessment
2. Accreditation standards are not published
3. Only an unreasonably short time is required to receive accreditation
4. A site visit is not part of the accreditation process
5. Permanent accreditation status is granted

The potential of any accreditation process to improve an organization's performance and enhance the quality of the industry as a whole depends on the willingness of the organization seeking accreditation to engage in a searching self-study and use the accreditation process as a powerful opportunity for self-improvement. When an organization invests in fully participating in a high-quality accreditation process, the results—for the organization, its clients, and the broader community—can be of extraordinary value.

Chapter Summary

1. Accreditation is the authoritative recognition that an entity meets established standards.

2. Accreditation is generally voluntary, and conducted by not-for-profit accrediting agencies.

3. Accreditation provides assurance to potential customers and others about the quality of an entity's processes and end products.

4. Outdoor program accreditation does not ensure absolute safety or customer satisfaction.

5. Deficient accreditation schemes may be replaced by government regulation.

6. Accreditation is a developing aspect of the outdoor industry.

7. The Association for Experiential Education offers accreditation for experiential adventure programs; the Adventure Activities Industry Advisory Committee in the UK also accredits outdoor programs.

8. Accreditation is available for outdoor specialties such as climbing and outdoor camps.

9. Practitioner accreditation is available in some outdoor disciplines.

10. The accreditation process generally features a self-study, peer review, site visit, and monitoring.

11. Organizations that invest in a searching self-study gain more from accreditation than those who do not.

12. Accreditation can take months or years to achieve, and can last for two to 10 years.

13. Standards may or may not be covered by accreditation or regulatory regimes.

14. A large accredited institution such as a healthcare facility or university may benefit from a specific accreditation of its outdoor program.

15. Signs of a quality accreditation scheme include comprehensive and rigorous standards, absence of conflicts of interest, well-qualified reviewers, a well-developed and deliberative accreditation process, and the absence of "accreditation mill" characteristics.

16. Outdoor programs can find extraordinary value in deeply investing in a quality accreditation scheme.

CHAPTER 23

SEEING SYSTEMS

LEARNING OBJECTIVES

1. The systemic nature of outdoor program incident causation
2. Direct causes (of incidents), indirect causes, and their interconnections
3. The management of risk as itself a complex systems issue
4. Underlying risks influencing direct risks which lead to incidents
5. Direct risk domains: Culture, Activities and Program Areas, Staff, Equipment, Participants, Subcontractors, Transportation, Business Administration
6. Underlying risk domains: Government, Society, Outdoor Industry, Business
7. Accident causation classifications systems and ongoing research
8. Interactions of risk domains
9. Considering direct and underlying risks, and their cumulative impact
10. The "pre-mortem" failure avoidance technique
11. Systems thinking in risk domains and risk management tools and systems
12. Strategic risks
13. Unintended consequences
14. Resiliency as a risk management tool

The 10 teenagers and their teacher hiked up the narrow steep-walled canyon on a rainy New Zealand afternoon, splashing through the stream that ran between towering cliff walls. The students, all 16 years old, had come with their 29-year old teacher from Elim Christian College to the Sir Edmond Hillary Outdoor Pursuit Centre, nestled in a wilderness area next to the Tongariro National Park, for a week of team-building and outdoor adventure. Scrambling or 'canyoning' through the Mangatepopo Gorge was an exciting opportunity to overcome fears and experience personal growth through adventure-based learning.

A group having fun canyoning.

The plan was for the group to walk, wade, and scramble perhaps 200 meters up the canyon, crisscrossing the stream, then turn around and return to the start. It had been raining throughout the day, at times heavily, but based on a reading of the morning's weather report, the canyon seemed safe to enter.

The water in the gorge was cold, and chest deep in places. Some students struggled. One student became frightened, began to cry, and wanted to turn back. Another student needed assistance; he had physical impairment from cerebral palsy, although this was not listed on his medical form. As they traveled, the current became stronger, and the water deeper. Near the turn-around point, one student was nearly swept away. In crossing deep areas of the stream, students had to jump in the water and catch the hand of someone who had already crossed.

Canyoning up a steep-walled gorge.

The water continued rising. It became brown and muddy. Travel became increasingly difficult. With the exit of the canyon—and safety—just about 135 meters away, the group took shelter on a ledge to wait out the flood.

But the water kept rising. It came over the ledge. It covered students' ankles, then tugged at their knees. The ledge was slippery, and students had to hold onto the rock face to avoid being swept away. The instructor, who has been at the center only three months and had not been fully briefed on gorge escape routes, had never seen the river in flood. She had no way of knowing if the water would continue to rise. She tried radioing for help, but the canyon walls blocked her call. The students were cold and uncomfortable. The instructor faced an extraordinarily difficult situation.

The water was now a roaring, raging torrent. The instructor explained her escape plan: she would jump in the river, swim downstream to safety, and every five minutes group members would follow, where from shore she would toss them a safety line with her throwbag and pull them to shore. The noise of the water was overwhelming, so she told her plan to nearby students, and tried to lip read as the teacher explained it to others farther along the ledge.

Some students were not confident in the water. The instructor knew some students would not make it alone, so she clipped them with webbing and carabiner to stronger swimmers, including herself.

The instructor courageously jumped into the water, floated through the torrent, and made it ashore just above a dam. A student soon followed, but came down the far side of the stream, out of reach of the instructor's throwbag. He was swept over the dam. He hit a log and rocks, lost his helmet, both boots, and a sock, but was able to get to shore.

Another student floated by, calling for help. But he was too far away to reach, and was thrown over the dam. His body was later found downstream. Others followed, but were unable to reach or keep hold of the throwbag. Within five minutes, six students and their teacher drowned. Bodies of two students were recovered more than two kilometers downstream.

How could this have occurred? The incident happened on April 15, 2008, and the organization had been providing outdoor programs since 1972. The Centre had safety management systems, risk assessments, and detailed safety policies in place. Safety procedures covered activities, staff training, emergency planning, rescue equipment, and more. The Centre repeatedly boasted of its "highly trained" instructors. They were led by a CEO with a PhD in Risk Management who had outdoor accident investigation experience and had been at the Center for over 20 years. On the surface, and on paper, things looked great.

But an external review and a coroner's investigation uncovered a complex system riddled with issues that contributed to the tragedy.

A partial list of findings and recommended areas of attention included the following:

Culture
1. The organization had a history of blaming staff for accidents, rather than addressing underlying issues.
2. Expectations to conduct activities "rain or shine" and to accept inexperienced, under-trained, and overworked staff leading potentially hazardous outdoor activities were not effectively addressed.
3. Management had an inappropriate over-confidence that safety systems were appropriate.

Activities & Program Areas
1. Participant swimming ability, required by Centre policy to be assessed, was not checked, nor was there any routine system to do so.
2. The Crisis Management Plan identified floods as a threat, but did not provide specifics or strategies to address the flood situation that occurred.
3. Managers noticed rising waters in the gorge, but did not at that point initiate or at any point effectively implement the Crisis Management Plan.
4. Rescue drills practicing rescue of groups in the gorge had not been conducted.

5. The philosophy of "challenge by choice" was not followed, where participants could choose to participate or not in the gorge trip.

Staff

1. Program management did not read the weather map supplied to the Centre by MetService (the national weather service), which would have alerted staff about heavy rain.
2. Program management did not access freely available updated weather forecasts, or subscribe to MetService's free Severe Weather Warning email notification service.
3. The instructor was not formally assigned a mentor, who could provide safety guidance, as described in the Centre's policies; the mentoring system did not appear to be in place.
4. Staff to participant ratios were inadequate. Solo instructing in challenging terrain was inappropriate. This had repeatedly been a problem with previous incidents but had not been addressed.
5. The instructor was permitted to lead the Gorge trip without having read and signed the Risk Analysis and Management System document describing Gorge risks and management strategies, as required.
6. The Centre's instructors in general were seriously inexperienced. The instructor had been working at the Centre for less than three months.
7. The instructor training and orientation (induction) system was too brief and was inadequate.
8. A map of the gorge with emergency escapes was available, but was never given to the instructor. Contrary to Centre policy, the instructor was never shown and familiarized with all the emergency escapes.
9. The group passed by a "high water escape" shortly before sheltering on the ledge, but due to inadequate instructor training and experience, did not take advantage of it.
10. In 1976 a girl on a Centre trip in the gorge was swept away and drowned. Over the years other incidents occurred where students were swept away by the current or trapped on a ledge due to rising water. However, these and other incidents were not effectively communicated to staff to be used as learning experiences.

Participants

1. Medical forms were not filled out completely, omitting the presence of cerebral palsy in one student.

Equipment

1. The radio was turned off, disassembled, and double-bagged, making communications to or from the group more difficult.
2. A radio communications system to eliminate spots of no radio reception in the canyon was not in place.
3. The throwbag was used in a manner and location in which it was ineffective.
4. Only one radio was present with the group, hampering communications when the group split up.
5. Radio procedures (regarding which channels to use) were unclear to rescuers, leading to confusion and inefficient communications.

Business Administration

1. Activity leader turnover was high. Activity leaders frequently reported feeling overworked and disillusioned with the organization.
2. Due to staffing issues, there was pressure to get new instructors into productive work mode as soon as possible.
3. The medical form did not ask about swimming competence.
4. The Centre boasted in its enrollment materials about its "highly trained instructors" with "extensive qualifications," but placed participants with an inexperienced instructor with insufficient knowledge of the program area. Parents were therefore unable to meaningfully give informed consent.
5. The Instructor Handbook was not sufficiently correlated with the Risk Analysis, and the Risk Analysis document was incomplete.
6. A documented history of problems with instructors with inadequate experience or program area knowledge, inadequate supervision ratios, and flood incidents was not addressed.
7. Competency-based assessments failed to ensure adequate knowledge of specific program areas.
8. The impact of financial pressure led to pressure to accept bookings even if suitable staff were not available.

Government

1. The weather report issued by MetService used by staff mistakenly omitted the word "thunderstorm," which could have alerted staff to heavy rains.
2. MetService did not follow up to address the error in its forecast.
3. The New Zealand government did not ensure safety standards for outdoor adventure programs were met, for example by a licensing scheme.

Outdoor Industry

1. An external safety audit was being conducted on the day of the tragedy. Despite the death and the many issues leading to it, those issues were not addressed in the audit.

About the Flood

The analysis noted that the flood was not unusual, happening on average every couple years. The rising water would have been predictable, if closer attention had been paid to MetService forecasts.

The water began receding just as the group left the ledge. Had the group stayed there—had the instructor had the training sufficient to know that was appropriate—it is very likely everyone would have survived.

23.1. INTRODUCTION

Incidents often have multiple direct causes. These causes themselves are brought about by other, underlying causes, or risk factors. All these elements interact with and influence each other in a complex system. To anticipate, understand, minimize and prevent these incidents, it's important to understand the systemic nature of the influences that bring them about.

Figure 23.1. Risk management systems are made of complex interconnected elements, just as are networks in the human brain.

We've left this important topic for the end of the book to emphasize its importance. It's easy—if wrong—to blame a single person when an incident occurs. The driver of the vehicle that crashed is at fault—or are they? Did the organization provide appropriate driver training? Did supervisors schedule the vehicle operator to drive late at night, through diminished conditions, after a long day of work? Was the expectation that drivers would speed, and

take mobile phone calls from managers while driving? Was the roadway properly maintained and signed?

A more accurate approach to understanding the reasons an accident occurred is to look at the direct causes of the accident, the factors influencing those direct causes, and the interactions between all those elements. Our understanding of accident causation remains incomplete. Accidents will continue to occur. However, looking at incidents from a systems perspective helps us see a more full picture.

We've broken the contents of the book into chapters—in Part II, eight chapters for eight risk domains, and Part III, eleven tools for approaching the management of risks. This analytical approach helps us closely examine and better understand individual system elements.

However, incidents with complex causes and solutions cannot be understood and addressed in isolation. Systems thinking reminds us that the components of a system will act differently when separated from the rest of the system. Therefore, no chapter topic here should be considered in isolation.

We must now begin the crucial step of stitching these elements together into an integral whole. It's only as an entire, interconnected network that the elements of a risk management system can be correctly understood.

23.2. FROM AVIATION SAFETY TO OUTDOOR SAFETY

Some of the best work in risk management systems is done in aviation safety and accident analysis. The frameworks and lessons there translate relatively easily into outdoor program risk management.

Figure 23.2. Research into causes of aviation accidents informs outdoor program risk management.

Airplane crashes are usually the result of multiple factors. In October 2018, Lion Air Flight 610 dropped 1500 meters in one minute to nose-dive into the Java Sea at over 700 kph, killing all 189 on board. The almost-new Boeing 737 airplane had experienced repeated equipment problems before the fatal flight and was reportedly unairworthy. The airline had a poor safety record and a reputation for a profits-before-safety culture. Airline maintenance crews were accused of faking maintenance reports. Pilots reportedly complained of overwork. The 31-year old pilot may not have received adequate training on the new airplane model. There may have been design flaws and inadequate training documentation on the new model from the manufacturer. And global shortages of aircraft engineers, mechanics and air safety regulators were cited as potential factors.

An example of an investigation exploring multiple systemic failures leading to an incident in the outdoor industry is found in the examination of a ropes course incident in Victoria, Australia. When a 17-year old boy died from falling off a home-made giant swing at a ropes course after a carabiner unexpectedly opened, causing him to fall 10 meters onto his head, the investigation found causes ranging from improper use of carabiners, lack of back-up systems (as required by the Australian standard for amusement rides), the participant inappropriately being positioned upside-down, and failure of the Victorian WorkCover Authority to identify and prevent unsafe operation of the giant swing.

The coroner also noted that voluntary organizations like the Camping Association of Victoria, which accredited camping venues, were unlikely to be able to prevent similar incidents in the future, in the absence of legislative jurisdiction to perform routine surveillance and enforce safety issues.

Because the giant swing was manually operated, it was exempt from certain occupational health and safety regulations, and the coroner recommended a change in legislation to remove this exemption in order to allow the workplace safety agency better awareness of the giant swing's design and operation before it became operational.

Finally, the coroner recommended the government establish a mandatory certification-type scheme and inspection system for adventure activities.

To address a case of an unclipped carabiner, recommendations were made addressing participants, staff, equipment, the industry association, the regulatory body and the legislature.

Systems Thinking and the Business of Risk Management

Characteristics of complex problems requiring systems thinking include 1) difficulty in achieving widely shared recognition that a problem even exists, and agreeing on a shared definition of the problem; 2) difficulty identifying all the specific factors that influence the problem; 3) limited or no influence or control over some causal elements of the problem, 4) uncertainty about the impacts of specific interventions, 5) incomplete information about the causes of the problem and the effectiveness of potential solutions; 6) a constantly shifting landscape where the nature of the problem itself and potential solutions are always changing.

In this light, we can see the endeavor of outdoor program risk management itself, embedded in a complex business management system, itself embedded in complex social and governmental systems, as a systems issue. With limited budget and incomplete knowledge, where to you put your risk management priorities? How do you drive down the severity and rate of incidents, but also keep program quality high, customer satisfaction high, financial performance acceptable? What is the right balance, as standards, technologies, expectations are ever-shifting?

23.3.   A MODEL OF THE OUTDOOR PROGRAM RISK SYSTEM

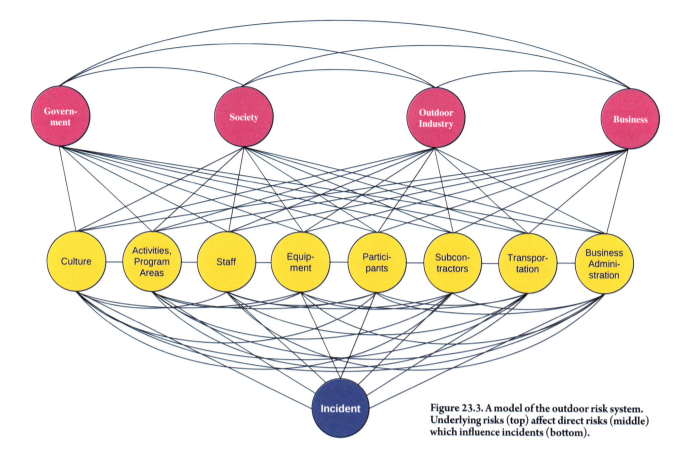

Figure 23.3. A model of the outdoor risk system. Underlying risks (top) affect direct risks (middle) which influence incidents (bottom).

Figure 23.3 illustrates an approach to understanding the components and interrelationships of domains that affect risk management in outdoor programs. This model is one of several (there is as yet no universally used standard), and shares some features with the well-respected Danish AcciMap accident analysis method (and its multiple variations) used in aviation incident analysis, outdoor safety, and elsewhere.

The model has three principal components:

1. Direct risk domains;
2. Underlying risk domains, and
3. The interconnections between them.

These three elements combine to influence the likelihood and severity of an incident causing loss.

Direct risks are found in the direct risk domains of Culture, Activities and Program Areas, Staff, Equipment, Participants, Subcontractors, Transportation and Business Administration. These proximate risks are also termed "operational risks" for their closeness to the operations of an outdoor program. Risk from multiple direct risk domains are typically factors in incidents.

(Terms here—such as 'proximate risk' or 'proximate cause'—are to be considered in the general outdoor safety context, not in specific legal and insurance contexts in which they might also occur.)

Underlying risks are also sometimes called root causes, or secondary, tertiary, etc. risks. Here they are found in underlying risk domains of Government, Society (such as in social norms and popular opinion), Outdoor Industry, and Business. These underlying risks influence direct risks, which in turn influence the nature of the incident.

Interconnections between the risk factors within the risk domains represent the ways in which the risk factors influence each other. These interdependencies show up, for example, when interventions designed to manage one risk have effects on other risk factors, sometimes unpredictably.

Ultimately, to understand why an incident occurred—and how its reoccurrence might be prevented—all of these elements must be considered, individually and together. Effective solutions must incorporate, rather than exclude, the complexity inherent in the system.

We'll now discuss each of these three elements in more detail.

23.3.1. Direct Risks

Direct risks arise from each of the direct outdoor program risk domains. Each chapter in Part II, Risk Domains, addresses one of these domains, and the discrete management of risks therein.

Examples of these direct risks well managed include (among many others):

1. **Culture:** just culture; culture of following safety rules
2. **Activities & Program Areas:** procedures to avoid falling down steep slope
3. **Staff:** good judgment
4. **Equipment:** safe camp stove operation
5. **Participants:** following directions
6. **Subcontractors:** adequately trained and equipped subcontractor staff
7. **Transportation:** defensive driving
8. **Business Administration:** accurate marketing materials

Direct Risks In Action. Let's consider the simple example of preventing ankle blisters while on a hiking trip. The formation of a blister is a relatively straightforward incident, but still benefits from systems thinking. Multiple direct risk domains can play a role:

1. **Culture:** Activity leaders foster a friendly, non-macho culture where it's okay to ask for help or stop to fix a problem rather than just push through pain and injury.
2. **Activities and Program Areas:** Activity leaders conduct a safety briefing including blister prevention before starting the hike. Leaders follow the procedure to do a "foot check" early on the first hours of the hike, checking for hot spots. The first days' route is planned to start with moderate distance and avoid rugged terrain.
3. **Staff:** Activity leaders have been thoroughly trained to understand and manage risk factors for blisters.
4. **Equipment:** Participant gear is inspected before departure, with attention to socks and hiking boots. A supply of extra gear or contingency plan is available if participants fail to bring the required equipment.
5. **Participants:** Hikers ensure their shoes and socks fit. They stop at the first signs of discomfort. Participants check for 'hot spots' that indicate rubbing and pressure that could lead to blisters.

6. **Business Administration:** Sales staff inform participants in enrollment materials how to select proper footwear, and to break in their boots before the outdoor program begins. Administrators ensure that program schedules and plans ensure activity leaders have sufficient time and resources to conduct safety briefings and foot checks.

With even a simple risk like that of contracting blisters from hiking, a system of multiple risk domains is clearly evident. With catastrophic failures such as fatalities, anticipate that a more complex network of risk domains will be involved.

23.3.2. Underlying Risks

Underlying risks, in this model, are divided into Government, Society, Outdoor Industry, and Business. Unlike as with direct risks, outdoor programs may have limited influence on these risk domains. However, they can have a profound influence on outdoor safety. Let's consider some examples:

Government. Examples of effective management of underlying risks relating to government can include, but are not limited to:

1. **Laws and regulations.** The presence of effective laws establishing and enforcing safety standards for outdoor programs.
2. **Funding priorities.** Sufficient funding for sustaining quality outdoor education and recreation programming.
3. **Emergency services.** Good access to search, rescue, emergency transport, and medical services.
4. **Economic models.** Economic models supporting equitable resource distribution rather than continued wealth accumulation of the already wealthy, leading to sufficient resources for education and recreation services.
5. **Enforcement of laws.** Effective enforcement of existing safety laws, leading to regular legal conformity.
6. **Corruption; rule of law.** Government priorities on enhancing social programs rather than enriching politicians and their allies.
7. **Governance effectiveness.** Skillful development and implementation of appropriate, effective policies.
8. **Availability of university-level training for outdoor professionals.** Well-developed intellectual and academic architecture in public universities to support quality and advancement in the industry.

Society. Examples of effective management of underlying risks relating to society can include, but are not limited to social values such as:

1. **Risk tolerance**. Appropriately reduced risk tolerance fostering managing risks more closely and minimizing major incidents.
2. **Education, recreation, health, personal growth.** Valuing these benefits of outdoor experiences leading to sufficient resources for well-managed outdoor programs.
3. **Valuing human life.** Prizing individual lives promoting incident prevention and close investigation of incidents.
4. **Character over superficial appearance.** Promoting the well-being of others and personal responsibility rather than self-interest and conspicuous consumption.

Outdoor Industry. Examples of effective management of underlying risks relating to the outdoor industry can include, among others, factors such as:

1. **State of industry collaboration.** Presence of extensive use of high-quality peer reviews, accreditation, conferences, and journals.
2. **State of industry standards.** Widely adopted high quality national-level standards (as seen in some areas of Oceania and Western Europe) with accompanying robust inspection regimes.
3. **Advocacy for support and professionalization.** Effective lobbying of government policy-makers for financial resources, regulatory uniformity, and compulsory safety standards.

Business. Examples of effective management of underlying risks relating to the corporate world, including large and politically powerful multinational corporations, can include, among others, factors such as:

1. **A strong "social contract"** leading to financially successful businesses giving back to the community rather than providing excessive compensation to executives and owners.
2. **Welcoming and support of appropriate business regulation** (in general), which can support the establishment (specifically) of regulations regarding outdoor program safety.
3. **Promotion of thrift and social investment** (in education and elsewhere) over ever-increasing consumption.

4. **Availability of university-level training for outdoor professionals.** Well-developed intellectual and academic architecture in private universities to support quality and advancement in the industry.

A Note on Classification. The division of global risk domains into Government, Society, Outdoor Industry and Business is one of multiple taxonomical approaches. Other valid constructions exist. Some might split out educational institutions, or address values promulgated by religious traditions, or call out the media (for example, regarding the role of a free press and investigative journalism). AcciMap, Systems Theoretic Accident Modeling and Processes model (STAMP) and the Human Factors Analysis and Classification System (HFACS) accident analysis models, and their variants, present other well-developed approaches, and research in this area continues. Overlaps and inter-relationships between risk domains, no matter their classification, are common.

23.3.3. Risk Domain Interactions

Examples of the interaction of factors in multiple risk domains may be clearly evident in the examples, such as the Mangatepopo Gorge tragedy (which has become a famous case study for systems issues in outdoor safety), provided earlier in this chapter.

In another example, explored in Chapter 16, Incident Review, a kayaking tragedy affected an entire country's outdoor programming. In March 1993, a group of schoolchildren set out on a two-hour guided kayaking trip along the shore of Lyme Bay in England. They became separated after encountering windy conditions. They were overdue, but the outdoor program management delayed calling for search and rescue for hours, and gave inaccurate information about the group when the call was made. After floating in cold water for hours, waiting for help that never came, four students drowned.

The kayak instructors were not highly experienced and emergency equipment was lacking. There were no governmental safety requirements for outdoor programs.

Following the incident, the United Kingdom passed legislating mandating licensing and safety audits for adventure activity providers. Outdoor businesses, staff, participants, government agencies, schools, and other groups were all affected.

23.3.4. Implications for Practice

How to put all this theory into practice? Here are ways to bring systems thinking alive in your outdoor program.

Consider Both Direct and Underlying Risks. In thinking about minimizing the probability and severity of incidents, address both direct and underlying risks. Direct risk issues are addressed in chapters in Part II. Approaches for addressing underlying risks might include:

1. Support mandatory outdoor safety standards developed collaboratively by industry and government
2. Support good information-sharing such as national or multi-national incident databases
3. Support professionalization of the industry through university-level training including advanced degrees, research, sustainable career pathways for outdoor activity leader professionals, and sufficient funding to support these initiatives

Consider the Cumulative Nature of Risks. In risk management planning, keep in mind that multiple small risks scattered throughout several risk domains can combine to make a significant incident much more likely to occur.

A camper at a nature-focused summer camp wandered into a wooded area in the middle of camp, and ate a handful of greenery from a plant growing by a stream. The plant was the deadly toxic poison hemlock (Conium maculatum), the same plant that killed Greek philosopher Socrates. The risk accumulation was:
1. The program area (summer camp) had a deadly hazard
2. Camp staff were not aware of the hazard or informed on what to do about it
3. Participants weren't alerted to the hazard. One participant made a silly decision to eat an unknown plant

If any of those factors hadn't existed, the incident wouldn't have occurred.

(We also see the cumulative nature of risk factors in other areas, such as health. If a person doesn't get appropriate exercise, have a healthy diet, maintain strong social connections, get sufficient sleep, minimize chronic stress, and avoid toxins such as nicotine, overexposure to sun, or urban air pollution, they are much more likely to get a serious illness.)

Employ Systems Thinking with Direct Risk Domains. Just Culture, covered in Chapter 5, Culture, reminds us to focus not on "good" workers and "bad" (unsafe) workers, but to see the systems that influence them.

In Activities and Program areas, another opportunity for systems thinking exists. When beginning a new program area or activity type (such as caving), avoid simply filling out a risk register (also known as a risk assessment) in order to think about direct risks of that activity (hitting one's head on a low ceiling) or area (the area is known to flood), and considering that your primary risk management tool.

Risk registers have their place, and they can be useful when planning for new activities or program areas. But they are not enough. A New Element Readiness Assessment (described in Chapter 6, Activities and Program Areas) and other tools can be used to address potential risks in all direct and underlying risk domains. Will we stress our Human Resources department staff and systems in attempting to hire and train new activity leaders for this new program? Is the business office able to generate accurate marketing materials and appropriately written risk acknowledgement forms? Do logistics staff know where and how to acquire and manage the new equipment? Are there authoritative, well-developed standards to help us develop appropriate activity procedures?

Visualize Catastrophe. The "pre-mortem" technique can bring a systems approach to risk management planning.

Visualizing Catastrophe

One systems-oriented approach to creatively anticipating and managing risks involves imagining the catastrophic failure of an outdoor program, or a component of an outdoor organization. A list of reasons why the disaster occurred is then generated—even though no such spectacular failure might have yet happened.

This project management technique is a form of prospective hindsight, popularized in business management literature as a "pre-mortem." This term is a twist on post-mortem, which is an analysis of the cause of death. The post-mortem provides an understanding of why the death occurred—helpful to everyone, except for the deceased.

The pre-mortem process uses structured brainstorming to reframe the perspective that risk assessments often take. A typical risk assessment asks what might go wrong. The pre-mortem approach assumes failure and asks what did go wrong—and why. Research shows that this technique increases the likelihood of accurately identifying causes of failure.

The technique can be employed at the beginning of a new initiative (such as starting to work with a new participant population, or a new activity or activity area). It can also be employed to strengthen risk management in an existing and successful program, or in the context of an incident review or risk management review.

The individuals participating in the process can be outdoor program managers, activity leaders, or individuals from any other stakeholder group. The procedure can be conducted with a small number of participants in focus-group style, or en masse with all staff or other large groups.

The procedure typically follows these steps (Figure 23.4):
1. Individuals participating in the exercise are informed by the facilitator that the program or project has experienced a devastating failure (such as a fatality).
2. Participants are asked to individually brainstorm every reason they can think of why this might have occurred. Participants individually write down their responses.
3. Each person shares their reasons with the group, and a master list of causes is generated. There is no discussion of solutions at this point.
4. The list of reasons is reviewed, assessed, and prioritized. This can be done immediately with the group, or at a later date by management team members.
5. The results are used to identify and make improvements to risk management systems.

Figure 23.4. Pre-mortem procedure.

A visualization of future catastrophe exercise was conducted by one outdoor program that had experienced a fatality. A group of activity leaders, in a process facilitated by the CEO, was asked to respond to the question, "Who will be the next person to die on our outdoor program, and why?" Responses included suggestions like adjusting activity leader compensation and moving from a seasonal to year-round model to increase the longevity and professionalism of field staff. Other potential issues that might be brought up range from loss of broad and enduring political support from organizational leadership for investments in risk management, to subtle and not widely known operational flaws such as cultural issues or time pressures leading to fatigue and error.

This retrospective hindsight activity has several benefits over standard risk assessments. It can:

1. Reduce the effect of over-confidence on individuals already psychologically invested in moving a project forward despite any obstacles
2. Raise awareness of valid concerns, despite peer pressure to express confidence in success
3. Help address the cognitive bias where individuals are overly optimistic about the probability of success (over-confidence bias)
4. Incentivize experienced, intelligent, and analytical individuals to speak up without fear of being perceived as overly critical or not a team player
5. Reduce reluctance to criticize programs or projects that have executive support
6. Shift organizational culture to pay greater attention to potential risks that may arise in the future

Employ Systems Thinking with Risk Management Tools and Structures. Risk management tools and structures are covered in the chapters in Part III. A classic systems thinking approach to incident review is root cause analysis, discussed in Chapter 16, Incident Review.

A systems approach is also evident when incident report raw data and synthesized information is distributed throughout all levels of an organization. This allows the entire organization to explore and learn from the incident. It is in contrast with a situation in which an incident report gets quietly filed away in a middle manager's office somewhere, with either no response to the reporting party, or a disjointed new procedure handed down later without context.

Consider strategic and emerging risks. Chapter 12, Business Administration, introduced us to strategic risks. How do we grapple with the fact that climate change is leading our activity areas to burn, or flood, while participants are present? Or that a changing climate causes more typhoons to occur in the areas in which we sail?

Likewise, changes in social risk tolerance and legal precedent, such as a large and precedent-setting financial judgment for an incident that might not have previously been brought to court, represent complex strategic risks.

From the perspective of evolutionary biology, humans are programmed to see immediate threats such as a lion in the grass. It's not as easy for us to act on long-term threats like those from a poor diet or climate change. In the outdoor program context, an example could be social forces that lead to underfunding of human development activities like outdoor programming, and thereby increase risk.

A scenario planning approach, in which long-term potential futures are considered, is an option for addressing these uncertainties.

Consider Unintended Consequences. Actions in complex systems often result in unanticipated responses. Examples in outdoor programming include:

1. A campaign to reduce incident rates leads to a perverse incentive where activity leaders suppress the writing of incident reports in order to (fraudulently) meet the rate reduction goal.
2. The establishment of a conservative immobilization and evacuation protocol for potentially spine-injured participants leads to large increases in dangerous airborne evacuations of patients without apparent medical benefit.

Beyond the outdoor program context, an example from foreign policy might be arming and training a rebel group to overthrow an undesired government, but then having the group turn around and attack the country that armed and trained it.

Build in Resiliency. This advice may sound obvious; however, many outdoor programs run on lean budgets, and institutional resiliency can be an elusive goal. Investigators cited a lack of staffing and other resources as contributing factors in the Mangatepopo Gorge tragedy. Backup systems and redundancy establish resiliency.

An example is the presence of multiple ways to identify emerging safety issues—program debriefs, incident reports, risk management reviews, and participant feedback.

For some organizations, it's easier said than done, but sufficient staff, equipment, financial and resources for the inevitable period of increased demand or reduced supply can provide a buffer that reduces the risk of a serious incident.

23.4. CONCLUSION

Complex systems share certain characteristics:

1. Incidents have multiple causes
2. It is hard to predict when next incident will occur
3. Personnel may not have complete control over all risk factors
4. Interventions may have unpredictable consequences

These circumstances apply to complex problems such as outdoor program fatalities, just as they apply to issues such as homelessness, global refugee flows, climate change, and corruption in government.

In addressing safety problems that occur in the context of complex systems, interventions that take into account the nature of the system of influences are most likely to be effective.

23.4.1. Return to Mangatepopo: Systemic Changes Since the Tragedy

What happened in the years following the Mangatepopo Gorge tragedy in New Zealand?

The Centre discontinued running programs in Mangatepopo Gorge, put new effort into its safety systems, created and hired for a new Safety Manager position, re-named itself, and continues providing outdoor programs. MetService now includes severe weather warnings in forecasts, provides the time of forecast production in forecasts, and sends updates in case of forecast errors.

Following the drowning of a 21-year old woman on a commercial whitewater river trip on New Zealand's South Island just two weeks after the Mangatepopo tragedy, the New Zealand government in 2009 began a review of the country's outdoor adventure sector. National Health and Safety at Work (Adventure Activities) Regulations were passed requiring safety audits and establishing safety standards.

The New Zealand outdoor industry, with funding from the government, created 'SupportAdventure,' a central resource for outdoor safety information, and created Activity Safety Guidelines outlining activity-specific good practice information.

These and other systemic changes have helped make New Zealand's outdoor adventure risk management systems among the best in the world.

Despite progress being made, outdoor professionals around the world still generally lack the training, career sustainability, and access to financial and other resources afforded to professionals such as professors or lawyers. Nevertheless, the example set by the New Zealand outdoor adventure sector can be a model of positive systemic change for outdoor programs world-wide.

Chapter Summary

1. Incidents have multiple direct causes.

2. Those causes are brought about by underlying factors.

3. Interconnections and interactions between those direct causes and underlying factors affect incident occurrence.

4. Effectively managing outdoor risks requires understanding how these three elements work in together in a system.

5. We don't yet fully understand why accidents occur.

6. The business of outdoor program risk management is itself a complex system.

7. A model of outdoor incident causation involves factors in underlying risk domains influencing factors in direct risk domains, leading to an incident.

8. Direct risks are found in the direct risk domains of Culture, Activities and Program Areas, Staff, Equipment, Participants, Subcontractors, Transportation and Business Administration.

9. Underlying risks are found in underlying risk domains of Government, Society, Outdoor Industry, and Business.

10. Other accident models, including AcciMap, STAMP, HFACS, and their variants, exist.

11. Systems-informed management approaches include:
    a. Considering both direct and underlying risks
    b. Avoiding accumulations of risk factors
    d. Applying systems thinking to direct and underlying risk domains
    e. Applying systems thinking to risk management tools and systems
    f. Considering strategic risks and unintended consequences
    g. Building institutional resiliency

TERMS AND DEFINITIONS

Terms are described here for the purposes of interpretation of wording in this document. While the descriptions below are intended to be standard, definitions vary across sources and contexts.

Guideline

A recommended, but not mandatory, way of doing something. For example: while camping in cold weather, encourage participants to eat fat-containing foods prior to bed to assist in keeping warm through the night. See also: policy, procedure.

Harm

Injury, damage, or other adverse effect.

Hazard

A source of potential loss.

Examples include physical hazards such as natural hazards (for example, lightning, avalanche, whitewater rapids, contaminated drinking water), and damaged or improperly maintained equipment. Hazards also include errors in judgment (such as confirmation bias or succumbing to peer pressure), carelessness, and fraud.

Interaction with a hazard generates a risk. For example, a cliff is a hazard; standing directly on top of the cliff represents a risk.

A prospective participant with an active, uncontrolled seizure disorder could be considered a hazard. Admitting such a person to a bicycling trip can represent a risk.

An activity location or activity type that is unfamiliar to an organization's staff can represent a hazard. Agreeing to provide a program activity the organization is not well prepared to offer represents a risk.

Incident

An occurrence of actual or potential nontrivial loss. This includes illness, injury, property damage, or other harm.

A near miss is considered an incident. Occurrences involving simple first aid (such as applying padding over a hot spot to prevent blister formation) are generally not considered incidents.

Loss

Injury, illness, death, property damage, or other harm.

Loss of program/activity time and loss of psychological well-being are included. Other examples of loss include damage to reputation, loss of goodwill, and loss of business.

Near Miss

A "close call" where a loss nearly occurred but was narrowly avoided.

Participant

A person enrolled in an outdoor program, during the time between the program commencement and program termination, and during a time in which program staff have a shared responsibility for the person's care or well-being. Persons are considered participants even during unstructured or "free" time if program staff during that period have a shared responsibility for their care or well-being.

Responsible persons may also qualify as participants for the purpose of risk management. While participants are generally considered the principal recipients of outdoor program services, responsible persons can typically be considered participants as well. These persons may be school group chaperones, Personal Care Attendants, or language interpreters, among others. They engage in the outdoor activities such as hiking, rafting, sailing, etc., along with other participants. They may accompany those other participants to areas with extreme environments (such as high altitude, avalanche terrain, or temperature extremes, among others) or with delayed or prolonged transport to care.

Observers who do not engage in activities, who are not present in activity areas with activity-related risks (such as rockfall zones at a climbing area), and who do not travel to extreme environments or remote locations, are generally not considered participants.

For participants who are legal minors and for vulnerable adults, parents or guardians need to be involved in certain circumstances, such as when receiving critical pre-program safety and preparation information, or when giving informed consent to taking risks associated with outdoor program participation. In these situations, involvement of parents or guardians is implied when referencing participants.

Policy

An over-arching mandatory directive. Policies are high-level rules where regular compliance is expected. For example, an outdoor program might have a policy that prohibits operating a motor vehicle while under the influence of drugs or alcohol. See also: procedure, guideline.

Procedure

An established way of doing something. Procedures should be followed, unless it is evidently safer or superior not to do so. For example, an outdoor program might have a procedure that requires a minimum of two activity leaders per group during remote wilderness backpacking expeditions. See also: policy, guideline.

Risk

Possibility of undesirable loss. Also, the probability of loss combined with the magnitude of the potential loss. Risk comes from interaction with a hazard.

A steep slope composed of loose rocks is a hazard. Hiking on that slope is a risk.

An activity leader not qualified to lead an activity represents a source of potential loss (hazard). Placing an inexperienced or improperly trained activity leader in charge of a group represents a risk.

Risk Management

A systematic, intentional, and ongoing process of maintaining risk at an acceptably low level. This involves identifying and evaluating hazards and their associated risks, and developing and implementing a plan to reduce, transfer, eliminate or accept those risks.

Staff

For the purposes of this document, staff indicates a person doing paid or unpaid work for an organization. Staff can include employees, volunteers, interns, assistants, apprentices, directors, and independent contractors. They may be on a full-time, part-time, year-round, or part-year/seasonal basis. "Activity leaders" are considered to be outdoor program staff with direct responsibility for conducting outdoor activities.

Vulnerable Adult

A person who has attained the age of majority and who has or may have a physical or mental disability, illness, or other diminishment of capacity for any reason, that significantly reduces their capability to make sound judgments, meet their basic needs, or protect themselves from exploitation or other harm, compared to the capabilities of an adult without such diminishments.

PHOTO CREDITS

Acknowledgements © serghi8/AdobeStock

Chapter 2
2.3 Courtesy of International Organization for Standardization

Chapter 3
3.1 Courtesy of International Organization for Standardization
3.2 Courtesy of Outdoor Learning and Adventure Education Association
3.3 Courtesy of Scott Andrews, Association for Challenge Course Technology

Chapter 4
4.1 Courtesy of Adventure Activities Licensing Service

Chapter 5
5.1 © fad82/AdobeStock
5.2 © Ingo Bartussek/AdobeStock

Chapter 6
6.1 © nakimori/AdobeStock
6.2 Courtesy of Lurens/Pixabay
6.3 © ma_studio/AdobeStock
6.4 Courtesy of Jeff Baierlein
6.5 © Svetlana Nikolaeva/AdobeStock
6.6 © nopporn/AdobeStock
6.7 © Courtesy of act suju/Pixabay
6.10 © BlueOrange Studio/AdobeStock
6.11 © JackF/Adobestock
6.12 © Andrea Izzotti/AdobeStock

Chapter 7
7.1 © Dmitry Naumov/AdobeStock
7.2 © ARochau/AdobeStock
7.3 © MAK/AdobeStock
7.4 Courtesy of Clker-Free-Vector-Images/Pixabay
7.6 Courtesy of Teddy Rawpixel/Rawpixel
7.7 Courtesy of succo/Pixabay
7.8 © THANAGON/AdobeStock
7.9 © salajean/AdobeStock
7.11 © WavebreakMediaMicro/AdobeStock
7.12 © Jitalia17/Getty Images
7.14 © 7.14 DCrane Photography/AdobeStock
7.15 © skynesher/Getty Images

Chapter 8
8.1 Courtesy of European Commission
8.2 Courtesy of Jeff Baierlein

8.4 Courtesy of Petzl
8.6 © Kotangens/AdobeStock
8.10 © gilitukha/AdobeStock
8.11 © Artranq/AdobeStock
8.12 Courtesy of Jeff Baierlein
8.13 Courtesy of Larry Hamilton
8.14 © Stringer Image/AdobeStock
8.18 © ARochau/AdobeStock

Chapter 9
9.1 © Solosupremoira/AdobeStock
9.2 © cromary/AdobeStock
9.3 © xalanx/AdobeStock
9.4 © michelangeloop/AdobeStock
9.5 © minicel73/AdobeStock
9.6 © Ourson+/AdobeStock
9.7 © EvgeniiAnd/AdobeStock

Chapter 10
10.1 Courtesy of FiluLeck/Pixabay
10.2 © fabio lamanna/AdobeStock

Chapter 11
11.1 © Tarquin/AdobeStock
11.6 © travelgalcindy/AdobeStock
11.7 © Monika Wisniewska/AdobeStock
11.10 Courtesy of Jeff Baierlein
11.12 © Antonioguillem/AdobeStock
11.14 © Rodica Nelson/AdobeStock
11.15 © dbvirago/AdobeStock

Chapter 12
12.1 Courtesy of Clker-Free-Vector-Images/Pixabay

Chapter 14
14.1 © pkproject/AdobeStock
14.3 © viperagp/AdobeStock
14.4 © dzmitrock87/AdobeStock
14.6 © WavebreakMediaMicro/AdobeStock
14.7 © Astarot/AdobeStock
14.8 Courtesy of Jeff Baierlein
14.9 © luther2k/AdobeStock
14.10 © LonelyTaws/AdobeStock

Chapter 16
16.1 © shapecharge/Getty Images

Chapter 17
17.1 Courtesy Jopwell x PGA/Pexels

Chapter 18
18.3 Courtesy of Wilderness Medical Associates

Chapter 19
19.1 Courtesy of paulbr75/Pixabay
19.2 Courtesy of Viristar LLC
19.3 © esalienko/AdobeStock

Chapter 20
20.1 © flucas/AdobeStock

Chapter 21
21.1 © SNEHIT/AdobeStock
21.3 © mnirat/AdobeStock

Chapter 22
22.1 Courtesy of Association for Experiential Education
22.2 Courtesy of Adventure Activities Industry Advisory Committee
22.3 Courtesy of bfu

Chapter 23
[Canyoning] © Ammit/AdobeStock
[Canyoning] © Ammit/AdobeStock
23.1 © adimas/AdobeStock
23.2 Courtesy of Murati/Pixabay

ABOUT THE AUTHOR

Jeff A. Baierlein has over 30 years of experience as an outdoor professional, ranging from trip leader to Executive Director. Jeff has led mountaineering, sailing, whitewater and flatwater canoeing, whitewater kayaking, sea kayaking, backpacking, rock climbing, canyoneering and caving trips, including international wilderness expeditions up to three months in length.

Jeff served as Executive Director of the Baltimore Chesapeake Bay Outward Bound Center and the Boojum Institute for Experiential Education. He was a member of the Board of Directors of the Association for Experiential Education and is an adventure program accreditation reviewer with AEE. Jeff has also conducted risk management reviews with Outward Bound and Viristar.

Jeff has been a Wilderness EMT since 1993, worked for two ambulance services as an EMT, and volunteered with four high-angle, technical and backcountry Search and Rescue teams, leading rescues in North America and Asia. Jeff has taught wilderness medicine classes with Wilderness Medical Associates on four continents since 1997.

Jeff holds two undergraduate degrees from Prescott College and a graduate degree from Antioch University. He has served as an expert witness with wilderness program fatalities, and is the Director of outdoor program training and consulting firm Viristar LLC.

Made in the USA
Columbia, SC
11 February 2025

53136917R00128